Rights to Language
Equity, Power, and Education

Rights to Language

Equity, Power, and Education

Celebrating the 60th Birthday of Tove Skutnabb-Kangas

Edited by
Robert Phillipson

LAWRENCE ERLBAUM ASSOCIATES, PUBLISHERS
2000   Mahwah, New Jersey   London

Lawrence Erlbaum Associates, Inc., Publishers
10 Industrial Avenue
Mahwah, NJ 07430

Cover design by Kathryn Houghtaling Lacey

The final camera copy for this work was prepared by the author,
and therefore the publisher takes no responsibility for consis-
tency or correctness of typographical style. However, this arrangement helps to make publication of this kind of scholarship
possible.

Librbary of Congress Cataloging-in-Publication Data

Rights to language : equity, power, and education : celebrating the 60th birthday of Tove
Skutnabb-Kangas / edited by Robert Phillipson.
    p.   cm.
Includes bibliographical references and index.
ISBN 0-8058-3346-3 (hc : alk. Paper)
ISBN 0-8058-3835-X (pbk. : alk. paper)
1. Language policy. 2. Language and education. 3. Language planning.
    4. Human rights.   I. Skutnabb-Kangas, Tove. II. Phillipson, Robert.

P119.3 .R54 2000
306.44—dc21   00-021044
                                                        CIP

Books published by Lawrence Erlbaum Associates are
printed on acid-free paper, and their bindings are chosen
for strength and durability.

Printed in the United States of America
10 9 8 7 6 5 4 3 2 1

Contents

Preface

This volume brings together cutting-edge scholarship in language, education and society from all parts of the world. It celebrates the 60th birthday of Tove Skutnabb-Kangas on July 6, 2000. The book is inspired by her work in the fields of minority education, multilingualism, linguistic human rights, and language and power. The contributors, all of whom are people whose work has influenced and has been influenced by Tove Skutnabb-Kangas, were encouraged to distil into relatively few words something of the essence of their professional experience. They were also invited to sketch out a vision of how the challenge of our multilingual diversity might be handled in a better world.

The fields named in the title of the volume serve to permit a thematic grouping of the papers into five parts of roughly equal size, starting with *Language* and *Rights*, and moving via *Equity* and *Power* to *Education*. Each part includes a range of chapters on these cross-cutting themes. The volume provides a provocative challenge to our ways of thinking about language, about how language rights are formulated and implemented, how speakers of all languages can be treated more equitably, and how multilingualism can be promoted in the wider society and more specifically in education. The rich mix of chapters serves to underline that the issues are comparable worldwide, that many apparently disparate topics can cross-fertilise each other, and that our understanding of the issues can benefit from coverage that is global, reflective, and committed.

There is considerable variety among the types of paper: retrospective and philosophical; comparative, local, and universal; activist and professionally iconoclastic; literary and visionary. The contributors come from many scientific specialisations, including anthropology, communication, economics, education, law, linguistics, literature, political science, psychology, and sociology. Collectively they exemplify how sociolinguistics has developed dynamic, multidisciplinary approaches to complex real-world problems. Such methods and insights are essential for language policy and language pedagogy in the contemporary world.

The book reflects the complexity and diversity of topics that are central to bilingual education, English as a Second Language, applied linguistics, and sociolinguistics. Many of the themes are bought together in the concluding 'integrated comment', which analyses the chapters in terms of the role of the critical intellectual, issues of scientific approach, monolingualism in a global age, seeing language dominance afresh, economic gospels, hopeful ways forward, and a broader vision of how some of our language policy utopias can be brought to life.

The strong coverage of the Nordic countries reflects Tove Skutnabb-Kangas's origins and primary professional base (Finland, Sweden, Denmark) and presents material that is not easily available in English. Many other regions are strongly represented: North America, India, South Africa, Australia, and many parts of Europe. There are papers on indigenous languages, sign languages, Esperanto, and Kurdish, all of which can be considered 'threatened' languages but which, for their speakers, are neither marginal nor 'minority' languages. In this way the book reflects a concern with the equality of all human languages, and a wish to promote a more democratic world linguistic order.

The book would have been even richer if it had included contributions by the following, also people who have influenced Tove Skutnabb-Kangas, who had hoped to write for the book: Alma Flor Ada, Mehmet Emin Bozarslan, Sertaç Bucak, Pirkko Carpenter, Rosario Diaz-Greenberg, Philomena Essed, Hartmut Haberland, Rainer Enrique Hamel, Eduardo Hernández-Chávez, Lachmann Khubchandani, Georgji Khruslov, Alexei Leontiev, Joe Lo Bianco, Chris Mullard, Mart Rannut, Olaug Rekdal, Máret Sárá, Miranda Vuolasranta, Kaarlo Voionmaa, Ruth Wodak.

Although the book represents a tangible personal tribute to Tove Skutnabb-Kangas, it is more than a collection of academic papers. Inscribed on a wall in St. Paul's Cathedral in London are these words about Sir Christopher Wren, the architect of this and countless other memorable buildings, 'si monumentum requiris, circumspice' - if you seek my monument, look around you. For Tove Skutnabb-Kangas this publication will only be memorable if it leads to greater respect for language rights globally and locally, not least in education, better implementation of policies informed by scholarship, and a more equitable and ethically accountable language ecology.

Acknowledgements

The first part of the paper by Ngũgĩ wa Thiong'o is from *Penpoints, gunpoints, and dreams, Towards a critical theory of the arts and the state in Africa* (Clarendon Press, 1998). It is reprinted by permission of Oxford University Press, © Ngũgĩ wa Thiong'o, 1998.

This book would never have come about without substantial support from many colleagues in the Department of Languages and Culture, University of Roskilde, Denmark, to all of whom I am very grateful.

Special and sincere thanks to Federico Decara for a remarkable feat in converting a set of files into camera-ready copy, for his patience and skill while we exchanged tales of the immigrant experience.

Naomi Silverman, Renata Butera and the team at Lawrence Erlbaum Associates have been wonderful to work with.

Many thanks too to the reviewers who recommended publication, and whose names now appear on the back of the book.

Tove's own influence on my own work and my life cannot be merely "acknowledged". I would not be what I am personally and professionally without her, I would not be without her. I lovingly hope our scholarly and private lives can continue to grow and age together, in peace and health. Let me join with all the contributors in wishing you

Happy birthday!

Grattis på födelsedagen!

Hauskaa syntymäpäivää!

Robert Phillipson

Transcultura, Trønninge Mose, Denmark, January 2000.

Tove

Francisca Sanchez

Truthseeker her life is an
Openhearted odyssey through the outrage of oppression
Voiceful visionary she is no variable star
Evening star instead navigating into twilight's

Storm always constant and vigilant she writes our own
Kalevala with the kaleidoscopic orthography of her life
Unabridged unapologetic unshakable
Treasured testimony tenacious against tyranny
Nourishes our struggle
Anchors our tapestry of advocacy
Border to border and
Braids new understanding with our breath

Knowlege and passion entangled
And afire leave a tesselated trail brilliant as a
Necklace of sapphires and rubies
Gifts to us of unflagging light and power
Ardent keepsakes of her strength
She burns with a sentinel's bright flame against the shadows

Part I. Language: Its Diversity, its Study, and our Understandings of it

The fewer speakers a language has, the more necessary it is for the children to become high-level multilinguals, in order to be able to obtain the basic necessities needed for survival. The mother tongue is needed for psychological, cognitive, and spiritual survival - cultural rights. All the other languages, including an official language of the state in which the children live, are needed for social, economic, political, and civil rights. A child must be able to speak to parents, family, and relatives, to know who she is, to acquire skills in thinking, analyzing, and evaluating. The mother tongue(s) is (are) vital for this. Further education, job prospects, and the ability to participate in the wider society require other languages. Thus high levels of multilingualism must be one of the goals of proper education.

Everybody, not just privileged elites or poor minorities, needs to be fluent and literate in at least two languages, preferably more. Everybody, not just minorities, needs to become aware of and acknowledge the importance of their ethnic and linguistic roots, in order to be able to develop, analyze, criticize, and reflect. Language rights for all are part of human rights. Language rights are prerequisite to many other human rights. Linguistic human rights in education are a prerequisite for the maintenance of the diversity in the world that we are all responsible for.

Tove Skutnabb-Kangas, 1999b, 58.

Such a Treasure of Knowledge for Human Survival

Kerttu Vuolab

Mother tongue - a treasure of knowledge

All children have a mother tongue. We human beings started to learn our mother tongue before we were born. The mother tongue is a chain that binds us to our own history. Each one of us is a ring in the chain of generations, a ring in our own mother tongue. If any ring grows weak, the whole chain will be weak. Every generation has to make sure that their ring is strong enough to add the next ring onto the chain. Our personal duty is to transfer the mother tongue to the next generation. By passing on our language, the mother tongue, to the next generation, we ourselves guarantee that life itself will continue into the future.

We would all like to live forever. By having children we make sure that our own life continues in them. I have no children, or else all the children in the world are mine. My life does not continue in my own children, but I write books. My life continues in my books, which is a very selfish reason for being an author. If I wished to be a mother to a daughter or a son, that would be as selfish a way to continue my own life in the future.

A language, a mother tongue, is the most valuable inheritance of human beings. Without it every generation would be forced to experience and discover how to protect itself against frost, storm, wind, snow, rain, sunshine and all the other life-threatening things in the world. Our imagination would not produce such an endless capacity for creating new ideas if we human beings had no language, no mother tongue. Without it a human being would not be able to explain or teach any idea or technique to the next generation. Without a human language no technical wonders would exist.

My mother tongue is the Sámi language. I call my mother tongue the Sámi language, because the words Lapp and Lappish do not respect our language on an equal level with other languages. My mother tongue Sámi is neither a poor nor a primitive language! No language in the world is poor or primitive. Every language is rich in some way or other. Sámi is a rich language: for instance it describes nature and the weather accurately and beautifully. It has almost 200 words for 'snow'. Every word explains the condition of snow: Is one able to ski on it? What temperature is it? Can it take the weight of walking on it? Is it going to change in the immediate future and in what way? All words in every language are prescriptions for human survival.

A language - a prescription for survival

If any language in the world dies, with it disappears great human wisdom, the experience of life over thousands of years. With a language disappears a treasure of knowledge that could save human life from the danger of destruction. The conditions for life are becoming progressively worse. Life on planet Earth cannot afford to lose any human language. Because knowledge for human survival is needed more than ever in the history of the Earth and life on it.

Human beings all over the world have passed survival knowledge on to the next generation by telling stories, singing songs (yoiking in our case[1]), reading poems, playing with words, chatting and telling jokes to each other. Every mother talks to her child with love and she hopes that life will continue in her child. All mother tongues are the unwritten history of human life. This history respects love, peace and life. You don't have to read much to realize what written history respects: money, war and killing, death.

Numbers have made people blind to understanding the value of things, especially in administration and government. Nothing seems to have a value before it has been measured or had a price put on it so as to gauge its meaning and importance. A language seems to have enough value when more than five hundred million people speak it. Big numbers have made the politicians and bureaucrats blind, they see the value of a language in terms of numbers. That is probably the reason why they do not respect minority languages. Small languages don't count for them. That is why most minority languages are in danger of being killed. The governments that respect only the major languages in their countries call to mind a herring: everyone is swimming in the same direction and nobody asks: 'Where are we going? What is threatening us?'

When I hear of 'minority languages', 'lesser known languages', or 'small languages' I am reminded of a fox cub. She is on her own, without a pack to protect her life. The fox cub must watch out and listen, be fully aware of any danger that could threaten her life. To stay alive the fox cub must be ready at all times to hide, run away, and take note of the other living creatures in the forest. A fox cub is a very alert living creature, eyes that see, ears that hear, with a sensibility for noticing what happens all around. With the wisdom of a fox cub the governments in the

---

[1] On yoiks and yoiking, see Gaski, this volume.

world could stop the destruction of nature. People should appreciate that there is real value in being alive, and their duty is to make sure that life continues.

Literature - the daughter of the mother tongue

Very often people think that we Sámi had no literature before books were written and published in Sámi. In fact we have a very rich oral literary tradition. Although I did not have books when I was a child, I had my stories, poems, jokes, fairy tales, myths, yoiks, legends. They were my books, and not only books, but also theatre. My libraries were my family, my home, and nature around the area of my home.

When I was a child, story-telling was not a separate ceremony like the evening stories on TV these days. When I was a child, stories for me were duty, hobby and fun, explainer, company and comforter. My family, especially my grandfather and my mother, told us stories from morning to evening, while they were doing their everyday work.

My literary events took place in our cowshed as we were milking cows. Or on the hill as we were walking to pick cloudberries. Or they happened in the middle of slaughtering. I remember one day my grandfather came home with a reindeer that was no longer alive but had yet to be skinned and have its horns removed. My grandfather was obliged to go back up the hill, because the reindeer had been penned into an enclosure. While my mother was skinning the reindeer she told us children the following story:

> A long time ago some animals in a forest
> decided to have a competition. There was a mouse,
> a wolf, a bear and a frog. The mouse,
> the wolf and the bear, each of them had a
> crossbow. But the frog had nothing, only her
> tongue. The first one to kill a reindeer
> wins. That was the competition.
> The mouse was the first to shoot at a
> reindeer. It took its bow and arrow and shot.
> But the mouse lives too near the ground, so
> the arrow didn't fly higher than the hooves of
> a reindeer. The arrow of the mouse did not kill
> the reindeer.

My mother was skinning the reindeer's legs and showed us that between the hooves there is a gland. The mouse's arrow.

> The wolf was a good runner, he fired a shot
> while a reindeer was running away from him.

The wolf's arrow flew to the rump of
the reindeer. It did not die.

My mother separated out the pieces of the reindeer's haunch. The arrow flew into
the muscles and formed them into a knot. The wolf's arrow.

The bear was a big animal. He was not afraid
to face a reindeer and shoot it. The arrow
flew to the middle of a reindeer's forehead,
but the reindeer did not die.

My mother was skinning the reindeer's head and showed us that there is a
depression in the bone of the forehead. The bear's arrow.

The frog was sitting alongside and asked:
'Can I try to catch a reindeer?'
The others burst out laughing:
'You don't even have an arrow or a bow!'
The frog just sat there. Suddenly her tongue
flew out of her mouth and the reindeer was
dead.

My mother cut the reindeer's heart in two and showed us that in the middle of a
reindeer's heart there is a little bone or knot of tendons. The frog's arrow.

Nature and life itself are illustrated in oral literature. We were able to see what
was portrayed, to hear it, to smell it, and to feel it. We experienced what was
illustrated in our own lives. The oral tradition explained nature and life to us.
Through stories we became familiar with animals, birds, fishes, flowers, trees,
insects, sunshine, rain, wind, snow, rivers, lakes, the ocean. Listening to the oral
stories we learned how we belong to nature as part of it. Oral literature taught us
human beings to respect nature, and then nature gives us security.

People have often asked me: 'Why do you bother to write in your own mother
tongue? There are so few people to buy your books - such a little language with
under 100,000 people who speak it.' My duty is to cultivate my own mother
tongue. I have to play my part so as to ensure that my ring in the chain of the Sámi
language is strong enough to add on the next generation's ring in the future. I have
to work for my mother tongue, because life on Earth cannot afford to lose my
mother tongue, such a treasure of knowledge for human survival.

In my young days people used to command us not to speak or use my mother
tongue, the Sámi language: We were told we would not even get as far as the
nearest airport, in Lakselv, if we used our native language. Now I can inform
people who hesitate to use their own mother tongue: the struggle is really
worthwhile. You can get to the other side of the Earth by being yourself. If it had
not been for me speaking and writing in my own native language, I would not be
traveling round the world speaking of the importance of the mother tongue.

Linguistic and Biological Diversity: The Inextricable Link

Luisa Maffi

> Culture and language are intrinsically connected to land and territory, and cultural and linguistic diversity are inextricably linked to biological diversity.
> Preamble, Code of Ethics of the International Society of Ethnobiology, adopted 28 November 1998

Still not too long ago, a statement such as the one above might have raised more than a few eyebrows. Uncomfortable echoes of discredited theories of geographical and biological determinism, romantic nationalism, and the like might have resonated in people's minds. Not so today. Today, as we step into the new millennium, it is becoming increasingly clear that all forms of the diversity of life on Earth - linguistic, cultural, and biological - are intrinsically related and interconnected, and that they share a common fate (Maffi, 1998, Maffi, ed., in press, Posey, 1999).

That the current rampant loss of biological diversity is having a profound negative impact on the viability of the human species (as well as of other species and entire ecosystems) has been apparent for several decades now; and so has the role of human agency in precipitating this loss. What has only more recently come to the fore is that the concurrent ongoing loss of linguistic and cultural diversity on the planet is largely due to the same global economic, political, and social factors that are affecting biodiversity, and that these two 'extinction crises' are convergent (Harmon, 1996a, b), one reinforcing and being reinforced by the other. It is also beginning to be recognized that, conversely, the persistence of vigorous, thriving linguistic and cultural diversity around the world may afford us our best chance of countering biodiversity loss and keeping the planet alive and healthy (Maffi, 1998).

This greater awareness is reflected not only in a growing number of researchers, practitioners, and activists embracing the new 'biocultural' approach, but also in the burgeoning attention now devoted to this perspective by international organizations, NGOs, and a host of other private and public institutions. The concept of biocultural diversity is becoming increasingly familiar in environmental conservation circles internationally, especially since the Convention on Biological Diversity (CBD) - elaborated after the 1992 Rio Summit (UN Conference on Environment and Development) - specifically acknowledged the role (and mandated the respect, protection, and promotion) of the 'knowledge, innovations and practices of indigenous and local communities embodying traditional lifestyles' for the conservation and sustainable use of biological diversity (Art. 8j). United Nations agencies such as UNESCO and UNEP are providing fora for advocates of this integrated approach (e.g., Maffi, 1998, Posey 1999, Maffi, Skutnabb-Kangas & Andrianarivo, 1999). Biodiversity conservation organizations are increasingly shifting their focus from the protection of individual species toward that of entire ecosystems and species interactions - as well as toward recognition of local communities, especially indigenous and other traditional peoples, as important agents and partners in conservation work (e.g., a current World Wildlife Fund, WWF, project involving the identification of the indigenous peoples living in the ecoregions designated by WWF as priorities for conservation, so as to highlight the value of these peoples' traditional ecological knowledge for conservation efforts, and thus the importance of sustaining their cultural traditions). Indigenous peoples and local communities themselves can only draw strength from the spreading of a perspective that affirms the interdependence of linguistic, cultural, and biological diversity (Maffi, ed., in press) - an interdependence long embodied in their world views and ways of life. Thus, they themselves have vigorously taken up the promotion of this perspective and the defense of their related rights at the international level (such as in the sessions of the UN Working Group on Indigenous Populations and at the Conference of the Parties to the CBD).

Observing these developments is a source of some personal satisfaction. When, in July 1995, at a Symposium on Language Loss and Public Policy held at the University of New Mexico in Albuquerque, a group of colleagues and myself began discussing the prospects for preservation of the world's linguistic diversity, and found ourselves in agreement on the need to stress not only the links between linguistic and cultural diversity, but also the connections with biodiversity, we felt that we were venturing into largely uncharted territory. Linking language and the environment in this way still seemed a rather quaint, if not outlandish, idea. Yet, in retrospect, it seems it was an idea whose time was ripe: that of the role of language, and of a rich diversity of languages, in sustaining a diversity of cultural traditions and behaviors, and in particular traditional ecological knowledge and practices, this in turn helping sustain biodiversity. From then on, it was a 'snowball effect'. About a year later, an international NGO, *Terralingua: Partnerships for Linguistic and Biological Diversity*, founded by participants in that informal discussion, was moving its first official steps, proclaiming as its goals:

- supporting the perpetuation and continued development of the world's linguistic diversity, and
- exploring the connections between linguistic, cultural and biological diversity

through a program of research, information, applied work and advocacy, and affirming as its basic principles:

1. That the diversity of languages and their variant forms is a vital part of the world's cultural diversity;
2. That biological diversity and cultural diversity (of which linguistic diversity is a major component) are not only related, but often inseparable, perhaps causally connected through coevolution;
3. That, like biological diversity, linguistic diversity (represented mostly by indigenous languages) is facing rapidly increasing threats that are causing a drastic loss of both languages and the knowledge of which they are carriers, including knowledge about the environment and sustainable resource use;
4. That the continued loss of linguistic, cultural and biological diversity will have dangerous consequences for humans and the Earth; and
5. That, therefore, the fate of the lands, languages and cultures of indigenous peoples is decisive for the maintenance of biodiversity and linguistic and cultural diversity.

Given these goals and principles, it quickly became clear to us that a major arena for our activities would be that of linguistic human rights. No sooner did we realize that we collectively lacked expertise in this domain than the name of Tove Skutnabb-Kangas came to mind. Tove responded to our appeal with what we would come to recognize as her trademark: enthusiasm. First cemented by a joint effort on a major piece of writing (Maffi, Skutnabb-Kangas & Andrianarivo, 1999), Tove's collaboration with Terralingua then led to her being voted our Vice-President in 1997. Her leadership in matters of linguistic human rights, as well as of language in education, has been central to Terralingua's ability to intervene with competence and effectiveness in these domains.

From the very beginning, Terralingua (TL) has been international and ethnically diverse, as well as interdisciplinary, in its (all volunteer) Board of Directors and staff, Advisory Panel, and membership at large. Its activities (so far based on volunteer work and a very small budget from membership dues) span all continents. TL is conceived as both a membership and a partnership organization. Members are those committed to supporting the aims and activities of TL (by contribution of money and/or effort). Members receive our quarterly newsletter and have the right to vote in the election of TL officers. Partners include like-minded individuals and organizations that choose to work with TL and its members on projects of common interest and mutual benefit, on the basis of an equitable agreement. TL already has several such partnerships with local, national, and international organizations throughout the world, and more are being sought. Additional members and volunteers to work with TL are also always welcome.

TL research has shown strong correlations between areas of biological megadiversity and areas of highest linguistic diversity, represented mostly by indigenous languages (Harmon, 1996a, b), suggesting that the cultural and biological manifestations of the diversity of life on Earth are mutually supportive, perhaps coevolved (Maffi 1998a, b). Research activities have included the organization of the international working conference 'Endangered Languages, Endangered Knowledge, Endangered Environments' (Berkeley, California, 25-27 October 1996), which sparked much of the current attention to the role of language in biocultural diversity conservation (see Maffi, ed., in press). We are currently collaborating with WWF on the indigenous peoples and conservation project described above. Collaboration is under discussion with the Smithsonian Institution concerning an initiative aimed at the integrated study of linguistic, cultural, and biological diversity.

Information services are provided via TL's web site and our electronic newsletter, *Langscape*, organizations of and participation in conferences and symposia, consulting, and interaction with a growing network of members and other correspondents. This includes putting members of indigenous/minority communities interested in language, culture, and environmental preservation in touch with like-minded organizations and/or scientists/professionals.

Advocacy activities include letter-writing in defense of indigenous and minority peoples' linguistic human rights and the right to linguistic self-determination. An official TL document on *Indigenous Peoples: Education and Language* (bearing the mark of Tove's expertise) was submitted to the UN Center for Human Rights' Working Group on Indigenous Populations (WGIP), on the occasion of the 16th annual session of WGIP, held in Geneva in July 1998. (Now officially available as UN document E/CN.4/Sub.2/AC.4/1998/2.) Also in July 1998, TL participated in the first Roundtable on Intellectual Property and Indigenous Peoples, organized by the UN World Intellectual Property Organization (WIPO) in Geneva, to advocate for protection of indigenous languages and traditional knowledge in the context of protection of indigenous peoples' cultural heritage. In addition, through Tove's involvement in the Scientific Council in charge of advising UNESCO on revision of the Draft Universal Declaration on Linguistic Rights, we can hope to influence the processes surrounding the first international instrument entirely devoted to linguistic rights. Also significant has been Terralingua's involvement in activities related to the processes concerned with the implementation of the Convention on Biological Diversity (CBD) such as, again in 1998, the Workshop 'The Interrelationships Between Cultural and Biological Diversity' at the Forum 'Biodiversity: Treasures of the World's Forests' in Germany. A final statement containing a clear reference to the need to protect linguistic and cultural diversity along with biodiversity was handed over to the Chair of the Subsidiary Body for Scientific, Technical and Technological Advice (SBSTTA) to the CBD.

TL applied work is currently being developed, including the organization of community workshops and seminars. The first of these, titled 'Supporting cultural and environmental diversity through indigenous language development and protection of linguistic human rights', was held at a Maaori Wananga (Center for Higher Learning) in Aotearoa/New Zealand, on the occasion of the 6th International Congress of Ethnobiology in November 1998.

In just a few years, and with virtually no other means than our brains, we feel we have come a long way already in furthering the cause of linguistic diversity and linguistic human rights. In this, we are sustained by our belief that linguistic diversity is one of humanity's most precious treasures, and that each and every one of the world's 6,000 to 7,000 extant spoken languages, no matter how small, contributes uniquely to this wealth. We also strongly believe that for each linguistic group and each individual on Earth the native language(s) is (are) a key element of their identity, dignity, cohesiveness, and well-being, the main carrier(s) of culture, knowledge, beliefs and practices, and that working to foster appreciation and support for linguistic and cultural diversity and respect for linguistic rights worldwide is one of the very foundations for equal and peaceful dialogue among groups and individuals.

We also feel we have made remarkable progress in promoting understanding of the connections between linguistic, cultural and biological diversity, and in suggesting that the cultural and biological manifestations of the diversity of life on Earth are mutually supportive and warrant integrated protection. Our work has helped elucidate the 'inextricable link', both material and spiritual, that indigenous and other local peoples who still live in close contact with, and vital dependence on, the local ecosystems, maintain between their languages (and the cultural knowledge these carry) and their lands and biodiversity - a link that traditionally fosters respect for and sustainable use of the natural world.

Yet, we continue to witness case after case of hostility and conflict in which linguistic and other cultural differences are seized upon as cover-ups for struggles over economic and political power, and/or in which linguistic human rights are curtailed or denied under the pretext of fostering national unity. Likewise, over and over again we continue to witness the disruption and ultimate breakdown of balanced, perhaps coevolved human relationships with the environment, whenever assimilation of indigenous and other local peoples by majority groups occurs, inducing language shift and loss of traditional ways of life and means of subsistence, and again often producing tension and conflict. As indigenous and local peoples lose a central element of their linguistic and cultural integrity and of their very livelihood, the world at large loses the many lessons it could draw from the solutions these peoples have devised for living mindfully and sustainably on Earth.

As we continue to work for the perpetuation of cultural, linguistic, and biological diversity, we must be constantly aware of these persisting challenges. And this is why research, applied work, and advocacy must go hand in hand today. This is not to say that basic research is no longer needed; it is to say, however, that it can no longer proceed in a vacuum, and that scholars need to educate themselves and others as to the nature and implications of what they do, and as to the broader social, political, and economic context in which they operate. It also means that scholars must become much better at listening to what indigenous and other local peoples around the world have to say about what they want and need, and be more prepared to ask if and how they may be of service.

Ecological economist Richard Norgaard has spoken of the 'NGOization' of the world, with NGOs moving in new directions and forging new alliances to respond to problems created by the institutions of modernity and that modernity itself is unable to solve. In retrospect, it is clear that my colleagues and I were unknowingly following this trend when we created Terralingua to promote an integrated perspective on linguistic, cultural, and biological diversity. It is also clear that, in advocating for the alliance of science and action, we are motivated by the conviction that, as anthropologist James Peacock puts it (letter to *Anthropology Newsletter*, October 1998, Correspondence section, p. 2):

> The division between knowledge and conveying or applying it is artificial; seminal knowledge is created through engagement with issues in the world and without such engagement at key junctures a discipline becomes inward-looking and archaic.

For additional information about Terralingua, write to:
Terralingua: Partnerships for Linguistic and Biological Diversity
P.O. Box 122
Hancock, MI 49930-0122, U.S.A.
Email: dharmon@georgewright.org

or visit the Terralingua web site at:
http://cougar.ucdavis.edu/nas/terralin/home.html

Rethinking Language Defense

Joshua A. Fishman and Gella Schweid Fishman

There are those who believe that all of sociolinguistics is 'applied linguistics'. Because of our own agreement with Kurt Lewin's dictum that 'Nothing is as theoretically promising as a good application', the above-mentioned belief does not worry us. Nevertheless, we do consider it to be a mistaken view, if only because it leaves out a necessarily corresponding recognition that any good application must be grounded in a good theory. Indeed, our major regret is that there is still relatively little sociolinguistics to apply[1]. Tove Skutnabb-Kangas is doubtlessly among the most outstanding 'applied sociolinguists' of our generation (see, e.g., her 1994 volume with Robert Phillipson). Her interest in fostering more mutually rewarding and stronger models of bilingual education and of defending the contextually weakest languages contributes tellingly to the foundations of theoretically informed language defense efforts.

Language defense

'Language defense' is a possible focus within both the status planning and the corpus planning halves of any all-encompassing language planning enterprise pertaining to contextually weaker or threatened languages. In line with Skutnabb-Kangas' interests, we will largely restrict ourselves here to status planning related types of language defense. Various types of language defense activities have been reported in the status planning literature by a large number of investigators. Along more global lines, the recent works of Fishman (1991 and 1997) have sought to derive more general principles of language defense from a multitude of cases throughout the world and even throughout history. Individual country or regional

---

[1] This is a paraphrase of Wilhelm Wundt's view, a century ago, that 'there is nothing wrong with applied psychology, except that there is really very little psychology to apply'. A century later, applied psychology may well have become the tail that wags the dog.

cases of language defense have recently been provided by Hamel (1997), Schiffman (1996) and Topolinska (1998). A careful review of the above and of a multitude of other studies which space limitations do not permit us to cite here, discloses that although they all devote attention to one type or another of language defense, these types differ quite substantially and should not lightly be lumped together. A systematization of the types of language defense might serve to bring some sort of order out of the hidden chaos of classifying disparate phenomena under one and the same label.

Permissive language defense

The most modest and elementary type of language defense is to seek or foster a 'permissive' stance on the part of the majority authorities. Such a stance does not obligate the authorities to overtly or constructively do anything on behalf of disadvantaged languages, but, rather, to abstain from particular types of oppositional or deleterious actions with respect to such (or any other) languages. The 'freedom of speech' provision in the Bill of Rights amendments to the American Constitution does not assist those who would like to foster non-English language use in the USA, but, on the other hand, it does prohibit the most obvious legislation against such use. Permissive minority language defense legislation would not render the English Only movement inoperative in the USA nor would it necessarily prohibit declaring English to be the only language of government. Such legislation would not even require suspending limitations in France on the assignment of minority ethnocultural names to newly born. Such restrictions now deny parents of newborn children in Brittany, Occitan, Alsace-Lorraine and the Basque Provinces the right to give their offspring names that are ethnoculturally specific (and, therefore, 'non-French'), even though freedom of speech is assured and a name 'speaks volumes'.

Note, however, that even the *Meyer v. Nebraska* decision of the U.S. Supreme Court (1922) which invalidated Nebraska's prohibition of using any modern spoken language as a medium for teaching children below the age of 12 (and has, therefore, been called the 'Magna Carta for the private nationality school [in the USA]' (Kloss, 1977, 73), neither the Court ruling nor that precedent led to any requirement or explicit encouragement vis-a-vis government support of any such medium for instructional purposes. Actually, such permissiveness is merely a hands-off policy and, therefore, it leaves functionally and contextually disadvantaged languages just as disadvantaged as they were before. These languages remain exposed to the Darwinian law of the linguistic jungle: the strong survive and the weak die off.

Basically, permissive rulings and legislation are largely symbolic gestures. They imply more than they deliver. At best, they prepare the ground for future support but in and of themselves they do not provide such support. Disadvantaged languages have been trifled with too long and they are not sufficiently robust to be trifled with further, particularly because time is of the essence where they are concerned. Most other matters that are assumed to require immediate attention are not merely given permissive nods. If education is assumed to be important, laws are passed requiring it, supporting it, fostering it. If language defense (and, therefore, a more multilingual/multicultural society and polity) is really considered to be in the public interest (rather than merely a private hobby or even a private passion), then it too cannot merely be permissively tolerated. A permissive policy alone even falls short of a symbolic treatment (see below) and, as such, it does not even begin to rise to the level of either active or preventive language defense.

Active language defense

Active language defense attempts to be therapeutic vis-à-vis disadvantaged languages. It is undertaken when danger is not only recognized but when ameliorative steps are implemented in order to counteract language endangerment. If we were to follow a medical metaphor, we might say that active language defense treats the patient in order to overcome whatever illness has been ascertained. But therapy is never as optimal an approach as the prevention of illness to begin with. To make matters even worse, most of the active language defense on record is more symbolic than substantive. Aggrieved language communities are soothed by having their languages declared 'co-official'. Activists for endangered languages are mollified by putting their languages on official letterheads or by having a song of theirs sung on an important public occasion. Even if such public occasions are frequent (like the daily opening of the school-day), such remedial steps are not only frequently too late but also commonly too little (as in the case of transitional bilingual education involving recessive languages). Effective language defense requires more than window dressing. Symbolic decorations are not what either daily life or language life are all about, not even for the healthy, let alone for those who are in ill health. In the absence of serious empirical supervision, experimentation, evaluation and follow-up relative to defined criterial achievements, it is very likely that even so-called 'action research' will be only symbolic rather than curative. Research may be informative, but by itself it is not curative. Many a sick language has been (and is still being) researched to death. An honorable burial is not effective language defense. An effective theory of remedial language defense requires a theory that fits all ameliorations to the nature and state of the debilitation. Subsidizing an adult film in a particular threatened language may be totally ineffective in terms of effective assistance to a language in which there is an inadequate and increasingly diminishing rate of intergenerational transmission. Unless very carefully channeled in concert with community language efforts, subsidizing concerts, plays, parades, and celebrations may merely foster symbolic recognition rather than overt language use among children or young adults of child-bearing age.

Preventive ('proactive') defense of threatened languages

The most effective assurance of continued physical health is preventive medicine. Similarly, demographically and functionally minoritized languages require preventive defenses well in advance of reaching any stage of definite difficulty. This view is recognized constitutionally in Belgium, where, in small pockets assigned to one or another of the two stronger languages, yet another one (German) is nevertheless recognized as meriting particular protection. Proactive language defense requires constant evaluation to catch possible difficulties before they reach the explosive, contagion or threatening stage. The 'sign inspectors' of the 'Office de la Langue Française' in Quebec might, most charitably, be said to be engaged in pro-active language defense efforts in a province in which 90-some percent of the population is francophone. In fact, the entire francophone movement in Quebec is proactive in the sense of being on behalf of a dominant language. Under such circumstances, there is little wonder that the efforts of this movement are considered by Anglophones to be anti-English rather than just pro-French.

A more balanced situation obtains in Barcelona and throughout much of Catalunya. There, the speakers of Castilian and the speakers of Catalan are quite evenly balanced in numbers. However, with respect to local functions, explicit financial and legal support is offered only to Catalan. Castilian speakers can request government forms and services (as well as attention to their personal needs in shops and in banks) in Castilian. Their individual rights to such services are constitutionally protected but they have no group rights (e.g., to government schools in Castilian) in this connection. Some have predicted that in the absence of continued immigration of Castilian speakers, the future of the national language (Castilian) is endangered in Catalunya. If it were suggested that pro-active steps be taken in defense of Castilian, Catalans are likely to reply that taking into consideration the national scene as a whole, it is Catalan and not Castilian that requires pro-active defense in Catalunya. Castilian speakers, however, answer that their linguistic future in Catalunya depends not on the national status but on the local status of their language. Thus, once again, pro-active defense appears to be problem causing in addition to (or rather than only) problem solving.

Another context in which pro-active language defense might be considered is that of the Italian cantons of Switzerland. Romansh, of course, is receiving supportive attention (without which some have speculated that it would soon cease to exist entirely), but Italian too is being spoken by fewer and fewer individuals in the officially Italian cantons. The economically stronger German and French cantons regularly attract thousands of Italian-speaking Swiss to leave the Italian cantons and to resettle in the French or German areas. In order to stem this outflow, which, due to Switzerland's long established 'territorial principle' invariably leads to the translinguification of the children of the outmigrants, would it not be a desirable pro-active defense to foster economic growth in the Italian cantons, thereby keeping more Italian speakers at home? Would such support be seen as unfair economic competition in the German or French cantons? Perhaps so, but *their* languages are growing all of the time and various governmentally sponsored 'focused economic encouragement' efforts have traditionally been undertaken throughout Switzerland, so why not do so in this pro-active linguistic context as well?

Given the possibly conflicted nature of proactive language defenses, they probably always require careful independent monitoring. But perhaps it is better to struggle with the problems such defenses may bring in their wake, than to constantly be pursuing reactive (restorative) defenses only after the horse is already out of the barn and matters are already at a 'last gasp' stage. Cases of long-term successful defense of threatened languages are few and far between and it is time to run the risk of erring on the side of caution (i.e., of somewhat burdening the strong rather than the weak), so as not to suffer further attrition in the ethnocultural and ethnolinguistic arena. That is done whenever any issue is considered to be a valued part of the national bookkeeping. We pave new roads for those that need them, not those that already have them. Much of social policy is not only protective but proactive and it is high time that defense efforts on behalf of threatened languages, *if they are seriously intended*, adopted this approach as well. This is what Tove has been saying for years to all who would but listen.

Maintaining, Developing and Sharing the Knowledge and Potential Embedded in All Our Languages and Cultures: On linguists as Agents of Epistemic Violence

Jan Branson and Don Miller

> When global control to an increasing degree happens via language, instead of more brutal means (despite some of the signs of the opposite today), the relativity which comes with the multihorizons of multilingual and multicultural awareness must be enhanced on a global scale too, if our planet and our humanity are to have a chance of survival. It is not only biodiversity which is a necessity for the planet. *Maintaining, developing and sharing the knowledge and potential embedded in all our languages and cultures*, supporting linguistic and cultural human diversity, is at least equally important for our survival as a species on this planet. (Skutnabb-Kangas, 1995, 17-18; emphasis added)

It was in the grey vastness of the Stockholm Town Hall, where Nobel laureates, though not those of peace, are honoured, that the small lady in blue with the twinkling eyes and rosy cheeks framed by golden curls entered our lives. This paper is a personal tribute. Many years ago E. M. Forster wrote: 'Two cheers for Democracy: one because it admits variety and two because it admits criticism. Two cheers are quite enough: there is no occasion to give three. Only Love the Beloved Republic deserves that' (Forster, 1965, 78). To be with Tove is to inhabit for a short while that 'beloved republic' where variety defines the richness of humanity, where criticism is the path to understanding, and where all is encompassed by a genuine love for her fellow beings, human and otherwise.

Like Marx, Tove is not interested simply in understanding the world but with changing it. In the process she demonstrates the vital links between language and education, language and society, language and culture, and language and politics. Her linguistics is of necessity sociolinguistics, her linguistic analysis never divorced from the politically charged environments in which language is used. Tove feels passionately about language and sees language, written, spoken or signed, as a living and vital part of each human being's identity and dignity. Linguistic diversity, linguistic equality, and multilingualism are for Tove the keys to peace in a world which must above all recognize linguistic rights as lying at the core of the achievement of human rights. Above all is the demand for the recognition of and respect for linguistic and cultural difference. Here we explore the parameters of those differences in a discussion of the epistemological differences that lie at the heart of linguistic difference.

Throughout our association with sign language linguistics, we have been particularly concerned with the intensely imperialist tendencies that dominate Western linguistic analyses of sign languages as they reshape the languages they study to fit their theories, their models of language, via their distinctly Western and inevitably imperialistic epistemologies (see Branson & Miller, 1992). From the late 1950s, a few, very few, linguists fought for the recognition, not only by governments but above all by their fellow linguists, of ways of communicating through signing as 'sign languages'. They stressed that these forms of communication were not simply mime or gesture creatively and momentarily used to deal with specific situations, but regular, structured ways of communicating, lexically and syntactically coherent. Above all they were at pains to stress that the signs used were not idiosyncratic mimicry, but arbitrary signs in the Saussurian sense. This was the ultimate test of linguistic coherence. These were languages, fully-fledged languages. 'Word order' became a central issue. What was stressed were the qualities shared by spoken and signed languages, not their differences. Dictionaries and grammars were developed and formal instruction in sign languages encouraged. But the sign languages were being formalised and moulded to satisfy linguistic criteria. Legitimate status was being bestowed on the 'colonised', on these linguistic minorities, via a linguistic legitimacy achieved through the transformation of their languages to fit the dominant linguistic moulds, through a form of 'epistemic violence', that unrecognised symbolic violence that 'effaces the subject ...' (Spivak, 1987), 'insidiously objectifying' the 'colonized' through a conceptual apparatus which robs people and their languages of their individual and cultural integrity, devaluing and distorting their differences (Branson & Miller, 1992, 1993).

But little note has been taken of these epistemological issues, essentially because the sign languages being analysed have on the whole been sign languages in use among urban Western communities, associated in the main with conventions developed and transmitted through deaf schools and urban deaf societies and clubs. Many of those using the sign languages in question are bilinguals in a sign language and the dominant spoken/written language. The impact of the written language through fingerspelling and initialisation, through the presence and imposition of manually coded forms of the dominant written languages, and through familiarity by signers with the formalised grammatical conventions of written language, were and remain strong. In addition, the sign languages studied operate in large scale societies in which language is geared to the management of communication with unknown 'faceless' individuals about often abstract rather than known and concrete situations and things, situations which demand the arbitrariness of the sign and the formalisation of linguistic conventions. The epistemic violence has been extremely subtle. Above all, the sign languages were studied by Western linguists who, in collaboration with Deaf communities, were intent on ensuring the unqualified acceptance of sign languages as languages.

What is the potential impact on the people we study, on their languages and cultures, of our own presence among these communities and of the epistemological and cosmological traditions through which we seek to document and analyse? If human rights involve above all the right to be different, what impact is linguistic analysis having on the human rights of those studied? Are we blocking access to 'the knowledge and potential embedded in all languages and cultures'? What brings these issues to the fore more forcefully than before is the small-scale but increasing engagement of sign linguists, including ourselves, with sign languages in non-Western societies, where the imperial implications are more overt and evident.

While most if not all academics will acknowledge the fact that cultural differences exist, that people from different cultures view the world and their place in it differently, Western academics have often seen their discipline-based activities as neither culturally determined nor culturally specific. The categories and models they bring to both the data collection and analytical processes are regarded as scientific and beyond culture. Pierre Bourdieu clarifies this acultural mode of analysis in relation to current Western linguistics:

> The entire destiny of modern linguistics is in fact determined by Saussure's inaugural act through which he separates the 'external' elements of linguistics from the 'internal' elements, and, by reserving the title of linguistics for the latter, excludes from it all the investigations which establish a relationship between language and anthropology, the political history of those who speak it, or even the geography of the domain where it is spoken, because all of these things add nothing to a knowledge of the language taken in itself. (Bourdieu, 1991, 33).

Language is culture, a product and manifestation of culture, but via Saussure is seen as separated from its cultural context to become an object in itself, to be examined as though it existed apart from its realisation in cultural practice.

If linguistics is as much a cultural construct as any other aspect of culture – kinship, religion, politics – then:

- Is its view of language tied to a distinctly Western cosmology?
- And if so, why should it apply unproblematically to languages in other cultures, including the sub-cultures of our own societies?
- Can linguists engage in the formal linguistic analysis of any language?
- Is such an aspiration, or assumption, necessary in the first place?
- Why do many linguists assume that they can engage unproblematically in the formal linguistic analysis of any and every language?
- What is the rationale for doing so?
- If such a process is assumed necessary for effective comparative analysis, then why must comparative analysis be acultural?

Linguists construct 'language' and its building blocks - morphemes, phonemes, nouns, and verbs, words and clauses, classifiers and signifiers. The assumed arbitrariness of the sign ensures the assumed viability of studying language 'in itself'.

Our work on the initial linguistic analysis of the sign language used in a village and its region in north Bali in Indonesia, a language referred to as Kata Kolok, seriously questions these linguistic assumptions. The linguistic ecology of the area is complex, especially with regard to the impact of the national language Indonesian (see Branson & Miller, 1998 and Branson, Miller, & Marsaja, 1999), but the distinctly Balinese cosmology and associated epistemology is one in which the link between on the one hand words, spoken or written, or concepts signed, and on the other the things they represent, cannot be conceived of as arbitrary. In many cases the utterance, the signing, or the written word is conceived of as powerful and often dangerous because of its explicit and inseparable relationship to the concepts expressed. Language cannot be conceived of 'in itself'. As Heryanto has pointed out, the concept of 'language' itself, and the identification of the word 'bahasa', an Indonesian word, with the abstract and generic concept of 'language', is not only a recent and distinctly Western import, or rather imposition, but is also integrally associated with the introduction of Bahasa Indonesia. Prior to its introduction, the term 'bahasa' referred more to the idea of 'culture', to an integral part of a person's identity. 'Language' did not exist. These were 'language-free communities' (Heryanto, 1995, 28ff)[1].

Our initial analysis of the Kata Kolok reveals integral links between the use of objects and their representation in sign language, especially in relation to traditional aspects of village life associated with agriculture, home life and ritual. Indeed what emerges is that there are, as is the case in spoken Balinese, no identifiable abstract signs for many objects, in fact in the case of the Kata Kolok, no sign for the 'noun' independent of its use or context. In addition, the equivalent of 'word' order is very free and there is in many cases no identifiable subject, verb or object. We require the use of nouns and verbs etc. in translating into English but this does not mean that they are present/required in the original.

The Kata Kolok, like most non-literate languages, is a language used in face to face situations among an active and known community, often within the confines of extended kinship networks and localised religious communities. The language has evolved within this communal context and has not been influenced by educational environments or written language. In such a known environment, the specific contexts within which objects feature in people's lives are experienced by all. Few clues are required. The development of abstract concepts is on the whole unnecessary. Gender-based differences in language used are also immediately understood and taken for granted. The people with whom a person communicates are known for all their idiosyncracies - personal, cultural, and linguistic. There are conventions associated with hand shapes which allow for a productive lexicon and a complex range of relatively frozen signs linked directly to experience where the

---

[1] The links with Mühlhäusler's treatment of the concept of linguistic ecology and with his preference for referring to 'ways of communicating' rather than 'language' are important (see Mühlhäusler, 1996).

people, animals, plants, and man-made structures – temples, houses, shrines, cow byres, etc - used in discursive processes are specifically known and named. Conventions also exist for levels of abstraction such as signs for 'man', 'woman', 'child', 'flower', 'fire', 'water', and so on. But the way these are used is very free.

How then should we approach the linguistic analysis of the Kata Kolok? Should we take note of the alternative epistemology associated with the use of Balinese languages and question if not reject, among many linguistic assumptions, the arbitrariness of the sign? To what degree has the analysis of sign languages, not to mention other minority languages, distorted those languages, moulded them to fit Western linguistic models, 'insidiously objectifying'? The process of studying and recording a language is fraught with the same problems as those faced by anthropologists studying 'other' cultures. The cosmology of the researcher, the epistemology through which they operate, and the specific paradigms of their discipline, all influence what is seen and what is recorded, let alone how it is analysed. All too often:

- We find what in Western and academic terms makes sense;
- We state that this is the case;
- We are in a dominant power situation – bestowing legitimacy;
- Our model is assumed correct;
- The model is taken on board by those studied as theirs;
- Rules become established;
- The language becomes formalised;
- The language is fundamentally transformed.

As we work for the achievement of linguistic human rights we must acknowledge that all linguistic research is potentially linguistic imperialism - imperialism via linguists and linguistics. If we are to take Tove's lead and orient our analyses primarily towards 'maintaining, developing and sharing the knowledge and potential embedded in all our languages and cultures', we must develop and share the epistemological diversity and difference integral to linguistic diversity. Linguists, and not just those on the fringes of sociolinguistics, must engage with the post-colonial critiques of Western scholarship such as those of Said, Spivak, and Trinh, among many, and recognize that linguistics is a cultural construct, that it is a way of thinking about communicative processes that is historically and culturally specific. We must not only revel in linguistic difference but cope with that difference analytically. Let us recognise the culturally specific nature of our own schemes and search for new modes of analysis that do not fit other languages into a mould but rather celebrate and build on their epistemological differences. Linguistic human rights involves not only the right to your own language but the right to conceptualize and study your own language in your own terms.

The Politics of A-political Linguistics:
Linguists and Linguicide

Amir Hassanpour

Writing in early 1999, I feel it is fairly superfluous to question the neutrality of linguistics or, even, 'exact sciences' such as physics and chemistry. However, the claim to a value-free, neutral or 'autonomous' linguistics is still a powerful one, rooted not only in the positivist-empiricist tradition but also maintained by the linguists' political and ideological preferences, the interests of the discipline, and the historical context under which this area of knowledge is (re)produced and utilized. It may be useful, therefore, to examine the ways in which linguists try to de-politicize their study of language, and, by doing so, engage in highly partisan politics.

I begin by examining a case - the linguistic study of Kurdish, a language that has been subjected to harsh measures of linguicide. The majority of linguists who have studied the language have kept silent about the deliberate killing of the 'object' of their research by the Turkish, Iranian, and Syrian states. The policy of linguicide, enshrined in the constitutions and laws of these states, has not only denied the Kurds linguistic rights but also seriously violated the academic freedom of linguists in and out of the countries where the language is spoken. An integral element of this policy has been the suppression of academic study of the language, its dialects, geography, and history. However, linguistic studies of Kurdish avoid documenting, let alone protesting, the ways in which this linguicide not only has destroyed the life of a people but also suppressed the discipline of linguistics. It is not difficult to see that this silence allows the machinery of linguicide to operate freely in its killing fields.

Ranking fortieth in the world in terms of the number of speakers (25 to 30 million), Kurdish has been forcibly divided, since 1918, among the neighbouring states of Turkey, Iran, Iraq, and Syria. It is also spoken by old and new exilic and refugee communities in Central and Western Asia, Europe, Australia and North America. Linguicide, the deliberate killing of language, has been the official policy of three states that divide Kurdish speakers - Turkey since 1925, Iran especially in 1925-1941, and Syria especially since the 1960s. Even in Iraq, where the language was tolerated as an official 'local language,' a policy of Arabization was practised as a means of containing Kurdish nationalism.

The harshest policy of linguicide in our times is probably practised in Turkey, where the entire state machinery is mobilized in order to eliminate the language in both speaking and writing. Under pressure from the European Union, which is reluctant to accept Turkey's application for full membership of the union, the Turkish government introduced, in 1991, a bill into the parliament in order to legalize the speaking of the language. Today, Kurds are legally free to speak in their native tongue in private spaces, but it would be considered a crime against the 'territorial integrity' of the state if a member of the parliament or a political party uses the language in political campaigns, or if the language is used in education or broadcasting. Turkey has also used its network of embassies in order to extend its linguicidal policy to the Kurdish immigrants and refugees in Europe and North America. Turkish embassies in Denmark and Sweden have interfered in the internal affairs of these countries by demanding that Kurdish should not be taught to immigrants and children in schools and day care centres. These practices and the policy behind them violate European and international covenants such as the *Charter of the United Nations* (1945), the *Universal Declaration of Human Rights* (1948), the *International Covenant on Civil and Political Rights* (1966), the *International Covenant on Economic, Social and Cultural Rights* (in force since 1976), the *Convention on the Rights of the Child* (1989), and the *European Charter for Regional or Minority Languages* (1995), some of which have not been signed or ratified by Turkey.

'De-politicized' descriptions of Kurdish

The two major works, in English, on Kurdish language, McCarus (1958) and MacKenzie (1961), do not refer to the suppression of the language in any of the countries where it is spoken. Both were excellent doctoral dissertations based on field work conducted in Iraq. The former is a study of the grammar of the Sorani standard in Iraq. The latter was intended to be a descriptive study of the Kurdish dialects of Iraq and Turkey. Since the Republic of Turkey does not allow linguists to conduct field research on the language, MacKenzie was denied a research permit. However, there is no information in the book about the suppression of the language in Turkey, although the author refers to the closure of the 'field' in depoliticized language that reduces it to an accident, a technical problem of communication: 'It was originally intended to spend an equal period of time in the Kurdish-speaking areas of Turkey and Iraq. In the event, permission not being forthcoming from the Turkish authorities, some ten months were spent in northern Iraq' (MacKenzie, 1961: xvii). The author notes, later, '[a]s it was found impossible to visit eastern Turkey no new material could be obtained concerning the Kurdish dialects of that area' (ibid., xxi).

A significant case of silence is the suppression of an internal study by the Turkish Army. In 1959, the Army, the U.S.A.I.D., and Georgetown University initiated a large-scale program of adult literacy training for recruits in Turkey's armed services. The rate of failure was high among non-Turkish, especially Kurdish, speakers. In order to investigate the problem, the American educationalists on the team asked for permission 'to investigate the range of Kurdish dialects at twenty training sites throughout Turkey' with the objective stated as 'the identification of major dialect types, their geographic location, and their relative proportions within the Kurdish-speaking population' (Bordie, 1978: 207). Data were collected through interviews and by mail. The latter included approximately 5000 short forms sent to teachers at the military literacy centres throughout the country. However, before the researchers were able to process all the collected data, the army confiscated the entire material. Only a few items at the home and office of one of the researchers were spared. Bordie is the only one, to my knowledge (my information derives from correspondence with one of the members of the research team, 20 March 1984), who has written about this event, although in a most ambiguous way. Referring to the 5000 short forms, he writes: 'Approximately 1500 forms were ultimately collected. Unfortunately, due to national difficulties, the remainder of the questionnaires remain unavailable' (Bordie, 1978, 209). One of the consultants on the research project, a well-known specialist in Kurdish language, has never written about the event, even in one of his published papers, which is a rather detailed survey of his career as a linguist.

Reference works are expected to provide a general picture of the structure of a language, its genealogy, number of speakers, geographical distribution, history, and status. The articles on Kurdish in *The Encyclopaedia of Islam* (MacKenzie, 1986) and the *Compendium of the World's Languages* (Campbell, 1991) make no mention of the violence against the language. The article in *The Encyclopedia of Language and Linguistics*, notes that the 'Republic of Turkey until the late 1980s banned the use of written Kurdish.' (Kreyenbroek, 1994). This information is not accurate however. Although Kurdish is now used in book and print journalism in Turkey, it is still *illegal* to write in the language. Most publications in Kurdish and about it are regularly banned and confiscated, and authors, translators, publishers, distributors, and even readers are punished by the state. The article in *The International Encyclopedia of Linguistics* notes that Kurdish is written and used in education and media in Iraq, but in 'other countries with a Kurdish populations, publication is either negligible or suppressed - except in Soviet Armenia, where it has been encouraged by the state' (McCarus, 1992, 289).

Linguicide, experience, and theorisation

I have experienced linguicide as a native speaker of Kurdish. Born into a Kurdish family in a Kurdish town, I had to get my education in Persian, the only official language in Iran, a multilingual country where Persian was the native tongue of only half the population. It was illegal to speak in Kurdish in the school environment or to own any writing in my native tongue. Fearing prison and torture of her children, my mother burnt, four times during my life, the few Kurdish books and records we had acquired clandestinely. At Tehran University, where I studied linguistics (1968-1972), my professors rarely referred to Kurdish, and when they did, it was always called a 'dialect' of Persian. Calling Kurdish a 'language' would be considered 'secessionism.' By contrast, in the United States where I continued my studies and wrote a doctoral dissertation on Kurdish, I enjoyed unlimited political and academic freedom to conduct research on the language. This freedom was, however, constrained by the conceptual and theoretical limitations of the discipline of linguistics.

While linguists and others had recorded cases of the repression of individual languages, the practice was not yet conceptualised and theorised as an aspect of the unequal distribution of social, political, and cultural power. No introductory linguistics textbook dealt with what I had experienced as a native speaker of a language subjected to state violence. I had to exhaust the excellent resources of the library at the University of Illinois at Urbana-Champaign in order to find, in the literature on particular languages, the use of concepts such as 'linguistic genocide,' 'language death,' 'dying language,' or 'language suicide.' Indeed, I discovered that the 'Association pour la défense des langues et cultures menacées' located in Brussels, Belgium, had, in 1976, protested to the Iraqi government about its Arabization policy in Kurdistan. However, these ideas were not yet integrated, theoretically, into the 'sciences of language.'

The question of language repression was integral to the topic of my dissertation, 'The language factor in national development: The standardisation of the Kurdish language, 1918-1985', which was later published (Hassanpour, 1992). I found a rather obscure publication, Rudnyckyj's essay *Language Rights and Linguicide,* published in Munich by Ukrainisches Technisch-Wirtschaftliches Institut in 1967. 'Linguicide' was the right concept for interpreting the experience of Kurdish under the modernising and centralising states formed in the aftermath of World War I in Western Asia. Cobarrubias (1983) elaborated a taxonomy of 'official attitudes' toward minority languages, which included 'attempting to kill a language' and 'letting a language die' as official policies. This still marginal but evolving conceptual repertoire allowed me to organise my abundant data about decades of repression and resistance. At the same time, Kurdish provided ample evidence for the indispensability of the concept 'linguicide' and the need for further conceptual refinement and theoretical advances.

Emotions and science

This opening in the rather closed conceptual space could, however, be slammed shut by academic requirements of 'neutrality' and 'objectivity.' While the members of my dissertation committee did not complain about 'researcher bias,' I was myself concerned. I sent the draft of the first five chapters to a friend, a non-Kurd who had finished a dissertation on the Kurdish language, particularly inviting comments about political overtones in my writing. Some of the comments were (private correspondence, April 10, 1985):

> ... it isn't 'dissertation style', which made what you wrote hard to read. There is anger in what you write. Anger against what happened to the Kurds. Although I suspect this anger gives you the energy to do what you are doing, I wish you could find a way to keep it from deadening and flattening your discussions and analyses... It is so difficult to write about things you care about deeply in that bloodless, academic style. If you have those strong feelings and then you try to push them out of your writing, they sneak in somehow.

If it was a problem for me to detach myself from feelings due to having experienced oppression as a native speaker of Kurdish, I think the problem for non-native researchers is for them to access at least some degree of emotional involvement in relation to a repressive system which they never experienced, but one which had killed the 'object' of their study, violated their academic freedom in many ways, constrained the development of the discipline of linguistics, and violated the dignity and freedom of millions of human beings.

Soon after receiving the comments from my friend, however, I was pleasantly surprised to see Tove Skutnabb-Kangas's book, *Bilingualism or Not: The Education of Minorities* (1984a*)*. The book had just been catalogued and put on the 'new books' shelf at the Modern Languages Library of the university. I did not expect any reference to Kurdish in a book on the topic, although I was interested in knowing what it had to say about standardisation, minority education and minority languages. Literature on such topics was rarely if ever used by theorists or textbook writers in linguistics, and most studies of Kurdish were written by philologists and linguists interested in the Middle East. I had never seen any reference to Kurdish in any linguistics textbook, except those dealing in some detail with the Indo-European language family.

In her book, Tove briefly recounted the story of how the Turkish embassy in Copenhagen had tried to prevent the teaching of Kurdish to Kurdish immigrants in Denmark. She referred to the language as 'oppressed' and 'forbidden,' and made a useful distinction between 'physical violence' and 'symbolic and structural violence' against languages and their users. Tove's work encouraged me to dig more deeply into all forms of violence committed by the state against a language and its speakers, writers, readers, and, researchers. I was, at the same time, able to record extensive resistance against physical, symbolic, and structural forms of violence in every area of language use.

Our knowledge of linguicide and language death has made a great leap forward since the early 1980s. Tove's work has been indispensable here. She and Robert Phillipson contributed the first article on linguicide in a reference work on language (*The Encyclopedia of Language and Linguistics*, Pergamon, 1994). She makes effective use of the Kurdish case in her flourishing work on language policy, language rights, and linguistic human rights. Her writings are permeated by a deep commitment to justice, equality, freedom, and democracy. In an evolving 'world linguistic order' which kills one language every two weeks, Tove's works contribute to our knowledge about the life and death of the miracle of language. Her academic research is inseparable from her practice of campaigning to save threatened languages, democratise the highly unequal and oppressive world linguistic order, and promote an egalitarian distribution of linguistic power. Tove's life is thus in the tradition of intellectuals such as Bertrand Russell, Jean-Paul Sartre, and Noam Chomsky who resist the status quo.

Globalization, the market, linguicide, and linguists

Language death, an ancient phenomenon, is complex and of multiple origins. In our times the dynamics of decline and eventual extinction is distinguished from previous periods by, among other things, the formation of a 'world linguistic order,' the increasing proliferation of new communication technologies, and unceasing globalization. I find it necessary, however, to distinguish, theoretically, between the killing of language by the state and the market, although the two rarely operate independently. The killer is, in the case of Kurdish, clearly the institutions of the state, and the international order that allows it to happen in Turkey, Iran, and Syria. By contrast, the *contemporary* killer of hundreds of small languages in North America or Australia is primarily the market. While the state, for instance in Canada or the United States, does not and cannot prevent a First Nation from publishing an encyclopedia or daily paper in its native tongue, the market does so, and always invisibly but ruthlessly. The political and legal freedom to teach in the native tongue or use it in media is almost completely constrained by the dictates of the market.

If Kurdish is killed by the institutions of the state in the killing fields of Kurdistan, the forces of the state and the market combine to constrain its study in the West. I focus here on the academic environment where the theoretical and methodological limitations of the discipline enter into complex relationships with the market and the state. The closure of the Kurdish speech area to field researchers discourages students from conducting research on the language; it deters, in turn, faculty members from supervising student research not based on field work; in like fashion, research grants cannot be obtained for such topics, nor is the resulting dearth of research conducive to course offerings; this environment prevents publishers from investing in books and journals on the topic; library collections for

Kurdish material are, therefore, necessarily poor. With a few exceptions, none of the Middle Eastern studies departments in European and North American universities offers any Kurdish language courses. The majority teach only the four state languages of the region, i.e. Arabic, Turkish, Persian and Hebrew. It is not easy to break out of this vicious circle, which is sustained by the highly unequal distribution of power between a non-state people, the Kurds, and the nation-state system. The Turkish state, one of the worst language killers, is a NATO member, and an indispensable ally of the United States and other Western powers. Linguists are, however, in a good position, theoretically and ethically, to resist the policy and practice of linguicide. Some students of genocide already treat linguicide and ethnocide as subcategories of genocide (Charny, 1994). Silence about the linguicide of Kurdish or other languages is, I contend, a political position which cannot be justified by claims to the neutrality or autonomy of linguistics.

Language Emancipation: The Finnish Case

Anna-Riitta Lindgren

Emancipatory policy is concerned to reduce or eliminate an illegitimate domination of some individuals or groups by others, so that justice, equality, and participation for all will become possible (Giddens, 1991, 210-212). The varying status of languages in societies leads to the constitution of linguistic hierarchies. By the emancipation of a language, I mean the improving of the position of an oppressed language through political efforts and language planning. If a language is used only in private life, and maybe in primary livelihoods, only orally but seldom in literate forms, linguistic human rights are violated, and the group identifying with this language is oppressed - and usually not only linguistically. Language emancipation is the process through which the oppressed language is brought into use in schools and in various sectors of public life, orally and in writing. Linguistic human rights (Skutnabb-Kangas & Phillipson, 1989, 1994) are at the core of language emancipation. Absence of these rights implies that there is a need for language emancipation.

A brief history: three stages

In the linguistic hierarchy of Finland, local languages[1] have been below the international power languages of western Europe since the arrival of Latin with the Catholic church in the Middle Ages. Before that there were communities speaking Finnish in the southern parts of the territory of present-day Finland, and north of them, communities speaking Sámi. In the Nordic countries, power became progressively concentrated around the Scandinavian dynasties[2] from the 12th century onwards. Swedish kings conquered much of present-day Finland and

---

[1] The position of Finnish, Sámi and Swedish will be analysed, and other languages ignored.
[2] The Nordic countries are Denmark, Finland, Iceland, Norway and Sweden. Geographically and linguistically the term Scandinavia excludes Finland.

converted the Finnish tribes in the 12th and 13th centuries. This meant that two dominant languages were brought to the area, Swedish and Latin.

In the 12th century, areas of the southern and western coasts of Finland were settled by Swedish-speaking farmers. In succeeding centuries the Finns and Scandinavians gradually expanded into the Sámi areas in the north. The northerly areas were considered as *terra nullius*, analogous to the 'Indian' areas in America (Niemi, 1997). The next European power language to arrive was German from the 14th century, through the trade of the Hanseatic League. German became a lingua franca in many Nordic towns, and was used among the aristocracy and in the courts of Sweden and Denmark (including Norway and Iceland) from the 15th to the 18th century.

The Reformation of the 16th century was implemented in the Nordic countries, and brought with it the principle of Lutheran language policy: Each and every one has to be able to hear God's word in their own language. This led to the first stage of language emancipation, which concerned four languages in the Nordic countries: Swedish, Finnish, Danish, and Icelandic. They came into use in the church sphere. This was the beginning of writing in Finnish.

The Enlightenment mentality of the 18th century further raised the status of Swedish and Danish. They replaced Latin in universities and schools, and German among the aristocratic elite. This was the second step in language emancipation.

The percentage of the Finnish-speaking population in *Sweden* was about one fifth, so that Finnish was quantitatively and functionally a minority language. In *Finland*, the period of the Enlightenment and the growing centralization of the kingdom made the position of Swedish even stronger than before: school was now in Swedish instead of Latin. In the 17th century there were still noblemen and - women who spoke Finnish with each other, but during the 18th century the upper classes began to speak Swedish only, and upward mobility required a language shift from Finnish to Swedish. Finnish became a language of the lower classes; it was not a sign of nationality, but a sign of social standing (K. Lindgren, 1997).

In 1809, Sweden lost Finland, which was ceded to the Russian empire and made into an autonomous Grand Duchy with its own administration, laws and religion. After the separation from Sweden, Finnish was numerically the majority language in the Grand Duchy; about 90% of the population was Finnish-speaking. However, the status of the Finnish language did not change. Finnish was spoken by the lower classes but the language of administration, formal education and elite culture continued to be Swedish. The only important exception was the bilingual church. The Russian language never became significant.

The third step in language emancipation came in the 19th century, when the *nationalistic movement* became strong and, after a range of ideological and political processes, independence was declared in 1917. One of the goals of the movement was to improve the position of the Finnish language, triggering strong language emancipation. The legal status of equality with Swedish was gained step by step between 1863 and 1922. Over these six decades Finnish was taken into use both orally and in writing in all domains of official, cultural, and business life, and at schools and the university.

Finnish and Swedish had been class languages for about two hundred years. One result of language emancipation was the emergence of two language groups in all classes of society. In the lower classes, there was a Finnish-speaking numerical majority, but Swedish-speakers were prevalent in certain areas. The upper classes became predominantly Finnish-speaking in two ways. Firstly, as a result of the overall thrust of language emancipation, a language shift from Finnish to Swedish was no longer expected of the sons of farmers (and gradually of daughters). Due to widespread upward social mobility in the 20th century, this was the most common way for the Finnicization of the upper classes.

The second way is more intriguing. From the 1860s, many families of the Swedish-speaking upper and middle classes shifted their language to Finnish, even if it was the language with inferior status. This language shift was a clear political choice by which the members of the upper classes redefined their linguistic and national identity. As a consequence, the upper class families who continued to speak Swedish also had to redefine their identity. In the spirit of *national romanticism*, both upper class language groups identified themselves with the agricultural population and spoke the respective languages. In this way, both languages changed their function from class languages to national languages (K. Lindgren, 1997).

There was nationalistic language emancipation of various types in the same period in Norway, Iceland, and the Faroe Islands, as well as in other European countries.

The fourth stage: recent emancipation processes

The flip side of nationalism was the birth of calculated assimilation policies targeting several *minorities* from the end of the 19th century. This tendency remained strong until the 1960s in Finland as well as in the other Nordic countries. Here the world-wide *ethnic awakening* began with the Sámi in the 1950s and 1960s as a single movement in Finland, Norway and Sweden, and spread to other minorities in the 1970s and 1980s. It has started a new wave of language emancipation, the revitalization of minority languages. I will refer here to the language emancipation of the Sámi and for reasons of space ignore two groups whose languages are close to the Finnish dialects in the northernmost Finland, the Torne valley group in northern Sweden (see Lainio, this volume) and the Kvens in northern Norway.

In the premodern world, minorities and indigenous people could often live so that their language(s) had a solid position in the central domains of everyday life. The younger generation were well educated in their own culture, and used the minority language(s) in their working lives. Modernization changed the linguistic environment in everyday life, so that new domains using the majority language became important: the state-run school system, mass communications, and official matters involving the use of written language. Nationalism and the development optimism of the first stage of modernism created a new value system. Assimilation was understood as emancipation, because 'democracy' was implemented in such a way that assimilation was seen as making the representatives of 'primitive' cultures equal. Under these circumstances, many accepted assimilation, and the minority languages became endangered.

The ethnic awakening began with the minorities starting to develop further the ideal of democracy: A minority should have the right to its own culture and to its identity without stigmatization or discrimination. From this point of view, true democracy requires pluralism, multilingualism, and also positive discrimination, which is essential for fighting the harmful consequences of hundreds of years of oppression. When the optimistic stage of modernism changed with the realization that one had ended up in a high-risk society, indigenous and ethnic cultures began to earn respect for new reasons. More pluralistic values and the emancipation of minority languages were substantially boosted by the results of scientific investigations of bilingualism. The most important Finnish linguist in this field is Tove Skutnabb-Kangas, who has also worked extensively to mediate scientific results to both minorities and majorities.

The revitalization of minority languages at the grassroots level means beginning to use the language in private life in contexts where a language shift from minority to majority language has already occurred. At the level of official and public life, it involves using the minority language in schools and universities, organizations, public administration, literature, and mass communications. Significant at the national level were the Sámi Language Acts in Finland and Norway in 1992 (see Magga, 1994). In Finland, the Act is comparable to the language act of 1863 when Finnish became an official language. In public life, minority languages are now used in domains where they never used to be (and the process represents emancipation more than revitalization). Revitalization and assimilation are now occurring in parallel in a dramatic race that co-articulates with globalization and rapidly changing values.

Some aspects of language emancipation processes

In the cases of language emancipation presented here, a similar pattern can be found. Through big social and cultural change, new domain(s) of language use arose. These domains came from a centre of power to a periphery, initially in the language of the centre. Later on, an emancipation of the language(s) of the periphery arose, bringing the language(s) of the periphery to the new domain(s). Christianity was brought to Finland initially in Latin[3], and Swedish and Finnish

---

[3] Religion was not a new domain, but the church as an international institution was.

were used in this domain after the Reformation. School, university, and science were new domains first in Latin; after one language emancipation Swedish was brought into use in these domains, after the next, Finnish and after the final one, Sámi. When the European state as a social institution reached the territory of present-day Finland, it came first as a Swedish-speaking kingdom. After nationalistic language emancipation, Finnish was used in politics, administration, law, economic life, and all sectors of public communication and cultural activities. Through modernization, new important domains came to the communities in the Arctic areas initially in the majority languages of the nation states. After the ethnic awakening, indigenous and minority languages are coming into use in these domains.

What is characteristic of the cases of language emancipation presented is that they are connected to an important ideological movement, from Reformation to ethnic awakening. Language emancipation is not the core of the ideology, but is a very important part of the movement. It is also typical that there is an ideologically motivated and well educated middle class group which starts the movement[4], from priests at the time of the Reformation to the ethnic activists of today.

What then of the ethics of the language emancipatory movements? The Lutheran sociolinguistic principle is egalitarian, but the churches have applied it in diverse ways; persecution of indigenous culture and nationalistic assimilation policies towards minorities have occurred. Language emancipation connected to the Enlightenment concerned the majority language in the Swedish kingdom in upper and upper middle class circles, whereas Finnish was neglected. Nationalistic policies included the oppression of minorities. The goal of the minority movement in the Arctic areas is a multilingual and multicultural community, where minorities have rights and where cultural variety is considered as a source of richness. For the individual, the goal is high-level multilingualism. The pluralism embraced by the minority movement seems to be more ethically grounded than earlier emancipatory movements. Its ethical sensitivity can be seen in its attitudes towards other minorities, especially those who are lower on the pecking order than themselves. Do the various minorities and groups within them compete with each other, or do they support each other so as to attain the common goal, a pluralistic society? I think the answer today is a mixture of both.

Is language emancipation a struggle for a place higher up on the pecking order, or is it a fight for justice? For the minority, both of these involve demanding rights. For the majority, it might be thought that giving up domination or some part of it means losing something. But this is a superficial view. Well-balanced multiculturalism and multilingualism can be useful and a great richness for the wider society, and oppression has well-known harmful consequences. Emancipation can sometimes be a cause of suffering too, but in the long run, it is therapeutic for the whole of society. Emancipation does not mean sacrifice for the dominant party but serves the well-being of the integrated whole.

---

[4] The Reformation in Sweden was initiated by king Gustav Wasa, but its realization, including linguistic realization, was the work of the clergy.

What can we learn for the future from the history of language emancipation? As is well known, there are many instances of language death around the world, and successful language emancipation does not in itself guarantee a good future. However, history does record some success stories, and even if the actual emancipatory processes were controversial at the time, when the emancipation has occurred and we can see the results, we never regret or miss the times when, for instance, schools were only in Latin or in Swedish. This is an important lesson for the future.

Linguistic Pluralism: A Point of Departure

D. P. Pattanayak

Linguistic pluralism has never served as a point of departure in theory building or state formation. The European nation states, built around unitary symbols, were modes for state formation for the developed world. While the nation state model has been collapsing in Europe, leading to the creation of new structures like the European Economic Community, later the European Union with its Parliament, the developing countries of the world have been trying during decolonisation to build their countries in the image of their former colonial masters. While the new structures in the developed world required the use of multiple languages, the developing countries were busy imposing restrictions on choice of language use. The new European structure operates with eleven official languages, and countries in Asia, Africa, and Latin America grapple with a three-language formula. Pressure to adopt a single colonial language became a logical development, whether as a neutral language or as a language of international communication.

The theoretical postures of scholars in the First and Second Worlds are directly opposed to the realities of the Third World. The developed world follows a mono-model approach in solving problems of a multi-model world. They not only deny the existence of mother tongues, they also deny dialects and sociolects. In describing languages they begin with ideolects, the ensemble of the total language repertoire of an individual. Scholars in the developed world never accepted a multilingual ideology. Theoreticians like Noam Chomsky searched for the ideal speaker-hearer of a language. After first rejecting bilingualism as subtractive and a burden, they finally came to terms with it. After refusing to accept multilingualism as an expression of multiculturalism in the world, they got stuck with bilingualism. The current slogans are Bilingualism and Multiculturalism.

After theorising that the bilingual competence of a person has to be set against the unilingual competence of two monolinguals, they reached a dead end. I am reminded of an incident at Uppsala, where I was presenting a paper on mother tongue teaching. A member of the audience stood up, pointed a finger at me and shouted: 'You people from the Third World, you make unsubstantiated generalisations. Can you give us one example of the distinction you are making between monolingualism and multilingualism?' I replied that for *you* one language is the norm. Two languages are a quantum leap, a hundred percent achievement over one. Three or four languages are intolerable, and many languages are absurd. For *us* many languages are the norm. Any restriction on language use is intolerable. Two or three languages are barely tolerable and one language is absurd. I further told him that Brian Weinstein, a political scientist had asked a question with reference to American culture: 'How much plurality can this culture tolerate?' I said if someone asks such a question in my culture, he would not be worth his salt as a social scientist. (S)he should rather formulate the question as 'how much uniformity can this culture formulate?'

Language borders are perceived differently by First and Third World scholars. The First World scholars theorise that 'borders are zones of loss, alienation, pain, death - spaces where there is a continuous potential for violence'. They further contend that 'living on the border is frequently to experience the feeling of being trapped in an impossible in-between'. In the multilingual Third World, borders are not razor-thin boundaries. They are spectrums or ranges where languages and cultures intermingle. Hybridisation is one result of such intermingling. The development of bi- or multilingualism is another. Two, three, or four languages operating with a single grammar is yet another manifestation of multiculturalism. As scholars of the First World refuse to recognise multilingualism, they ignore the underlying homogenising process which imposes recognition of a Language, a Linguistic or Cultural Area.

Binary opposites such as We : They; East : West; Here : There; Subject : Object; Centre : Periphery; Core : Margin; are characteristic of First World thinking. They operate on a binary Either : Or scale. The multilingual pluricultural world operates on an inclusive scale of Both : And. This includes We, You and Me; and Here, There and Yonder. In this world there is neither centre nor periphery, core nor margin, but a network of relationships. Social and communication relationships can be understood properly when seen in networks and not through polarisation.

One of the major consequences of colonialism in India and the Third World is the separation of cognition from perception. By declaring cognition as scientific and in consequence the rest unscientific, in one stroke large chunks of life and living in the Third World were thrown out of consideration.

By luring people to opt for globalisation without enabling them to communicate with the local and the proximate, their cultures are destroyed. By the outright purchase of national products and processes, and appropriation of traditional knowledge systems through patents and similar mechanisms, the Third World is impoverished and drained of self-respect. Many languages and many cultures, which have been their only defence against centralised control, are being systematically destroyed. Only acceptance of multilingualism and pluriculturalism as a point of departure can save the world from self-destruction.

Birch - Wind - Looks

Lilja Liukka

Koivu

Olen koivu
Oksani rönsyilee
mahlassani pisara
villiä vapautta.
Juureni kaukana
Vanhassa metsässä
vahva yhteys
esiäiteihin
voimani alkulähteisiin.

Tuuli

Tuuli hyväili koivua
tanssitti lehtiä, oksia.
Koivu kuiski
rakastan sinua
mutta syksyllä olen lehdetön.
Tuuli koivulle
hyväilen sinua
vihreänä, mahlaisena, lehdettömänä
huurteisena ja lumisena.

Katseet

Helmassa
Helliä sanoja
turvallista
ensi askel, sanat
ympäristön ihailua.
Askel kauemmaksi
Katseita paljon
helliä, tuttuja.
Mitä on nämä
Kylmät katseet
kauempana?

Birch

I am birch
My branches stretch out
in my sap, drops
of wild freedom.
My roots deep
In the ancient forest
strong connection
to my foremothers
primal sources of my strength.

Wind

The wind caressed the birch
made leaves, branches dance
The birch kept whispering
I love you
but in the autumn I lose the leaves.
Wind to birch
I caress you
when you are green, full of sap,
leafless, hoarfrosted and heavy with snow.

Looks

Lap embraced
Tender words
secure
first step, words
admiration from environment.
A step further
Many looks
tender, well known.
What are these
Cold looks
further away?

Culture, Sharing and Language

Probal Dasgupta

Resources are resources when you make and remake them. That your labour, your contexts, and the resources are shared turns it into a remaking. The 're' of remaking marks a repeated return to what gradually grows on you. This process, at every level, gives you a home, an *oikos*, the Greek word with which Ecology begins. Sharing happens in language. Knowledge of language, knowledge as language is handed down to children.

Kwa-kwa, says baby to duck. Duck-ducks, she says as a regularizing English-speaking child. Goose-geese, she says as she grows into a relaxed settlement with some morphologically irregular enclaves. Please cut corners and (tactically) accept this stereotypical language acquisition curve. (Quibblers welcome to do their proofreading - elsewhere!)

Project this curve on to social acquisition over a different age spectrum. Immature child naively affirms all she surveys. Angry young individual negates injustices, anger fuelled by regularizing impulse. Allegedly mature person sagely settles for some social arbitrariness.

Why do this projection? It gives you a simplistic dichotomy to begin with and then resist: university students, always potential radicals. Drawn to an Enlightenment that applies rules universally. Versus a 'mature' contemporary world. Which has outgrown the macho radicalisms. And foregrounds movements for women. For environmental conservation. For indigenous peoples. For the handicapped. For the elderly. For many disenfranchised and displaced categories.

The macho radicalisms had pleaded for efficient global arrangements. And argued that even purely technical arguments based on a scientism would usher in a generalizably just social order. Versus the post-macho one-issue lobbies proposing that arrangements are locally satisfying only when they spring from the cultural, from sharing. The cultural must have primacy over the technical. A version of mind over matter.

These excessively local, extremely one-issue efforts are beginning to join hands. To share resources. The environmental consciousness is still steeped in the mind-set of scientism. (Technique first; culture an obscure and intuition-bound second.) Its emphases are still technologistic and thus manipulatory. Today's greens are slowly going through a late-private, early-public personal process of learning that pollution reflects the technically motivated, culturally implemented manipulation of some kinds of workers and work by other kinds. Pollution can only be managed, not reversed, if you just modify ways, means, and types of manipulation.

From this juncture, environmentally minded people can return to, remake, reshare a feminist discovery: the patriarchal stereotypes enshrined in the English 'neutral pronoun *he*' could only be cleaned up through public action by private citizens. Reexamine that discovery, won't you. Draw your conclusions about the cultural, about sharing, about communication resources and their effects, in a sustainable global network of local knowledges and the languages providing living subsystems for these.

Suppose an ecologically aware public has done this reexamining. Won't what applied to *he* in English now strike them as applying to English in Languageland as an ecosystem? Won't the newly aware public wish to do to the *English*-carried industrial-chauvinist stereotypes globally (in favour of the industrious industrial Northerner and against those lazily living it up, in the poverty they deserve, in their teeming, dumb millions down South, etc.) what their ancestors did to the *he*-carried male-chauvinist steoreotypes in an America or a New Zealand?

Such wishes seem to follow, once a project of serious sharing is taken up, to the point of trying to move from contemplation to action. Subjective preparation, providing a format of narrative that makes sense of sharing across identity boundaries, needs to precede and ground the political will to formalize - sustainably and therefore transsubjectively - a pan-global human fellowship.

A public that keeps faith with desires on this scale, after scaling both the one-issue mountains and the (as yet unexplored) alliance-seeking valleys of the environmental Age of Aquarius, will obviously need to touch base with the textual adventure of the planetary linguistic visualization. This adventure has taken the form of the inter-local language Esperanto. For it is in this language that imaginative citizens have really seen themselves, and ably shown themselves in their speech and writing, as responsible, sharing earthlings first and as hedonist shareholders of national stock only secondarily.

Some of this sounds quixotic? To all observers who have cared to examine the evidence, however, it is clear that the exchangeworthy diverseness of human work continues to receive a quiet and serious articulation in the strong and growing literary visualizations of our ubiquitous, unowned humanity in the 1887-launched language-ship Esperanto. Made of more than just wood from many forests, Esperanto's planetary texting of shared humanity has used pieces of bonding that originate in local minicrafts that ground a portable between-community (not above-community) linguistic-literary rationality. Academics of language and of literature or 'cultural studies' will notice once they stop replicating nationish opacities and heavy panoplies (defying old fortresses but glorifying new ghettoes) in their self-congratulatingly decanonized, principled reasonings.

Of such are the backgrounds of hope and of despair; one can even look forward to some leading scholars of language choosing to be accountable for a change (breaking with a long tradition of hegemony-backed non-accountable behaviour masked by 'radical' talk), and facing the challenge of learning the language of *espero* - hope, Esperanto, and joining its discourses. If this breakthrough happens, the 'academic' discussion of smaller languages and their speakers' rights will never be the same again.

References

You will inevitably look at what the Esperanto movement in your region provides. It may put you off: there has been some ghettoization. But if you are accountable, you will want to work your way through this to the real inheritance. If you get lost on the way, feel free to ask; some quick signposting follows. In Esperanto, one anthology, Auld, 1984, and two significant texts, Auld, 1980 and Montagut, 1993. About Esperanto in English, Dasgupta, 1987, and in Bangla/Bengali, Sircar, 1991 and Dasgupta, 1998.

'Spirit of the Earth'

Constance M. Beutel

I have an especially beloved photograph of Tove Skutnabb-Kangas. In it she is standing in the meadow of her home, Transcultura, near Roskilde, Denmark. It's an early summer morning and Tove is dressed in her favorite color, blue. Sunlight washes over Tove, the meadow, small trees and the greenhouse in the background.

The photo is special because it reminds me how Tove's activism and scholarship about languages is deeply rooted in her understanding of the complex, organic vitality of our earth. Her dedication in preserving each person's right to her Mother Tongue, in all the diversity of the thousands of languages needed to express ourselves, relates, I believe, to the ecological preservation of the earth itself. Paulo Freire once remarked on the sacredness of language by reflecting on how our languages have passed through the minds and hearts of millions of people - from one to the other - through the ages. The power of saying a true word does transform the world.

I spent a major part of my career working in the field of telecommunications for a large U.S. corporation. The language and vocabulary of business is not necessarily complex nor subtle. This language of market economies is filled with military metaphors of deadlines, targets, strategies, tactics, missions, takeovers, assaults, and so on. This web of enterprise also casts the lives of so many, workers, consumers, haves, and have-nots.

It was while working in this environment that I met Tove. I had begun a program that made university undergraduate and graduate studies available to my colleagues after work hours on corporate premises. I was deeply concerned by the massive restructuring of industry in the 1980s and the resulting consequences to co-workers who were not able to transition to the new economy. At the same time I was disturbed by the potential of education to ço-opt. Did this education have the potential to transform as well?

I began my dialogue with Tove by writing in the margins of her book *Bilingualism or Not: The Education of Minorities* (1984a*)*. Much of what she wrote about was new and troubling to me. She made me think in new ways about the power and politics of languages. Of dominance, fear, ignorance, and control. With her persistent and passionate voice, she also spoke eloquently of the lives, histories and futures of the language minorities who are being engulfed by language majorities.

You can be overwhelmed by the engine of corporate worlds pursuing market economies and bottomline greed. Yet, working within my chosen field of telecommunications, I see emerging possibilities of a world of sustainable Mother Tongues. There are students at my university today talking to their families and friends in Indonesia through internet telephony – video, voice, and text. In addition to those 'communities of interest' that George Gilder, Esther Dyson, and others describing people who are using the internet to form communities related to their interests, another new phenomenon is occurring. Families, long separated by distance, are reuniting on-line. I have recently experienced this reunion myself when my cousins, aunts, and uncles have recently re-connected with me by e-mail.

Computers and internet access are expensive and won't address, for a long time, 60% of the people of the world without telecommunications access. Yet, these technologies are creating new pathways around borders of 'monolingual stupidity'.

I have learned from Tove that the destruction of language, linguicide, is more than the death of memories of millions of people alive today. This destruction, if not stopped, is also intricately woven into our futures on the earth.

Now it is our time to join with Tove, standing as she does, passionate and committed to our living, beautiful, complex earth.

Part II. Rights: Language Rights, their Articulation and Implementation

The scope of linguistic human rights

A UNIVERSAL DECLARATION OF LINGUISTIC HUMAN RIGHTS
SHOULD GUARANTEE AT AN **INDIVIDUAL** LEVEL,
IN RELATION TO

THE MOTHER TONGUE(S) (MTs),
that everybody can

- identify with their MTs (first languages) and have this identification accepted and respected by others;
- learn the MTs fully, orally (when physiologically possible) and in writing. This presupposes that minorities are educated through the medium of their MTs;
- use the MTs in most official situations (including schools).

OTHER LANGUAGES,

- that everybody whose mother tongue is not an official language in the country where s/he is resident, can become bilingual (or trilingual, if s/he has 2 MTs) in the MTs and (one of) the official language(s) (according to her own choice).

THE RELATIONSHIP BETWEEN LANGUAGES,

- that any change of MT is voluntary, not imposed. This presupposes that alternatives exist, and enough reliable knowledge about long-term consequences of the choices.

PROFIT FROM EDUCATION,

- that everybody can profit from education, regardless of what her MT is.

Tove Skutnabb-Kangas, 1998, 23.

Language Maintenance as an Arena of Cultural and Political Struggles in a Changing World

Naz Rassool

National language policy, historically, has represented the grand narrative through which the national imagery has been constructed. In the pluralist nation-state, it has served to legitimize the incorporation of discrete social groups into the 'common' (dominant) culture. This form of cultural assimilation has often led to the positioning of minority languages and their speakers at the periphery of cultural, social, and political life. The relationship between cultural imperialism and linguicide, ratified by colonial language policies, has already been well documented. Whilst many of the linguistic inequalities generated during the colonial period, and those embedded in the social relations of the nation-state still remain unresolved, new, more complex ones are emerging within the globalized cultural economy. This chapter seeks to examine the nature of some of the changes taking place, and their potential impacts on the way in which the concept of linguistic rights is conceptualized.

Globalization and transnational power frameworks

The nation-state as the basis of citizenship, national identity, and party-political interests is in the process of being fractured by transnational 'networks of wealth, information and power' (Castells, 1997, 342). This de-centering of state power has contributed to the fact that transnational power ensembles such as the European Union (EU), transnational corporations (TNCs), the International Monetary Fund (IMF) and World Bank now represent influential policy sites. Transnational power blocs such as the EU will, potentially, impact on the language rights of minority groups through the specific meanings attached to the concept of citizenship as this relates to non-indigenous population groups. For instance, although *gastarbeiter* now form a regular feature of the cultural landscape within several metropolitan societies in Europe, they generally remain excluded from the right to citizenship. Deprived thus of a political identity within the host nation-state, they lack the power to define themselves. Although most are multilingual this has not necessarily empowered them in terms of having access to power in the countries in which they would spend most of their adult lives. The past two decades have also witnessed increasing levels of mass migration as a result of civil war, ethnic conflict, political destabilization, poverty, and natural disasters in many 'developing' countries. These people are the refugees and political exiles, the socially displaced and disenfranchized who, as stateless people, also have no political identity within the boundaries of asylum countries. Having no voice, no power to define their own futures, they are forced to live uncertain border lives within largely exclusionary metropolitan countries. Moreover, Fortress Europe is building ever higher walls to exclude them. What are the linguistic and cultural choices available to this group of people? How are the language rights of this group of people to be defined?

Elsewhere, in the under-developed world, the regulatory controls built into external donor-aid/loan packages of the IMF and World Bank represent powerful mechanisms by which the language rights of minority groups in developing countries are curtailed. This is particularly the case where policy regulation intersects with literacy provision in social development programmes such as the World Bank's Structural Adjustment Programme (SAP). Decreases in public spending framed by neo-liberal economic policies have been integral to structural adjustment in borrowing countries. This has contributed to overall cuts in education and literacy provision in many of these countries - thus intensifying already existing social inequalities. Some of these inequalities are heightened by broader cultural changes taking place within the global terrain.

Multiple realities and multi-identities

Within the global cultural flow facilitated by the shifting finance-, techno-, ideo-, media- and ethnoscapes (Appadurai, 1993) of the late twentieth century, the very concept of the nation as an 'imagined community' (Anderson, 1980), grounded in the principles of sovereignty and territoriality, is being powerfully contested by global flows of money, people, and information. Within this dynamic global arena, local (heterogeneous) cultural particularities are simultaneously converging and colliding with universalizing (homogenizing) cultural processes and practices, giving rise to an intricate web of social relations within a global sphere. Language as primary mediator of 'reality' plays a key role in this process.

For instance, the ubiquity of American films and the global marketing of English language-based popular culture represent powerful means through which the 'second-order universes' that we increasingly inhabit in the modern world are constructed. This extends also to the dominance throughout the world of English broadcasts via cultural sites such as the BBC World Service, CNN Television, and the Voice of America. These communication practices represent key cultural definers operating within a discursive terrain to construct social meaning.

Constituting powerful signifying practices, their hegemonic value lies in the potent yet subtle means by which they influence the shaping of Americanized/Westernized cultural identities, aspirations, life-styles, dreams, and desires of culturally and linguistically differentiated groups of people across the world. In the process, homogenized cultural meanings, values and linguistic 'norms' are imposed on diverse communities and societies. 'World' languages embody a potent form of hegemonic cultural capital representing 'that which we all must have' in order to be successful global 'citizens'. Representing the languages of the economically and politically powerful, they now have the potential to redefine linguistic aspirations as well as to refract the cultural imagination of larger groups of people across the world. But underlying the image of a 'classless', 'global' identity is the powerful ideological force of assimilation and the legitimation of new forms of cultural imperialism.

Technological change, cosmopolitan identities, and linguistic diversity

The rapid transfer of information between countries and continents, and especially the application of information technology in banking and financial markets have also transformed the global economic base. New economies of space and time have not only improved capital and information flows, they have also redefined work practices and the labour process within the global terrain. The rise of information industries has de-centred the notion of the 'work place' with 'knowledge' workers increasingly 'outsourced' to transnational companies. As a result, cross-cultural interaction is increasingly becoming an integral part of everyday working life, at least for high-status 'knowledge' workers at the core of information technology-based industries. Global flows of money thus operate in tandem with global flows of high-skilled knowledge workers who are increasingly required to have multilingual skills as well as a working understanding of other cultures. This notion of flexible language users underscores the increasingly popular notion of cosmopolitanism as a reflexive lifestyle choice. That is to say, multilingualism is seen as central to the forging of a cosmopolitan identity, and thus it represents a strategic life-style choice.

The concepts of cultural hybridity and linguistic flexibility feature strongly in postmodern theorizations of contemporary social change, and especially, in the notion of the borderless 'hi-tech' global community. The Internet, computer bulletin boards, and e-mail facilities, offer not only cross-cultural communication possibilities and opportunities but also new 'worlds' to inhabit in cyberspace, and new multiple, flexible identities to adopt. Free-flows of information and open access thus seemingly bode well for the opening up of opportunities for transnational interaction, empowering citizens to participate in the democratic process within nation-states as well as participating in discussions on a variety of global issues. This opening up of para-national participatory possibilities and opportunities, at least on the surface, lends further credence to the concept of a burgeoning classless, borderless *laissez faire* cosmopolitanism. However, what is not usually emphasized is that this notion of cosmopolitanism infers a relative freedom of choice, political power, and parity in status amongst different language users. But freedom of choice and movement are available generally only to those already politically and economically enfranchised. This was illustrated in the discussion earlier of the restrictions imposed on the lives of refugees, asylum seekers, and *gastarbeiter*.

Increased levels of access to information and debate in the interactive global environment have obvious empowering potential. However, the fact that English dominates information technology textual environments inhibits access to non-English speakers. It also brings the possibility of structuring new - and reinforcing older - language inequalities. The high economic currency of information technology in the world today has implications for the ability or motivation of many developing countries to sustain the emphasis that some of them have placed on the maintenance of local literacies as part of the process of supporting social development in a culturally meaningful way. It would also impact negatively on the extent to which technological diffusion can take place effectively in rural areas where people speak and/or are literate predominantly in local languages. English language dominance thus would serve to intensify already existing social inequalities, and increase the separation of the information-rich from the information-poor; the economically powerful core countries from the politically and economically disempowered periphery. Linguistic imperialism as 'the promoter of one-way learning, the flow of knowledge and information from the powerful to the powerless' (Mühlhäusler, in Phillipson, 1998, 104) thus continues to circumscribe cultural, economic and political possibilities in the developing world.

Conclusion

This chapter explored the discursive ways in which language impacts on everyday life within the rapidly changing global cultural environment. The discussion has shown the extent to which already powerful economic and political definers are exerting control over cultural and political meaning on a global basis. Language maintenance is now, perhaps more than ever before, an arena in which the struggle for control over social meaning is being played out. Two key issues have emerged for consideration in terms of our conceptualization of language rights within the global cultural economy.

The first relates to the extent to which language and literacy are central to the text-dominated and information suffused social world. This focuses attention on the exchange value of language in everyday life and foregrounds the argument that language as a means of communication frames, and at the same time, is embedded in discourse both literally and symbolically. In a literal sense, it highlights the importance of linguistic capital to individuals, placing emphasis on having a knowledge of discourse norms and conventions as a necessary prerequisite to being able to participate in the interactive text-dominated social world.

Second, I want to link this idea further with Pennycook's (1998a, 79) view of the 'right to language'; that is, 'the notion of language as an active process of naming the world'. As a means of cultural expression, language has potent symbolic power. It constitutes an important group and self-identifying variable; it represents *different ways of being in,* and *ways of seeing the world.* Language not only mediates reality; it also characterizes the means by which different groups of people define themselves in relation to both the social and material world; it provides the means by which they *name* the world. And, in the process of naming, the world itself is transformed. This underlines the importance of the need to find a 'voice' as an integral part of political and cultural self-definition. If we take account of these complexities, it follows that the concept of language rights needs to incorporate a view of language as a multidimensional social practice. The right to individual languages is as important as to be 'languaged' adequately in the global cultural economy.

Human Rights: The Next Fifty Years

Cees Hamelink

In 1998 the 50th anniversary of the Universal Declaration of Human Rights was celebrated. One of the depressing features of this exceptionally far sighted moral catalogue is the gap between morality and reality. The lack of implementation of human rights standards poses the most serious challenge to the international human rights regime. The most important issue for the significance and validity of the regime is the realization of the standards it proposes. It is urgent to make a concerted effort toward a more effective implementation of the human rights regime in the 21st century. If we fail, there will be no reason to celebrate the centenary of the Universal Declaration of Human Rights.

The challenge for the next fifty years to secure that human rights are respected across the world is particularly vital for the category of rights that suffer the weakest forms of enforcement, cultural rights.

Cultural globalization

Attention to the protection of these rights is especially pertinent at the time of the rapid commercialization, consolidation, and globalization of the cultural industries. A worldwide process of cultural erosion is today reinforced by international trade agreements that perceive of independent cultural policies as unfair barriers to international trade. In this process of cultural globalization the right to language is under serious threat. The forces that drive toward the cultural homogenization of the world, transform a highly diversified cultural landscape into the pattern of a Disney theme park and toward a Hollywood-inspired common language that becomes the universal vehicle particularly in such new communication platforms as the Internet.

Today's process of cultural globalization has the characteristics of a fundamentalist religious movement. At its core is a set of normative doctrines that needs to be propagated as widely as possible through persuasive techniques and formats and with the assistance of professional missionaries. The global communications market provides the effective vehicle for the worldwide proliferation of today's most powerful cultural movement that shapes the live environment for increasing numbers of people around the world, directly and indirectly: global capitalism. The missionaries for this movement are the cultural industries that create consumer practices worldwide. At the core of their propagandistic mission is the aspiration to establish the ultimate global shopping mall. One of the strategic cultural instruments that advanced capitalism deploys is linguistic imperialism. When this is succesful, 'the dominant ideas can more easily penetrate the minds of the dominated, and the full development of other languages is forestalled, impeding the development of diverse counterhegemonies that are necessary for querying the rationality of a monocultural, monolingual cosmology based on economic "efficiency"' (Skutnabb-Kangas & Phillipson, 1997, 63). The propagandistic mission of the global cultural industries does not augur well for the sustainability of the world's variety of living languages.

Cultural tribalization

In response to the global spread of modernity and its icons, ethnic identities are often re-defined in very aggressive ways. There is worldwide a trend towards entrenchment into forms of tribalism (such as nationalism or religious fundamentalism). This tribalism not only rejects the values of modernity, it also promotes the primacy of the values of collective belonging, racial and ethnic identity, national chauvinism, and religious and moralistic revival. At its core, tribalism is driven by the 'tribal instinct', a powerful force that has shown its devastating potential throughout human history and in recent times in former Yugoslavia, the Russian Federation, and Rwanda. The 'tribal instinct' represents the strong belief in the superiority of the value-system of the clan to which one belongs and the dedication to defend if not expand this by physical force. Its ultimate scenario is the total refusal of social cooperation with outsiders, the fragmentation of the world into separate local communities that have no common ground unless one of them manages to impose its set of supreme values upon all others and locks all up in the oppressive irrationality of 'Holy Terror'.

Tribalization represents the extreme differentiation into separate cultural identities that often violently clash with each other. For tribal cultures the cultural identity of others can be very threatening, to the point where it needs to be eliminated. Tribalization refuses dialogue and this tolls the death knell for a living and dynamic culture, inclusive of its language. Moreover, the tribal instinct fosters ethnic conflicts of a very violent nature; the oppression and elimination of other tribes and their cultural values and practices (including their language) is seen as essential to the defence of tribal identity. Minority cultures have often been the victims of ethnocide and with the onslaught against their identity their languages have often suffered irreparable damage.

The need for public interest intervention

The protection of cultural rights cannot be delegated to the powers of states and markets. It needs a robust intervention in the international and national political arena by forces that actively represent the interests of ordinary people. Since 1991, a movement has emerged to promote the constitution of a global civil movement that addresses the quality of our cultural environment. Some of the essential aspirations of this movement have been articulated in a text called the *People's Communication Charter* (PCC). The *People's Communication Charter* is an initiative of the Third World Network (Penang, Malaysia), the Centre for Communication & Human Rights (Amsterdam, the Netherlands), the Cultural Environment Movement (USA), and the AMARC, the World Association of Community Radio Broadcasters (Peru/Canada).

In the early 1990s academics and activists associated with the Third World Network in Penang and its affiliated Consumers Association of Penang initiated a debate on the need and the feasibility of a global people's movement in the field of communication and culture. One of the first steps in this process was the drafting of a basic charter that expresses the various dimensions of the human right to communicate.

Core principles

From the first draft text in 1993 the text was seen by the initiators as an open and dynamic document. Numerous people and institutions around the world became involved in commenting upon and editing the text. The present text reflects the input from a great variety of supporters in many different national and cultural situations. The following core principles emerged in the debates around the Charter:

1. All forms of information handling - collecting, processing, storing, distributing, etc. - should be guided by respect for basic human rights.
2. Communication resources (such as frequencies) should be considered 'commons', should be accessible to all in fair and equitable ways, and cannot be regulated by market forces alone.
3. Communication in society cannot be monopolized by governmental or commercial forces.
4. People have a right to the protection of their cultural space.
5. Information and communication providers should accept accountability for their products and services.

Implementation

The realisation of the people's right to communicate cannot be a homogeneous project. It will take different forms in different socio-cultural and political contexts. There may the establishment of an Ombudsman office for the quality of the cultural environment, or a civil society campaign to rescue public broadcasting. The focus may be on the protection of children against advertising or on actions against media stereotyping of people with a handicap. This is really the business of ordinary people. It is also the ultimate test case for the significance of the Charter. The whole initiative in the end only makes sense if people themselves begin to be concerned about its implementation.

Another recent development is the call and proposal for a global civil campaign by which sectors of civil society and non-governmental organisations form an international alliance to address concerns and to work jointly on matters around media and communications. The campaign has been called 'Voices 21'. Voices 21 is inspired by:

- the awareness of the growing importance of the mass media and communication networks for the goals they try to achieve;
- the concerns about current trends in the field of information and communication toward concentration, commercialisation, privatisation, and liberalisation;
- the lack of public influence on these trends in both 'developed' and 'developing' countries, in democracies and under dictatorships.

The central focus of the campaign is to address problems and demonstrate solutions to one of the greatest challenges of our time: that the voices and concerns of ordinary people around the world shall no longer be excluded!

In spite of all the solemn declarations about information societies and communication revolutions, most of the world's voices are not heard. In today's reality most people neither have the tools and skills to participate in social communication nor a say in communication politics. The preamble of the *People's Communication Charter* (see http://www.waag.org/pcc) states:

> All people are entitled to participate in communication and in making decisions about communication within and between societies.

In spite of all the developments and innovations in the field of information and communication, this standard has not yet been realized.

In order to put the Charter on the public agenda, a series of international public hearings is being undertaken that will address violations of the provisions of the Charter. The first of these hearings focussed on 'Languages and Human Rights'. The pertinent article 9 from the *People's Communication Charter* (on Diversity of Languages) reads:

> All people have the right to a diversity of languages. This includes the right to express themselves and have access to information in their own language, the right to use their languages in educational institutions

funded by the state, and the right to have adequate provision created for
the use of minority languages where needed.

The PCC Public Hearing on Languages and Human Rights was held in Amsterdam
on 1-3 May 1999, with support from the World Association of Christian
Communication (whose journal *Media Development* reported in depth on the
Hearing, volume 4, 1999; webpage: www.wacc.org.uk). A panel of judges heard
how the language rights of Kurds in Turkey, Berbers in North Africa, Sign
Language users, Creole speakers in the Caribbean, and minority language speakers
in California are violated. The panel, which included a professor of international
law, a community radio organizer, a sociolinguist, and an eminent bilingual author,
was chaired by Tove Skutnabb-Kangas. The organizers of the Hearing wanted to
demonstrate their respect and appreciation for her work on issues relating to
linguistic rights. It would be very much in the spirit of her lifelong academic work
and moral commitment to hope that the hearing can contribute to raising the world's
awareness of one of the most critical challenges to its rich and diverse cultural
heritage.

Tolerance and Inclusion: The Convergence of Human Rights and the Work of Tove Skutnabb-Kangas

Fernand de Varennes

Introduction

International law is highly specialised. Scholars in this area of law rely almost exclusively on legal sources in their work and, as a general rule, seldom take into account the insight of non-legal experts.

This has also to a large extent been true of my own work involving minority rights and linguistic minorities, with one notable exception: when I began examining these issues as a doctoral student at the University of Maastricht I was deeply influenced by the work of Tove Skutnabb-Kangas. At a time when most legal scholars were probably uneasy with the idea that individual human rights had any relevance to issues of linguistic diversity, I could find inspiration and understanding in the views and content set forth in Dr. Skutnabb-Kangas' publications.

Today, some 10 years after I first started to explore how international human rights law touches on matters of linguistic preferences and freedoms, it seems to me that there is an increasing acknowledgement in legal circles that language not only can but must be respected and accommodated because of fundamental human rights principles. This has also been Dr. Skutnabb-Kangas' message, though from a non-legal position, and it now seems there is widespread acceptance of this when one considers how legal instruments in Europe and at the international level have evolved and tried to address 'linguistic rights' issues.

'Linguistic rights' in international law

> French law does not, as such, give everyone a right to speak his own
> language in court. Those unable to speak or understand French are
> provided with the services of an interpreter. This service would have been
> available to the author had the facts required it; as they did not, he
> suffered no discrimination under Article 26 on the ground of his
> language.   (United Nations Human Rights Committee, *Dominique
> Guesdon v. France*, UN Document A/45/49, 1990)

Dr. Skutnabb-Kangas' call for 'linguistic rights' about 20 years ago did not initially
find a great deal of support among legal scholars. To understand why this occurred,
one has to explain from the outset that from a strictly legal point of view there is no
'right to language' in international law. The traditional position exemplified in the
above extract has been that only individual rights are recognised in international
law. There is therefore for legal purists an almost inherent difficulty, at least in the
past, when even suggesting such a thing as 'linguistic rights' which seem to imply
some kind of a collective nature.

It may seem difficult to reconcile this rejection of a 'right to language' with the
appeal Dr. Skutnabb-Kangas has consistently made for 'linguistic rights', but in fact
the contradiction is more apparent than real. To better appreciate why the
international legal approach is in fact quite amenable to recognising the right to use
minority and indigenous languages in various situations, one has to better
understand how it is possible to deny the existence of a 'right to language' in
international law.

In the *Dominique Guesdon v. France* case mentioned above, the author had
attempted to argue that legislation in France making French the only language to be
used before criminal courts constituted discrimination based upon language, as they
were not permitted to use Breton, their primary language, before the courts. The
UN Human Rights Committee rejected this argument, essentially saying that to
have one official language in court proceedings could not raise any issue of
discrimination, since 'everyone was being treated equally', unless of course one
could not understand the language of the court.

The Committee's reasoning was perhaps based on one of the most frequent
misconceptions involving non-discrimination in international law, which is the
assumption that a state measure imposing a single language for all signifies that
everyone is treated the same and that therefore there is no active differentiation
being made between individuals. Since everyone can attend the same school
classes, or receive the same administrative forms and services - in only one official
language - everyone is therefore treated equally within the meaning of the principle
of non-discrimination. Although it would take too long to fully explain how this
position has very gradually changed in international law, one can summarise by
stating that there are in fact many 'linguistic rights' which are protected within
existing individual human rights:

> Language preferences or restrictions by a state may breach fundamental
> human rights such as freedom of expression, non-discrimination, and the
> right of members of linguistic minorities to freely use their language in
> community with other members of their group. In practice, specific
> situations may involve a combination of these rights, as in the case where
> public authorities adopt measures which restrict an individual's use of his
> or her minority language with other members of his group and, at the
> same time, conflict with that person's freedom of expression. Despite
> some overlapping, the various human rights do provide a degree of
> protection in respect to language matters in distinct areas of activities. (de
> Varennes, 1996, 174)

In other words, Dr. Skutnabb-Kangas' basic principle that 'linguistic rights should
be considered basic human rights' (Skutnabb-Kangas & Phillipson, 1994, 1) is not
as objectionable from a legal position as it might have seemed until relatively
recently.

Regardless of what may have been the initial unease at trying to reconcile her
non-legal perception and approach to the more technical nature of international law,
there has undoubtedly been in recent years a convergence of the two approaches.

A gradual convergence

> The importance of language rights is grounded in the essential role that
> language plays in human existence, development and dignity. It is
> through language that we are able to form concepts; to structure and order
> the world around us. Language bridges the gap between isolation and
> community, allowing humans to delineate the rights and duties they hold
> in respect of one another, and thus live in society. (*Re Manitoba
> Language Rights*, 1985, 1 Supreme Court Reports 721, 744, Canada)

As early as 1983, Dr. Skutnabb-Kangas had proposed a provisional declaration on
linguistic rights which would eventually serve as a model for the Declaration of
Recife, adopted at an international seminar on Human Rights and Cultural Rights
held in 1987 and organised by the International Association for Cross-Cultural
Communication and UNESCO. While this must have seemed like a pipedream 20
years ago, developments which began in the 1980s would eventually lead to the
adoption of treaties and other instruments which to some extent have given a legal
shape to the views of Dr. Skutnabb-Kangas, although not always exactly in the
form she might have envisaged.

At about the same time as Dr. Skutnabb-Kangas had presented in 1983 a
provisional declaration on linguistic rights, there was a movement in Europe to
grant some kind of legal recognition to the rights of linguistic minorities. There
were for example at the European Parliament level a *Resolution on a Community*

charter of regional languages and cultures and on a charter of rights of ethnic minorities and the Council of Europe's *Recommendation on the educational and cultural problems of minority languages and dialects in Europe.* From a strictly legal point of view these documents had no binding effect, but they did however represent tentative first steps in the direction of greater tolerance for the use of minority or indigenous languages by governments as envisaged by Dr. Skutnabb-Kangas. There emerged from that point on an increasing number of documents from rather disparate sources such as the Organisation on Security and Cooperation in Europe (OSCE), UNESCO, and the United Nations and others, which all appeared to signal a basic agreement on the fundamental principles dealing with the 'right' to use minority or indigenous languages.

While the 1980s for the most part signalled an increased acceptance of 'linguistic rights' from a social or moral point of view, it took somewhat longer to see an evolution in legally-binding terms. But that is what finally occurred in the 1990s with the creation and entry into force of two legally-binding treaties, the *European Charter for Regional or Minority Languages*, and the *Framework Convention for the Protection of National Minorities.*

Although there are differences between the two, beginning with the point of view and wording each adopts to address matters such as public education in minority languages or the right to use these languages in contacts with public officials, the essential fact remains that they agree in most areas. The same principles are also to be found in specialised documents commissioned by the OSCE known as the *Oslo Recommendations Regarding the Linguistic Rights of National Minorities* and *The Hague Recommendations Regarding the Education Rights of National Minorities*, as well as in United Nations documents such as the *Declaration on the Rights of Persons Belonging to National or Ethnic, Religious and Linguistic Minorities.*

Despite differences in emphasis and terminology, there is for example acceptance of fundamental principles which Dr. Skutnabb-Kangas has repeatedly promoted such as an entitlement to public education in minority or indigenous languages, although this is 'according to the situation of each [language]' (*European Charter for Regional or Minority Languages*), 'in areas inhabited by persons belonging to national minorities traditionally or in substantial numbers' (*Framework Convention for the Protection of National Minorities*), or 'wherever possible' (*The Hague Recommendations Regarding the Education Rights of National Minorities* and the *UN Declaration on the Rights of Persons Belonging to National or Ethnic, Religious and Linguistic Minorities*). Despite the differences in wording, all of these documents show a convergence, an acceptance in political and legal terms of the 'linguistic right to education' so strongly espoused by Dr. Skutnabb-Kangas since the 1980s.

Conclusion

> Does not the sun shine equally for the whole world? Do we not all equally breathe the air? Do you not feel shame at authorising only three languages and condemning other people to blindness and deafness? Tell me, do you think that God is helpless and cannot bestow equality, or that he is envious and will not give it? (Saint Constantine, quoted in Fishman, 1968, 589)

What Dr. Skutnabb-Kangas had first proposed at the beginning of the 1980s seems to have become increasingly accepted in legal circles. Although it has taken quite some time and the legal approach is not completely in accord with the approach she would have preferred, it is undeniable that international law has embarked on the path of recognising certain rights to the use of minority or indigenous people's languages.

The principles of tolerance and the call for 'linguistic rights' espoused by Dr. Skutnabb-Kangas and the rights afforded in international law to individuals in areas of language use and preferences have in many ways become strikingly similar, if not altogether identical. It is as if there is agreement that human dignity and respect for human differences can and must be accommodated whenever possible as part and parcel of human rights within a democratic framework, and that in practice means some degree of use of minority and indigenous languages by public officials and entities in appropriate circumstances. From a moral - and legal - position, Dr. Skutnabb-Kangas has been right all along.

Unity in Difference - Belonging

Pirkko Leporanta-Morley

Unity in difference

Te, joille samankaltaisuus
on itsestäänselvyys
vahvistamattakin vakio
ette voi tietää
kuinka erilaisuuteen
kasvetaan, kasvatetaan
kuinka katoavan tiedon
kantaminen
meidät yhdistää.

You for whom being homogeneous
is self-evident
an axiomatic constant
you cannot know
how one grows up,
is brought up to difference
how being bearers of
disappearing knowledge
unites us.

Belonging

Jag har uppfostrats
med den evakuerades kunskap
om hur man avstår
från de älskade trakterna
utan at glömma
om hur man skiljs
från sin släkt
utan at förlora kontakt
om hur man tillhör
folk och kultur
som rotas igen
i den nya jorden.

I was brought up
with the knowledge of the evacuee
knowing how one leaves behind
the beloved landscape
without forgetting
how one is separated
from family
without losing contact
how one belongs
to a people and culture
rooted again
in new earth.

Discourse and Access

Teun A. van Dijk

If there is one aspect of language, discourse, and communication Tove Skutnabb-Kangas has studied in her scholarly work and stood for in her personal life (the two inextricably combined), it has been people's access to talk and text. Linguicism not only involves being barred from using your own language, but also being excluded from or marginalized in communicative events. You may be allowed to use a 'foreign' or a 'minority' language as immigrants or as children of immigrants, but what if your talk or text does not count, is not credible, or nobody listens to or reads you?

Thus linguicism, broadly understood, is to be studied in a framework that also critically examines all forms of discursive discrimination and marginalization. What does it mean if we are allowed to speak only in everyday conversations, or may only passively use the mass media, but have no active access to, or control over, elite discourse such as political speeches, news articles, textbooks, scientific discourse, or corporate communication?

In this small tribute to the work of Tove Skutnabb-Kangas, I would therefore like to briefly reflect on 'access to (public) discourse' as an important aspect of linguistic human rights.

Discourse access as social power resource

Differences of power between different groups are reflected in their differential access to public discourse. Ordinary people only seem to have active control over very few discourse genres. They have active access as speakers and listeners only to everyday conversations with family and friends. For most other discourses in their lives, such as those of teachers, bosses, or the media, they have little opportunity to 'talk back' in some kind of equal interaction.

On the other hand, members of various elite groups have much greater scope for discursive control and access. Indeed, people's power is not merely measured in money, land, income, position, or knowledge, or other material or symbolic resources, but also by their access to public discourse. Professors have much broader scope for access than their students, journalists a broader one than their readers, and politicians a more extensive one than their voters.

This is true both for the number of discourse genres controlled, as well as for the amount of control over each text and its context, including the audience. Thus presidents and prime ministers have access to many forms of political discourse, including those of the media, and even textbooks and everyday conversations in which he (and less often she) may have access as a person often spoken *about*. Journalists come running to them. Few people and positions are so powerful. Thus, access to public discourse in contemporary society may be a direct measure of social and political power.

Analyzing power

To understand the role of discourse access in social relations of power and domination, we need a preliminary understanding of power which can only be briefly summarized here. Defined basically as a form of social control of one group (organization, institution) over others, such control seems to apply primarily to action: We have power over others if they do what we want, or what is in our (and not in their) best interest. Such action control may be based on force, and hence be a form of coercion (as in male violence against women, or military or police violence against citizens), or on other resources of control (such as money, a job, position) that allow us to 'make' people do what we want.

Many forms of modern power are more subtle though. They control action indirectly and symbolically, for instance by persuasion. Such power is exerted by mind control. And since the mind is primarily controlled by text and talk, access to discourse as a power resource becomes essential. In other words, if minds are controlled by discourse, control over discourse is an important, though indirect, condition for mind control. Control over influential public discourse implies more power over other people's minds, hence more symbolic power. The processes involved in 'mind control', such as communication, interaction, discourse production and understanding, thought, judgement and decision making, among others, are vastly complex, but this is the overall picture of how access to public discourse is related to power.

Critical scholars are especially interested in *power abuse* or *domination*, when the exercise of power violates basic principles, norms, agreements, and ultimately people's human rights. If some groups have preferential access to political, media, educational or scholarly discourse, and abuse that power by ignoring or being derogatory about women, minorities, refugees, or the poor, we speak of discursive or communicative power abuse or domination. This power is subtly exercised in many forms of everyday social practices, and in text and talk in particular: non-dominant groups are excluded, marginalized, or treated as problems not only socially and economically, but also cognitively and discursively.

Fortunately, the same analysis also permits an understanding of counter-power and resistance. As soon as dominated groups gain access to various forms of public discourse, primarily that of politics, the media and education, we have the beginnings of effective forms of resistance and challenge. Analysis of access to public discourse is essential both for dominant and dominated groups, and facilitates understanding of the dynamic and dialectic interplay of power abuse and resistance.

Types of access

There are many forms of 'access' depending on how it is defined. The basic question we need to examine may be summarized - still informally - as follows:

Who may/must talk/write/read/listen (to) whom, when, where and why?

A first distinction is between access to discourse *production* and *reception*, examples of which have been given. Access may be voluntary and 'free', that is, people may decide for themselves whether to speak/write or read/listen, or they may be obliged to do so. In interrogations in a police station or courtroom, suspects or witnesses may be obliged to speak; a secretary of a board meeting may be obliged to be silent, or to speak only when spoken to. Students may be obliged to read textbooks or texts and to listen to teachers, etc. In other words, access to both production and reception may be *free* or *obligatory*.

We may have access to discourse largely controlled or produced by others. In everyday usage, 'access' mostly refers to the way we contribute to discourse controlled by others, for instance when a politician has better access to media discourse produced by journalists. It sounds strange to state that we have 'access' to our own conversations or letters. Yet, technically, that is what is involved: one has some degree of control over one's own discourse, thus students have access to oral or written exams, but their contribution is significantly controlled by their teachers.

One typologically interesting criterion is therefore whether people have *full* or *partial* access to or control over their own or others' discourse. I may fully control the content and style of a lecture or a letter, or this paper (though the editor has *some* influence over it). But as soon as I contribute to a conversation or text largely controlled by others, my production and control is only partial, for instance in a talk show, a lesson at school, or a courtroom.

Similarly, access or control over one's own or others' discourse may be *exclusive* (*individual*) or *shared* (*collective*). In most oral discourse we speak for ourselves, individually, but in many forms of institutional or written discourse, talk or text may be jointly produced, typically so in the media, but also in organizational documents, brochures, and the like. Obviously, shared control implies limited individual control. Virtually no journalists have full control over a newspaper report, and even less over a television program - if only for technical reasons. There are many different *discourse production roles* that people engage in, and they may only have access to, or control over the dimension of discourse that is associated with a particular role, such as providing ideas, prescribing a topic, checking style or images, recording, and so on.

These various types and examples also show that access or control over discourse may be more or less *active* or *passive*. Both cognitive psychology and current media studies emphasize that there is no such thing as 'passive' discourse reception: Listeners and readers actually *do* something, not merely listen or read. This 'active' role of recipients explains why discourses do not always have the intended effects: readers or viewers are no communicative 'dupes'. They do with discourses what they like or prefer, up to a point. Yet, the distinction makes sense for several reasons. Thus, my contribution to a newspaper article, talk show, or political speech may be passive, for instance when others speak or write *about* me. We could call this topical access: I am a topic of talk. Similarly, others may cite my work in theirs, or an expert opinion in a news report, without my having any control over that - again, that would mean a form of passive access. This would typically be a gradual distinction, because I may volunteer - actively - an opinion about some event when interviewed by a reporter, but whether or not the reporter or editor will include what I say is up to them, and largely beyond my control. There are numerous types of more or less passive or active forms of access to both production and reception. I may be an active listener when wanting information, or I may be forced to listen to what others have to say, which could be described as more 'passive'.

These and other examples show that there are fuzzy borders between *control*, *access* and *influence*. I may not control a news item, or have active access to it, but if I am powerful or interesting enough I may influence its production. In the same way, my ideas may influence other scholarly work, even when I do not have direct access to, or control over it.

An elementary typology of discourse access and control leads to a very complex array of properties of communicative events, the role of participants in these events, and the way participants - and others - are represented or addressed in such discourse. Thus, each type of communicative event or genre, such as a everyday conversation at home, this paper, a lesson in school, a job interview, news report, talk show, board meeting, police interrogation, doctor's consultation, novel, and so on, may be characterized in terms of the kinds of control over or access of the participants - writers, speakers or readers, listeners - to (part of) such discourse. Since we are dealing with the roles of participants in discourse, there is a *contextual* dimension.

What we seem to be dealing with here is various forms of *intertextuality*, such as when news reports cite opinions, eyewitness testimony or reports. The same holds in court or the classroom. A theory of intertextuality involves not only relations between texts per se, but also access to complex contexts, which requires a theory of context.

Access to text and context

Finally, and most crucially, then, access may be analyzed in terms of (partial/complete, sole/collective, etc.) control over *text* or *context*.

What is involved in *context control* depends on our theory of context, and since such a theory barely exists, we need to improvise the relevant categories involved in the production, reception or uses of discourse in social situations. Leaving aside the nature of context, I shall simply assume that contexts are abstract structures that define what in communicative situations is *relevant* for the production, forms, content or reception of discourse. In other words, cognitively speaking, contexts are 'constructions' of participants. These constructions may be represented as subjectively variable mental models represented in episodic memory (the storehouse of our personal experiences).

Thus I may control how people see, interpret or model the social situation in which they talk, write or read (e.g. 'This is not an interrogation, but a friendly chat') and this should also influence the way they speak or listen, write or read. Or, more directly, I may influence the social situation itself, e.g. by establishing the domain, time, place, occasion, goals, purpose, and so on. I may decide who may participate and in what role, when, and where. Thus professors and doctors tell their students and patients when to meet for a test. Discourse control is not limited to the verbal dimension of communicative events, but also involves social aspects of the situation.

Finally, access to discourse most crucially manifests itself in the ways people (groups, institutions, organizations) control the various properties of *discourse 'itself'*. Thus, we may have more or less, partial or complete, control over the topics, local meanings, coherence, lexical style, and rhetoric of a discourse. And since the structures of the text build on an understanding of how people's minds are controlled, discourse control is also, indirectly, control over the mind.

Mind control

Control by persuasion requires access to the mind. Since discourse is a form of interaction, however, discourse control is a kind of action control if we have access to others' discourses. If we - as a group - are able to have people say what we wish, we control at least part of their verbal actions. In other words, when controlling discourse, influencing action and mind seem to coincide.

More specifically, we control others' minds by writing or speaking in such a way that people's minds are changed (or not) more or less as we wish. Since minds are very complex, so are these influences. We may thus influence the construction or activation of mental models, knowledge, attitudes, ideologies, or values. Headlines may be used to establish overall coherence and interesting topics, which may influence the mental model that interprets the real-word events. Local meanings supported by lexical style may influence social attitudes and ideologies, and so on. In this way, discourse control may lead to 'preferred models' (as persuasion can be understood).

We have thus come full circle. People or groups are powerful because of their access to social resources, including public talk and text. Once they have access to public discourse, they obtain indirect access to people's minds, which may further confirm dominant group power.

Research on discourse access needs to focus on all the elements mentioned, such as control over participants and their roles in context, how contexts are constituted, and so on. The same is true crucially of the ways discourse influences the mind. Why are some people (groups) often more credible than others? Which groups influence our knowledge, attitudes or ideologies more than others? Apart from existing work on persuasion, much research is needed on how (the processing of) specific discourse structures influences changes of mental models and social representations.

Conclusion

I have argued that an analysis of patterns of access to public discourse is a useful means to understand power and domination. If using one's language is a linguistic human right, then there are particular rights which have to do with discourse and communication and their control. Depending on group membership, position, and other factors, some people have greater control over (various) public discourses. I have briefly examined various types of access, and shown how each communicative event may be analyzed in terms of a set of access properties, depending on who is speaking/listening, and who is under partial or full control of production or reception. Access may be associated with context features as well as text features. Indeed, access *is* a crucial property of text and context, influencing how participants are able to control the structure of the social situation, as well as the structures of discourse, and hence, indirectly, those of the mind.

Language Rights for the Language of Norfolk Island

Peter Mühlhäusler

One can look at views about the inherent value of languages and their being worthy of protection from two perspectives. First, there have been considerable changes in the absolute number of languages thought worthy of protection (and indeed scholarly linguistic study), i.e. to the classical languages Hebrew, Latin and Greek were added over time European national languages, dialects of European languages, traditional indigenous languages, and Pidgins and Creoles. What has not changed is the perceived hierarchy of languages. Whilst much time and money continues to be spent on classical and nation state languages and in particular world languages, resources benefiting other languages are unimpressive. Whilst on paper all languages might have the same rights, in real life, a few are very privileged and most are underprivileged and in danger of dying out. What has contributed to an enhanced status of certain languages is their perceived purity - conversely languages whose impure, mixed or incomplete character was common knowledge continued to be excluded from the rights that are afforded to 'normal languages'. Among this group we find Pidgins, Creoles, immigrant mixed 'jargons' such as Cocoliche in Argentina, and similar non 'standard' forms of powerful language such as English. Whilst a great number of English-related languages are spoken in the Pacific region for instance, only very few have a proper name (e.g. Bislama and Tok Pisin but not informal English of Milne Bay, Bass Strait English or Palmerston Island English) and even fewer have any formal recognition. The principal aim of this paper is to highlight a few aspects of the history of the language of Norfolk Island and its socio-political status.

Norfolk(ese)

In 1854 the descendants of the mutineers of the Bounty and their Tahitian partners were resettled from Pitcairn Island to Norfolk Island in the South Pacific (an island of 35 square kilometres located about 1,600 km from Sydney or Brisbane by plane) which, after half a century of having served as the penal colony, had become vacant. By 1854 the Pitcairn Islanders had developed a linguistically distinct form of speech which most of them used side by side with English as a language of everyday spoken discourse. Its status on Pitcairn Island was ambivalent and affected by two conflicting sources. On the one hand, Islanders' ways of speaking reinforced their feeling of uniqueness and special identity; on the other, acrolectal standard British English enjoyed enormous prestige which was enhanced by the arrival of two Englishmen in 1823, one of whom, John Buffett became the island's first school teacher. Pitcairn prides itself as having been the first place in the English-speaking world with compulsory primary education in English. The informal language continued to be spoken and passed on to new generations of speakers but it had no name, was not written (and very rarely written about) by the islanders and was characterized by visiting outsiders in fairly unflattering terms: Broken English, a clipping of English words, an extraordinary patois, and bastard jargon, characterizations which have persisted until the very recent past, and have to some extent also been adopted by the speech community.

Once transported to Norfolk, the diglossic (English high, Pitcairn/Norfolk low) situation persisted but the increase of contact with the outside world - first with the British-run Melanesian Mission which established itself on Norfolk in 1858, and increasingly Australian administration, the state of the Pitcairners' ways of speaking began to deteriorate. The trend to administer religion and teaching in standard English strengthened and the missionaries of the Melanesian Mission held the languages of the Pitcairners in contempt. Norfolk began to be administered by Australia and when the school system of New South Wales was adopted after 1913, deliberate steps were taken to eliminate the Norfolk language. Its use was forbidden in the schoolgrounds and many of my older informants told me of physical and psychological punishment for using the Norfolk language. In addition, the education system reinforced the negative stereotypes about the language as 'a haphazardly constructed medium, originally adopted for talk among people who were either unable or too lazy to speak English properly' (Harrison, 1985, 137).

The outcome has been that many islanders were now ashamed of using the language in public and the growing number of mainlanders and visitors to the islands saw no reason to acquire any knowledge of Norfolk.

Today not only are the islanders of Pitcairn origin outnumbered by Australians and New Zealanders (about 900 against 1,500) but the members of the Pitcairn descendants no longer have a good grasp of their own traditional language.

Types of language right

The story told thus far differs little from that of many other English-related languages, for example the Creole of the West Indies, West African Pidgin English, or Solomon Island Pidgin. However, there are some interesting differences as well.

The Pitcairn society came into being as an act of mutiny and there are strong indications that their mixed English-Tahitian language had its origins in a deliberate act of defiance. Whilst the ontological status of Pitcairn/Norfolk is far from sorted out (Mühlhäusler, 1998), it is clear that we are not dealing with a Creole or indeed, as was thought in the past, a mixture but a language that exhibits many traces of deliberate creation. The very strong sense of identity has survived to the present, which has led to recent attempts to have the Pitcairn/Norfolk community recognized as an indigenous people and their language declared an indigenous language.

It is interesting to note that indigenous Australians, when faced with this prospect, dismissed it as they have dismissed the claims that Kanaka English, the language spoken by some of the descendants of the Melanesian sugar plantations workers in Queensland, be given recognition. The claim to be an indigenous people speaking an indigenous language is also perceived as undesirable by most mainlander residents and members of the Pitcairn descendant community on Norfolk. It is one thing to give the language some legal status as a quaint dialect of English, another proposition to recognize it as an independent language.

The question of the relative official status of English and Norfolk remains to be answered but whatever answer will eventually be given will not be of great consequence for its survival. That Norfolk will be recognized as an indigenous language either in the Pacific context or by virtue of the fact that Norfolk is governed by Australia is unlikely. The reasons for this are economic: Recognizing Norfolk in this way would give it access to funding currently shared by 'recognized' indigenous languages. The funds needed to institutionalize Norfolk would need to be channelled away from recognized indigenous languages in Australia and the Pacific and would also require a reallocation of considerable amounts of public funding on Norfolk away from English to Norfolk. Particularly critical would be claims for money to be spent on reclamation and restoration of the Norfolk language which, as a consequence of past policies favouring English, has lost much of its viability. Equal rights with English thus appear unlikely to materialize.

At present, there are no official rights for the language but a debate has begun as to what rights there might be in future. An aspect of this debate is whether it should be recognized as a heritage language or an official language and in what domains and functions. Can Norfolk become a language of education, public speaking, law, politics, church etc.?

The tacit agreement of most players appears to be that whatever rights Norfolk obtains should not be at the cost of English. Knowledge of English has been a prerequisite for full membership in the Pitcairn/Norfolk community from its beginnings and at no time in the past was there a monolingual Norfolk-only community. By the same token, for most of the history of the Pitcairn/Norfolk community there were members who were monolingual in English only.

Unlike in other cases, one cannot argue for rights for Norfolk and its speakers on grounds of communication or its educational disadvantages (certainly not today - there may have been some sound arguments in the past). Rather one has to argue for the right of the community to have in addition to a medium of communication a medium of signalling identity (or indeed non-identity with outsiders). But in acknowledging this, there is another twist. For most of its existence, Pitcairn/Norfolk has been an esoteric insider language, and outsiders, even those who married into the community were discouraged from learning it. Giving the language new status and rights in education and public life will inevitably diminish its esoteric nature. As with other indigenous languages of Australia the question of language ownership arises: Should its speakers keep the exclusive rights to speaking and learning it? Should outsiders be permitted to learn it? Should information about the language be restricted to a few selected by its indigenous speakers? Should different peer groups have the right to deep subtle differences?

There are at present no answers to these questions. Talking about rights is relatively easy for named exoteric and straightforward old languages but in the case of Pitcairn/Norfolk there are issues that remain to be resolved. As I write this I am preparing, at the request of Norfolk Islanders, a draft language plan for the Norfolk language in which these issues are considered. I share the fear and sadness of the Norfolk Islanders that their way of speaking will disappear. And like them I hope that sorting out these issues will not only promote rights but promote the continued well-being of the language.

Tove's work on linguistic human rights (e.g. in Skutnabb-Kangas & Phillipson, eds., 1994) has done much to increase awareness of language rights around the globe. I hope that her ideas will thrive in the fertile soil of Norfolk Island.

The Latvian Language Law Debate: Some Aspects of Linguistic Human Rights in Education

Ina Druviete

The Latvian sociolinguistic scene

The civic and linguistic integration of minorities is a core public issue in post-communist states that affects both domestic and international stability. A policy of cultural pluralism is being pursued in Latvia that recognizes the language rights of minorities while at the same time seeking to forge a common civic identity. Over the last three years there has been an increasing number of publications that deal with the issue of civic society in general and with the linguistic integration of minorities in particular. As with any state that is truly independent, Latvia is inexorably evolving into a civic nation. In Latvia's case the integration process is complicated by the ethnic diversity of Latvia and poor Latvian language skills among certain groups of inhabitants, who therefore cannot fully participate in the life of the nation.

The education system in Latvia plays an increasingly important role in facilitating competence in Latvian as a second language for children of other (i.e. non-ethnic Latvian) nationalities. In 1998 the Latvian Saeima (Parliament) worked on two new laws which include special provisions for the linguistic integration of Latvian society – the Education Law and the Law on State Language.

According to the draft laws, in primary schools three types of bilingual education program will be offered. All high schools which are financed by the state or local government will become state language (i.e. Latvian) schools by the year 2005, but primary schools may also be national and ethnic minority language schools or offer minority language classes. The principal language of higher education establishments will be Latvian.

The population of Latvia comprises 2,450,000 people. 55.5% of this number are Latvians, and 44.5% are representatives of other nationalities, of which 32.4% are Russians, 3.9% Belarusans, 2.9% Ukrainians, 2.2% Poles, 1.3% Lithuanians, 0.4%

Jews, 0.3% Gypsies, 0.1% Germans, 0.1% Estonians, and 0.9% others (Data from State Statistical Committee, January 1998). There are 4 types of schools in Latvia at present:
1. with Latvian as the language of instruction,
2. with Russian as the language of instruction,
3. integrated schools with Latvian and Russian sections,
4. ethnic minority schools.
In the school year 1997/1998 there were 1074 schools in Latvia – 719 with Latvian as the language of instruction, 199 – with Russian, 150 integrated schools, 6 ethnic minority schools (minority classes are not included in this calculation; data from the Ministry of Education, May 1988). Nevertheless, the number of students educated in a language other than Latvian or Russian is still insignificant. In the school year 1997/98 there are 1043 pupils being educated in languages other than Latvian or Russian – 753 students studying in Polish, 215 – in Ukrainian, 31 – in Lithuanian, 44 – in Belarusan (Ministry of Education, 1998). Practically all Russian and other minority students still continue to attend Russian-medium schools. Hitherto, a large proportion of the young people graduating from these schools had poor competence in the Latvian language, this hampering the integration process. This has led to a political decision to terminate the system of separate education, which hinders not only the linguistic but also the cultural and civic integration of the society.

Respecting linguistic human rights

Both laws have sparked debate about linguistic human rights in education. The question that needs answering is whether international language rights standards include a provision that a minority such as the Russian-speakers has the right to receive education in Russian at every level.

As regards the primary school, what is considered by the Latvian government to be the main task is to ensure adequate opportunities for instruction in the mother tongue not only for Russians but for all the minorities in Latvia,. At the same time the second language - the official language - will be added in various bilingual education programs. Secondary education will be provided basically in Latvian, with optional study programs for national minorities. It is difficult to see how integration can be achieved when there is still a system of separate education and students of different ethnicities meet one another for the first time in higher education establishments. It is also a duty of the state to provide an education that will allow school graduates to be fully employable and to continue their studies in higher educational establishments. As to the language of instruction in these, I fully agree with the analysis of the Russian sociolinguist Diachkov:

> An attempt by certain groups of the non-Latvian population (those not
> interested in inter-ethnic integration or the formation of a political nation
> in Latvia) to use the Russian language as the only or predominant

> language of instruction at the higher educational level for non-Latvian
> students ... seems to contradict the provisions of the European Charter for
> Regional or Minority Languages and is absolutely senseless and even
> detrimental to inter-ethnic relations within a small European state. Such a
> practice would promote the ethnic disintegration of the country, and
> estrange Latvia from the European and world community of nations
> rather than facilitate its integration into it (Diachkov, 1998, translation by
> ID).

It could also be mentioned that the draft laws provide for a transitional period
leading to secondary and higher education in the official language. Also none of the
laws contain articles about the language of instruction in private higher education
establishments or those financed from abroad.

Thus we can conclude that the principle of mother tongue education has been
respected in Latvia and that there are no violations of linguistic human rights. As
regards the transitional situation of the language hierarchy in Latvia, the right and
duty of minorities in Latvia to learn the state language is important not only because
it ensures that the linguistic rights of Russophones do not result in linguistic self-
sufficiency and the segregation of this minority. The logic of a democratic language
and education policy is to protect the weaker languages and the languages of
minorities.

In the case of Latvia this meant that Latvian had to be promoted to reassert the
language rights of the indigenous nation, and the languages of smaller minorities
had to be recognized in schools and cultural life. The case of Latvia illustrates a
two-track policy whereby one policy track aims at enhancing the use of an official
language as a tool of state-building and formation of a civic nation, and the other
track maintains minority language space, in this case primarily in the schools. A
pax linguistica is possible only if all groups feel that their languages are
safeguarded. This is especially true in cases where one deals with a territory that
represents the only place where a certain language is used; groups using a language
that is used in kin-states tend to be culturally less anxious (Karklins, 1998, 249-
250).

Tove Skutnabb-Kangas was one of the first foreign experts who stressed the
relevance of the sociolinguistic context when choosing educational models. She
wrote in 1992 (see 1994b, 178):

> In my view, during several years to come, the Russian language in the
> Baltics must during a transitional period be treated as a majority language
> for all educational purposes ... whereas the Baltic languages must for
> educational purposes be treated as minority languages, in need of
> protection. Russian is thus a majorized minority language (a minority
> language in terms of numbers, but with the power of majority language),
> whereas the Baltic languages are minorized majority languages (majority
> languages, in need of the protection usually necessary for threatened
> minority languages).

This principle has been observed in the Latvian education system up to now.

The Latvian state has developed legislation which establishes a foundation for the integration of Latvian society as well as for future integration into the European Union. The country has been very active in ensuring that Latvian laws are in accordance with international standards and human rights principles. The education system presents the greatest challenge to Latvian sociolinguists and politicians: strategies are needed to ensure that decisions are well grounded politically and scientifically and based on long-term ethnic and language policies.

Use of Language Rights by Minorities

E. Annamalai

Constitutional rights and their exercise

Legal provision of language rights may be a necessary condition to sustain linguistic diversity, but the ways in which and the purposes for which they are used are crucial for the maintenance of minority languages. The laws may be ignored or subverted by the State on some administrative, financial, or political reasoning, which is made possible by the way laws are formulated so as to permit administrative laxity and contingencies (Skutnabb-Kangas, 1998). The minority linguistic communities may demand application of the laws under certain political and historical conditions and not under others. The community may use the law for a purpose which it deems to be in its interest but which may not be the intent of the law. This chapter examines how different minority linguistic communities in India make or do not make use of the language rights provided by the law and how they perceive their interests when they use them.

The Indian Constitution explicitly provides the right for any section of the citizens having a distinct language, script, or culture of its own to conserve the same (Article 29(1)). This is a right to preserve a language and its script. Their use is a prerequisite for their preservation. Therefore, the right to the preservation of language entails its use. The minorities, religious and linguistic, also have the right to establish and administer educational institutions of their choice (Article 30). It is left to the minorities to decide about using their educational institutions to preserve their language and culture in whatever manner, and to decide on use of their languages in education for the purpose of their preservation.

As far as the role of the State in schooling is concerned, it shall not deny admission to any educational institution maintained or aided by it to any citizen on grounds of language among other grounds like religion, race, and caste (Article 29(2)). The right to admission is not the right to have equal access to education for the children of linguistic minorities. To enable this, it is enjoined upon the State that it should endeavour to give education in the mother tongue of the child at the primary level (Article 350A). The administrative proviso to this is a condition on the number of minority students in a class and in a school. Use of mother tongue in primary education is not a right of the citizen, but is an obligation of the State. The annual reports of the Linguistic Minorities Commission give a number of instances of representations by linguistic minorities about states not fulfilling their obligation.

With regard to language in government administration, every citizen is entitled to submit a representation for the redress of any grievance to any officer or authority of the State in any language used in the state (Article 350). The State is not, however, obliged to respond in the same language. In legal proceedings, the accused must be given their charge sheet in a language known to them.

Besides these Articles with specific reference to language, the Constitution guarantees certain fundamental rights for equality before the law (Article 14) and for non-discrimination (Article 15). Though language is not included as a ground for non-discrimination, the courts have interpreted this Article in conjunction with Article 350A with regard to primary education and decided that it is discriminating the child of a linguistic minority if the State denies primary education in the minority language (Annamalai, 1998).

Linguistic minorities cannot be taken as one undifferentiated entity with regard to their use of these laws to realize their language rights. They have different political and historical characteristics, which play a role in their desire and action to use language rights and in the success of their actions. At the national level, every language in India is a minority language with no language having speakers in excess of 50% of the population. For the use of any language of India in the administration of the federal government, the rights issue is not an issue of minority languages versus a majority language but is an issue of appropriation of that use between minority languages. English gains in this conflict because the communities of some minority languages, which claim cultural distinctiveness on historical and political grounds, perceive their political interests to be with English at the national level.

At the level of the states, there are a majority language and many minority languages. These minority languages are of two kinds, viz. Endogenous and exogenous. The former do not have speakers of their languages in other states (other than those living contiguously across state borders and migrants in pursuit of employment), and the latter have a majority of their speakers in another state or their speakers distributed in many states with no majority in any state. These two kinds have different historical and cultural relations with the majority language of the state in which they exist. The former have another state where their speakers are in a majority to extend moral and political support for them. The minority languages also differ in their demographic characteristics. Their population size makes their political presence different and it enables them to function differently as political constituencies. They also differ in their economic (mainstream v. marginal economic activity) and geographic base (urban v. rural residence), which makes a difference to their position in the centre-periphery axis of political power in the state. These differences contribute to the differences in their perceptions of their interests and in their use of language rights to realize their perceived interests.

The minority linguistic communities make different demands with regard to their language and may be classified broadly under the following headings.

1. Development of language: This covers codification, publication, and literary and cultural activities for which a claim on the resources of the State is made. Codification includes, depending on the need level of the language, having a script or standardizing it, making a dictionary, and translating basic documents relating to government welfare and development programmes. Publication includes printing and purchasing for local libraries and schools books and magazines produced in the language. Literary and cultural activities include support to community organizations involved in such activities and sponsorship of such organizations by the government.

2. Use in the media: This relates to allocation of radio and television time that is under government control for programmes in minority languages, mostly music and news. It may also include public signboards locally displayed, and naming public utilities in the locality after the community's personae.

3. Access to education: This includes establishment of educational institutions and government approval of them, provision for the minority language in the language policy in education as a subject and as a medium at levels depending on the status of the minority language, and installation of compensatory mechanisms in admissions and examinations in educational institutions to redress the linguistic disadvantage of minority language students.

4. Access to employment: This includes requiring proficiency in the majority language in recruitment and having a relaxed proficiency level in the majority language for jobs in the public sector, and affirmative action reserving jobs in this sector not on the basis of language but on the basis of socio-economic disadvantage, which may or may not correlate with the minority status of a language. It also covers having the status of additional official language for specified regions or purposes depending on the position of the minority language in the state.

It may be noted that access to information including that related to consumer products and services, access to legal proceedings, and access to governmental administration to redress grievances in the minority language do not figure in the above categories. They do not figure prominently in minority community discourses on language rights. The majority language community also has problems in these areas, where the rule of English persists.

The minority linguistic communities differ in which demands they make, and in their success in achieving them. These differences correlate with political, historical, and demographic characteristics. Sometimes mere symbolic recognition is considered adequate by elites seeking to enhance their political status. The success potential of demands increases when the language is conflated with other primordial symbols like religion and ethnicity to identify and mobilize the minority community.

Some examples of the implementation of language rights

The political goals and strategies followed to realize language rights vary between
the linguistic minorities. When there is a critical demographic mass, geographic
contiguity, and distinct ethnic identity, the demand may be for political autonomy
for the language territory as a separate state within the country or as a separate
district with special powers within a state. The formation of the states of Nagaland,
Meghalaya and Mizoram, whose people are speakers of Tibeto-Burman languages,
tribal, and Christians, out of Assam, whose speakers of the majority language are
Indo-Aryan and Hindus, is an example of the former. The formation of the
autonomous districts of Karbi for the speakers of Karbi, a Tibeto-Burman language
in Assam, and Darjeeling for the speakers of Gorkhali, a dialect of Nepali in West
Bengal, is an example of the latter. Both took place after violent agitation for
political autonomy to protect, among other things, the language and culture of the
communities concerned. The use made of their language in public domains after
political autonomy, however, varies.

Urdu, which is identified with Islam and has sizeable populations in some
states, is a second official language in Uttar Pradesh and Bihar, and in Andhra
Pradesh in a few districts.

With regard to the use of minority languages in education, exogenous minorities
have succeeded in having their languages included as a medium at the primary level
and as a subject at higher levels. It is one means of checking the dominance of the
majority language (Annamalai, forthcoming). Thus Telugu, Tamil, Malayalam, and
Marathi figure in the school curriculum in Karnataka, as well as Urdu. However,
the urban middle class in the minority community may prefer English-medium, fee-
paying schools.

The endogenous linguistic minorities who are economically advanced and
culturally assimilatory at the level of high culture, like, for example, the speakers of
Tulu, Kodagu, and Konkani in Karnataka, do not generally claim their language
rights in the domains of education and administration. They perceive that their
bilingualism in the majority language has not undermined their economic and
political interests and they do not see much advantage even symbolically in
demanding the use of their languages in public domains. What they demand is
language development for linguistic, literary, and cultural activities.

Political factors at the national and caste levels may be responsible for
differences in perception and action with regard to the use of language rights within
one endogenous linguistic minority community. Mythili in Bihar in one census
count (1961) had six million speakers. It is grammatically different from Hindi and
has a literary history. After a sustained campaign, Mythili was accepted for use as a
medium in primary schools, but some elites identify with Hindi and regard Mythili
as a dialect of Hindi; some at lower levels of the social hierarchy perceive their
interests to lie in aligning themselves with communities of the same caste speaking
dialects of Hindi rather than with Mythili speakers of higher castes (Brass, 1974).

Political and linguistic interests correlate with social divisions, and demands for minority language rights do not get popular approval.

Small endogenous linguistic communities do not have the political muscle to have their language demands heeded. Their elite may be at the margins of the political structure of the state, or there may not be an elite at all in the community to make their case. Non-governmental voluntary agencies intervene in some such cases to broker with the government on their behalf or to run schools in which the minority languages are used. They, however, struggle with the government to get those students who do not drop out at the primary level into the mainstream of education after the primary level. In some cases, the Tribal Welfare department of the government takes an interest in education and co-ordinates with the Education department to make the situation slightly better. When there is no political visibility of a linguistic community, bureaucratic commitment to the legal provisions of language use in education becomes vital for any progress in realizing language rights. Bureaucrats generally hold the view that the tribal minority languages are dialects that are not worthy of use in education, and the interests of their speakers will be served best by learning the majority language and by their ignoring their mother tongue. It is these small politically and economically marginalized linguistic communities that are totally deprived of use of their language rights. The government, in the name of language promotion, may provide for teaching small endogenous languages and doing research on them at university level, when their speakers become politically conscious. This has been done for some larger tribal languages in Bihar. This may help elite formation in the tribal communities and confer some status on their languages but it does not give direct benefits to the communities at large with regard to access to education and employment.

This sketch of linguistic minorities and the realization of language rights shows that the communities vary as regards consciousness, goals, and strategies of action to achieve language rights. Language rights, in other words, are not perceived and acted upon universally by linguistic minorities, since political, historical, and demographic factors influence success in achieving language rights. These are, however, not immutable. The situation becomes favourable to linguistic minorities when there is a de-centring of the political, bureaucratic, and economic structure of the State. It changes the perception of the linguistic minorities about the value of their language integratively, and dilemmas and dichotomies between their cultural and material interests cease to be a problem. The development of political consciousness to bring about this structural change is crucial for maintaining linguistic diversity through the use of language rights. This is what the language rights movement can hope to achieve in the next century.

(Un)Writing the Margins: Steps Toward an Ecology of Language

Mark Fettes

Many would say she is a margin-dweller, our Tove: an explorer of tidal pools, perhaps, perched on weathered rock with surf foaming at her feet; or a streetwise fox, prowling backyards where the suburbs meet the forest; or a stubborn cloudlike dandelion, scattering seeds of life on concrete plains. To the city dweller such lifestyles appear irrelevant, annoying, potentially inimical. The imagination of the urban world embraces logical order and enforced civility. Wilderness is to be cherished only at a distance, or behind bars.

The linguistics of the city is our common heritage: it has its place. Yet beyond the Pale its 'rage for order', as Paul Friedrich (1985) terms it, is little more than a blueprint for urbanization. To understand the beach (let us adopt it as our central metaphor), we must come to terms with an ecology adapted precisely to the unending struggle between tide and land. What the city perceives as debris and desolation is for others a home. It is, moreover, *our* home. We are all strand-dwellers by origin and nature, salt water mingled with air and earth, dark currents swirling at the edge of daylit pools. Waves murmur in our poetry and dreams; or sometimes crash and roar, sweeping towns away.

To perceive and foster the specific *homeness* of both beach and city, we need a linguistics of the margins, an interpretative science that transcends the logical-literal to embrace the *eco*logical-littoral. Let me tell, briefly, of my own sojourns among waves and sand, and my ongoing efforts to integrate them in a panoramic vision of sea and shore.

Take, first, Esperanto, ironically categorized as 'planned' or 'artificial' within the linguistics of the city. I first encountered it, as many do, in the pages of a textbook - in the building yard, as it were. But the design is not that of a skyscraper, static and monumental; think rather of a ship (Dasgupta, 1987), or perhaps a fleet of rowboats, in which disaffected urbanites can slip out to reacquaint themselves with the rhythms of the sea. For the exuberant linguistic freedom of which Claude Piron has written so well (1994) is not unique to Esperanto: it is part of our premodern heritage, from before the era of 'taught mother tongue' and the disciplines of empire (Illich, 1981). Of course, how far one ventures in such a small, seemingly vulnerable craft is a personal decision: some stay in the harbour (or even the shipyard), others shuttle back and forth to nearby cities, and some discover the sea and shore to be their second home.

More on such *homeness* in a moment. I want first to locate the little languages of the world in this metaphoric shorescape, for their ecology has much occupied my imagination in the past few years. Think of them as the web of relationships constituting the living world in a particular bay, exquisitely adapted to the tidal pulse and the turning seasons, the dance of earth and moon and sun. To know this ecology one must live it, as few linguists are prepared or equipped to do; the city's laboratories work mostly with snapshots, specimens, classifications, blueprints for development. In their theoretical schemes the future can only be urban. Yet because they take the streetmaps of the city for reality, they misconstrue the very world under their feet, as Marx long ago observed in *The German Ideology* (Smith, 1990). Indigenous philosophies, lacking the technologies of industrialization, have gone deeper.

Central to this multi-millennial heritage of thought, as I understand it, is the idea of awareness, an active spirit or personhood characterizing all sorts of unities in the world, whether individual beings or their communities or the ecosystems of which they form an integral part (Cajete, 1994). One of the clearest distinctions between this and the modernist tradition is a deep respect for the uniqueness of every member of a family or community, their moral and cognitive autonomy, and thus the specificity of their journey in the world. Urban social science works in terms of structures and categories, fitting individuals into them; indigenous philosophy points to a science of processes and relationships arising from the individual's quest for self-realization. This is the ecology of the shore, where castles crumble at each rising tide but life bobs, burrows, clings, and thereby sustains a system more complex and robust than the city can understand.

Within such a system, each and every person occupies a unique location, a singular node: their experience of language is part and parcel of their participation in particular personal relationships and communal traditions of imagining and acting in the world. Thus the natural ontology of language is not an abstract private competence externalized, but an ecosystem of public acts - *language devices* (Millikan, 1984), used by embodied beings to co-order their awareness of and action in the world. Over time, in partially or wholly closed communities, multiple intersecting genres and discourses bring forth 'a language', a kind of local currency for communicative trading, the germ of a terrestrial lifestyle. Yet the sea surges around and through such apparently stable, referential systems, because of the need for each individual to make them their own: to walk the tightrope between experience and description, embodied knowledge and discursive knowledge, poetry and prose. In its drive towards Cosmopolis, modernity has tended to idolize the latter half of each pair: the androcentric pole, yang over yin. But idolatry has never been a viable strategy for the long term.

Three alternatives, then, intertwine in my own work. The first is a quest for a theory of language ecology which can integrate naturalist and critical traditions across many disciplines. Beyond the sunlit demesnes of Bakhtin and Vygotsky, I have discovered other realms of gold: Ruth Millikan's naturalist epistemology (1984), Dorothy Smith's feminist sociology of knowledge (1990), Edward Reed's ecological psychology (1996). These and other works point clearly to the possibility of an emancipatory human science that interprets, not legislates; enables, not constrains; discovers homes, not constructs margins. By its nature, such a science will be reflexive and therefore self-limiting and adaptable to local needs. It will also be permanently incomplete, as open to remaking and reshaping as the systems that it studies. But for this to become the accepted way of doing science, much will have to change.

The linear notion of development, for one, must go. If the urban legacy is not sustainable in its present form, it behoves us to learn from the cyclical indigenous vision of life and all that sustains it. There on those developer-ravaged shores, ancient processes of decay, renewal and rebirth are underway. What part in them will language play? I am deeply skeptical of models that call for the reenactment, tribe by tribe and community by community, of the standard development paradigm. This raises, then, the second challenge of language ecology: to engage with the complex, often agonizing realities of contemporary life in indigenous communities, not only to discover how language is implicated in their spiritual and cultural ecology, but to inform and empower the process of linguistic *healing* as it fits with the myriad alternative therapies now being worked out in such areas as justice, health, and education. Doing so may change both the way we think about language and the linguistic realities themselves.

What will come of this global indigenous renaissance, I cannot say. The cities will surely endure, in one form or another; all futures hang on whether their ecology can be altered. The third challenge, therefore, is to make the city more like the shore. I know of no better technology for this than the Esperanto rowboat: adaptable, economical of resources, personal yet seaworthy. A city of seafarers and marine biologists, a city of Toves, is very different from a civilization that shuts the sea out and thus walls itself in. For the generations raised behind such parapets, Esperanto offers a glimpse of the curving, wave-wrapped world: not an end, but a beginning. The voyage is not the vessel; nor the chart of its journey; nor the tales that are told. In the doing is the knowing. That which cannot be spoken, in the deep ecology of language, is still more precious than that which can.

Not fare well,
But fare forward, voyagers.

Part III. Equity: Justice for Speakers of All Languages

Equality is misunderstood if the demand is that everyone should use the same *methods* to reach the collective *goal*. Pressure to assimilate from the majority is often one such wrongly interpreted idea of equality. If migrants have to live on the majority's terms, they are in a poorer position than the majority in education, cultural services, etc.

Tove Skutnabb-Kangas and
Pertti Toukomaa, 1976, 82.

Writing for Diversity

Ngũgĩ wa Thiong'o

The first part consists of the summing up of the book *Penpoints, gunpoints, and dreams, Towards a critical theory of the arts and the state in Africa* (Clarendon Press, 1998), which builds on a series of lectures given at the University of Oxford. This is followed by the answers to three questions put to Ngũgĩ wa Thiong'o by Robert Phillipson.

The writer, the state, and linguistic and cultural diversity

In these four lectures I have talked a great deal about the state of art and the art of the state. I would like to close these lectures on the artist's response to the power of the state and to the challenges of interpretation. The artist can of course choose to withdraw into himself, become silent, self-censor himself, or simply join the ranks of the worshippers at the shrines of the state. In all those he or she would be negating him or herself as a writer for, as I said in my first lecture, a mirror that did not reflect would be negating itself as a mirror. Writers have no real choices other than to align themselves with the people and articulate their deepest yearnings and struggles for change, real change. Where the state silences, art should give voice to silence. Where, for instance, there is no democracy for the rest of the population, there cannot be democracy for the writer. Where there are prisons, the artist is also in prison. Where people are marginalized into ghettos and slums, the artist is also marginalized. Hence it is obligatory for writers in Africa, Asia, South America, and the world over to keep on fighting with the rest of the population to strengthen civil society, expressed in the capacity for self-organization, against encroachments by the state. Hence the struggle for the economic, political, and cultural empowerment of peoples is also a necessary task for the artistic endeavour. The real empowerment of the peoples is the only solid basis for the freedom of the artist. I often sign my book *Detained: A Writer's Prison Diary* for people with the message of my hope for a world without prisons and detention camps. It is the hope, in other words, for a world which will have eliminated the necessity of prisons, detention camps, the army, and police barracks, in short, eliminated the conditions which make the state as we have known it necessary in the organization of human life. It is only then that human civilization will cease to resemble that of the pagan idol described by Marx as drinking nectar only from human skulls.

This may go against the grain of so much of post-modernist rhetoric where hybridity, ambiguity, indecision, the blurring of choices have been elevated to a universal condition. The element of doubt has always been integral to art. Art explores connections even between seemingly unrelated entities. And it is important that human beings become wary of any certainties, particularly those preached and promoted by those with state power. It is important to see, for instance, the connections between the wealth of a few and the poverty of the majority within a nation and between nations. But we should be wary equally about any rhetoric that promotes Hamlet-type indecision about what to think of our societies which produce today baggers of millions on the shoulders of millions of beggars. Or be wary about the language-use that may blunt human social sensitivity to suffering because begging, for instance, is an exercise in free speech or where democratic freedoms are equated with freedom of finance capital. The ascendance of capitalist fundamentalism and the Darwinian ethical system which this is generating poses a singular danger for the world. It is the mother of all the other fundamentalisms, religious and nationalistic, which are developing in opposition to it or in alliance with it. When confronted with the havoc it is wreaking with its religious catechism of 'privatize or perish', it wears the mask of innocence of Graham Greene's Quiet American, or that of one of the comic characters in the American TV comedy *Family Matters,* who will wreak any amount of havoc and then ask, 'Did I do this?' Rather, there should be no ambiguity about the necessity to abolish the economic and social conditions which bring about the need for charity and begging within any nation and between nations, and language should sensitize human beings to that necessity.

There will always be conflicts between the artist and the state for as long as the state continues to be a supervisor of stabilities erected on gross inequalities within and between nations. Echoing Joubert and probably Shelley, Matthew Arnold once said that force and right were the governors of this world but that force would remain the legitimate ruler until right was ready.

> But right is something moral and implies inward recognition, free assent of the will; we are not ready for this right, - right, so far as we are concerned, is not ready, - until we have attained this sense of seeing and willing it. The way in which for us it may change and transform force, the existing order of things, and become, in its turn, the legitimate ruler of the world, will depend on the way in which, when our time comes, we see it and will it. (Matthew Arnold, 'The Function of Criticism', in *Essays in Criticism,* New York: Chelsea House, 1983, 9)

Paving the ways of seeing and willing a moral universe of freedom, equality, and social justice within and among the nations of the earth is surely the special mission of art. Art is dreams of freedom and creativity.

It is to be hoped that time will come when the state will have been so subjected to the power of civil society that it will wither away, as predicted by Marx and Engels, and simply become a machinery for the administration of conveniences of human social existence. It will wither away in its character as an instrument of class coercion of the majority. And just as it was the case in some pre-capitalist societies, it is possible that in such a postcapitalist society, where production will be geared not towards social domination of others but towards meeting human needs, culture and creativity will reign. But that is in the future. For me, now, art can only play the role of a John the Baptist in the coming-to-be of such a world. It behoves art to join all the other social forces in society to extend the performance space for human creativity and self-organization and so strengthen civil society. It was again Marx who talked about the point of philosophy not being so much to explain the world, as had been the trend hitherto, but to change it. And Martin Carter of Guyana has talked equally eloquently about all those who sleep not to dream, but dream to change the world. The question is, change it to what and for whom? For me, dreaming to change the conditions that confine human life is the mission of art, and it is often in conflict with that of the state as we have known it up to now, in Africa and the world. In such a situation art has the right to take up penpoints, to write down our dreams for a world in which, at the very least, there are no prisons and gunpoints.

Policies for greater equality among languages

Q: You have written a blockbuster in Gĩkũyũ, which is due to be published simultaneously in both Gĩkũyũ and Swahili. What do you hope publication of this book will achieve?

The novel I have just finished, at least the third draft, is called *Mũrogi Wa Kagoogo*, which literally means the Wizard Who Could Bring Down Birds From the Sky. It is quite substantial; it is estimated that the printed edition will be about 700 pages. It will therefore be one of the biggest novels, in size at least but I hope also in content, in an African language. It is certainly the biggest novel or book ever written in Gĩkũyũ language. Now I am first and foremost a novelist, an artist, who is obviously interested in writing an interesting story that can capture the attention of the reader. The size is therefore not of paramount significance since some of the most enduring stories, like those of Æsop, Andersen, the Grimm brothers, or those of the classical African orature, are only a few pages long. But nevertheless if the book which I have written fulfills the requirements of art, the size will then become important in drawing people's attention to the potential and capacity of African languages. Here the image is as important as the content. African languages are often associated with slim texts, on very poor quality paper, and shoddy editorial and production work. It is important, even for the African users of their own languages, to associate positive images to productions in African languages. In this case I am also glad that the sweep of the novel is wide geographically and culturally as well as deep in terms of time. India, Latin America, USA, Europe, and Africa come into it. The ancient cultures of Egypt and the Mediterranean, the African diasporic scene, are all visited, alluded to, however briefly, but the center of the novel remains Africa in a fictional country called Afurõõria. So I hope that the novel will be one more indicator of the possibilities in African languages and, by extension other currently marginalized languages. The Kenyan publisher, East African Education Publishers, intends to bring out Gĩkũyũ and Swahili editions simultaneously with the English edition probably a year later. We shall thus be privileging African languages at least in terms of which editions come first. In the same spirit, Africa World Press wants to bring out an American Gĩkũyũ edition.

Q: You are involved in a journal in Gĩkũyũ, *Mũtĩrĩ*, which has literary and socio-political content. What role do you see this publication playing in future?

I view *Mũtĩrĩ* journal in the same way. *Mũtĩrĩ* is a journal of modern literature and culture written entirely in Gĩkũyũ language. Between January 1995 and July 1999 we shall have produced 7 issues, each of 160 pages of prose, poetry, essays on different subjects ranging from history to science and technology. The journal, financed by a small grant from New York University, is housed in the Department of Comparative Literature, and it is currently published by Africa World Press and distributed in Kenya by East African Educational Publishers. Once again the hope is that the journal will become both a model and a testimony. There has never been a journal of this magnitude and range of ideas in Gĩkũyũ language and I am assuming that since Gĩkũyũ language is in the same position as other African languages, intellectuals of the other languages will be able to say that what *Mũtĩrĩ* has done and accomplished, they can do as well, if not better. I see a situation in which such journals begin to exchange articles, to share through translations, and in the process help initiate a dialogue between African languages and between African languages and others. Already *Mũtĩrĩ* has managed to attract writers who used to operate in English only as well as people versed in Gĩkũyũ language but who had not thought that there was a platform for their output in the language. The journal then has already given a platform to first time writers but who write exclusively in Gĩkũyũ. The journal also carries translations from other languages, Spanish for instance, and it is hoped that this will continue.

Q: Your most recent book, *Penpoints, gunpoints and dreams,* clarifies the nature of the struggle between an independent writer and the state. It also pushes forward the analysis of decolonising the mind to show how language policy in typical postcolonial contexts estranges people from their mother tongues and cultures. This message is similar to what Tove Skutnabb-Kangas has been fighting for for decades, namely use of the mother tongue and the right to maintain cultural diversity in the face of globalisation and rampant finance capitalism. How far do you feel your message is getting across, both in postcolonial contexts and in the US, the belly of the beast which your exile has taken you to?

I admire the work of Tove Skutnabb-Kangas and particularly the running theme in her work, which is about the equal worth of all languages, big and small. In a sense there is no such a thing as a small and a big language, the difference is simply in the number of people who speak a particular language at any one time. I share in this, and that is one of my basic assumptions in both *Decolonising the mind* and *Penpoints, gunpoints and dreams*. It is difficult at this stage to gauge the impact of these two books and indeed of Skutnabb-Kangas' work and your work as well. But there are signs that there is movement in this area. I have seen some publications too with Native American languages where the phrase 'Decolonising the mind' crops up a great deal. And wherever I have spoken, at Hawaii for instance, the question of language crops up. There is a soul-searching going on among the intellectuals of marginalised languages and I hope that this will end in a change of language practice among these writers.

In Africa it is important to mention the conference, 'Against All Odds: African Languages and Literature into the 21st Century', being held in Asmara, Eritreia, in the year 2000. This conference will bring together writers in African languages and scholars and publishers who want to face the challenge posed by the reality of African language communities. The conference should give visibility to writing in African languages; pose a challenge to scholars in and outside Africa to change their attitudes to African languages; and also celebrate the fact that despite all the odds against African languages, these languages have thrived and they refuse to die. The theoretical assumptions and democratic concerns in the work of Tove Skutnabb-Kangas are absolutely in consonance with the spirit and the letter of the conference as well as that of my book, *Penpoints, gunpoints and dreams*. The conference is a defiance against linguistic imperialism, which you talk about, an affirmation of the validity of linguistic and cultural diversity. Real unity of cultures and species is found in their very diversity.

On the Financing of Language Policies and Distributive Justice

François Grin and François Vaillancourt

Introduction

The purpose of this chapter is to briefly examine some aspects of the distributive dimension of language policies. The distributive dimension remains among the least-explored in language policy, including in the growing economic literature on the subject, which for a number of reasons has tended to prioritise the allocative dimension. In this chapter, we shall not attempt to provide a full coverage of the question, about which much has never been investigated. Rather, we shall attempt to posit a few basic notions, leaving necessary elaboration for further work. Nevertheless, we hope to provide some of the necessary orientation into the issue.

This set of issues is not just significantly under-researched; it also coincides, to a large extent, with some of the strategically most important questions in the analytical combination of distinct traditions and perspectives in research on language policy. More precisely, the distributive dimension and its linkage with the allocative dimension is the locus where the technical, often (though not necessarily) top-down perspectives on language policy meet issues of democratic citizenship and linguistic human rights. These have long been among Tove Skutnabb-Kangas's central concerns, and it is therefore fitting that a paper on economic aspects of language policies included in a Festschrift honouring her work should address these issues. Hence, this contribution, in addition to expressing our indebtedness to Tove Skutnabb-Kangas's unyielding scientific and social commitment to these issues, aims at signalling some of the socially and politically important points of articulation between complementary perspectives on the evaluation of language policies.

The first section of this chapter contains some definitions. In the second we present the essentials of the economic approach to the problem of 'distribution' in public policies. The third section moves on to the more specific problem of the financing of public policies. In the fourth, these tools are applied to language polices, particularly those aiming at the maintenance and promotion of a possibly threatened minority language. The final section provides a brief summary and conclusion.

One key (and paradoxical) result from this preliminary examination is that financial support for minority languages, if financed, in whole or in part, by members of a majority community, will often be easier to justify on allocative than on distributive grounds - that is, in terms of efficiency rather than justice.

Some definitions

Since this chapter combines considerations on language policy and economic issues, definitions of notions encountered in both fields are required.

No distinction will be made between 'language policy' and 'language planning'; both terms will be used here interchangeably, to refer to a 'systematic, rational, theory-based effort at the societal level to modify the linguistic environment with a view to increasing aggregate welfare. It is typically conducted by official bodies or their surrogates and aimed at part or all of the population living under their jurisdiction' (Grin, 1999).

The field of investigation of economics as a discipline can be broken down in various ways, such as micro v. macro-economics, but one fundamental distinction is that between the *allocative* and the *distributive* dimensions.

They can be easily contrasted with each other in terms a general definition of economics as a discipline. Although there are several views of what economics is about, we adopt a broad definition, according to which economics is first and foremost about the *efficient allocation of scarce resources which have alternative uses*, no matter the nature of the ends pursued or of the resources used. Hence, economics is not confined to the study of the production, exchange and consumption of goods, services and factors; rather than being defined as a subject area, economics is defined as an approach. Whenever there is a problem of allocating scarce resources, the problem has an economic dimension. Of course, this in no way implies that it does not have *other* dimensions as well, nor does it mean that the economic dimension so defined is always important. Depending on the issue examined, the problem of the allocation of scarce resources can be more or less salient.

However, the pure allocation problem is only one side of economic inquiry. If we agree that, by and large, social actors do allocate their time, money, energy, influence, etc. in a way that is advantageous to them, we may have a general framework for the analysis of behaviour, but two important comments must be made.

First, *efficient* allocation of their own resources by actors does not necessarily result in *overall* efficiency. This would be the case if the 'invisible hand' *did* work perfectly[1]; however, this result is predicated on the existence of perfect markets for everything - the so-called 'non-market' commodities included (Grin and Vaillancourt, 1997). However, mainstream economists recognise that there are cases of *market failure*, that is, situations where markets are either missing or incapable of yielding efficient outcomes. This is usually the case for the natural environment and for the 'linguistic environment, justifying government intervention in language matters even from a purely allocative standpoint): all that is needed is agreement on the idea that linguistic diversity is valuable, just like a pleasant natural environment is valuable.

Second, the resource allocation process by actors (whether in a pure *laisser-faire* universe or with some degree of government intervention to overcome inefficiencies resulting from market failure) results in an *ex post* distribution of resources about which comparatively little is known. In particular, there are no grounds for asserting that this distribution is intrinsically fair or not. Economic liberals espouse the view that the distribution resulting from a *laisser-faire* policy is 'natural', and it is only one step away to call it 'fair'. We shall not enter this debate, which is one of the most fundamental in the social sciences and would far exceed the scope of this paper. Rather, placing ourselves in the context of government intervention (which, as pointed out above, can be justified in language planning on *allocative* grounds *because* of market failure), we shall attempt to explore one side of the distributive implications of such intervention.

In a distributive perspective, the various outcomes of the process of production, exchange and consumption imply a different level of welfare for different social actors - whether individuals or groups. Hence, these different outcomes can be evaluated in terms of 'fairness', 'equity' or 'justice' -no distinction is made here between these notions. From a public finance perspective, distributional implications can be examined at two levels. The first is that of the financing of policy intervention - that is, who should pay for it; the second is the identification and measurement of gains and losses resulting from it (and hence the identification of winners and losers). In addition, from a welfare economics perspective, one may also examine the issue of possible systems of compensation whereby winners can compensate losers, while still reaping a net benefit from the policy - consequently, the policy still yields an overall increase in welfare and hence does deliver allocative efficiency gains. In this paper, we focus on the first of these distributive issues, that is, the question of *who should pay* for policies.

---

[1] Adam Smith is credited with the expression 'invisible hand'; however, the concept itself can be found (with a much more crisp analysis of its social meaning) in Mandeville's earlier work such as the *Fable of the Bees* which first appeared (under a different title) in 1705 - that is, well before Adam Smith's *Wealth of Nations*, which appeared in 1776; see Simonnot, 1998, chapter 4.

Financing public policy

The study of the role of the state in society (and thus of the financing of the state's activities) runs through the history of economic thought and predates the emergence of classical and neo-classical - now mainstream - economics. Over time, the field of public economics has emerged and the following principles have appeared.

The concept of 'user-pay'

Mainstream economists hold that the best solution for financing publicly provided goods and services (such provision being, of course, one typical activity of 'public policy') is to have the beneficiaries or users pay for it. The reason for this claim is that user-pay is a mechanism similar to the market mechanism; as such it is expected to ensure that the appropriate amount of publicly provided goods and services will be produced, given the costs of the policy. An insufficient output will be increased to meet the unfulfilled demand, while excess output will not be financed and thus not produced.

User-pay is easily applied to publicly provided meterable goods such as water, airport services, or road access. It is less easily used for non-meterable goods such as public television which, once broadcast, can be consumed by anyone who has access to a television set. The traditional 'Lindahl solution' of asking each individual to reveal his or her preferences and to pay tax accordingly is, in this framework, analytically correct, but not very operational, since each individual has an incentive to lie, hoping to benefit freely from a service paid by others. This behaviour, known in the field of public economics as 'free-riding', leads to the underprovision of the public good.

However, even if the goods and services considered are meterable, one may not want to make users pay for them in total or in part, if the consumption of these goods has an impact on the well-being (or 'welfare') of others. For example, if schools provide meals to underprivileged children, which increases their school performance and thus enhances their capacity to acquire skills, higher skill levels will eventually translate into higher overall economic performance, from which society as a whole will benefit. Hence, schools meals generate *positive external* effects, which should be taken into account when pricing them. In other words, school meals should not be billed fully to parents, and subsidising them (which implies a transfer from all taxpayers to poor families) is economically justified.

Taxation

Given the above, governments resort to taxation, that is, to the compulsory contribution by citizens of a share of their private output, without regard to their consumption of publicly provided goods and services. Such financing is justified in a democratic setting by demonstrating that it reflects the choices of a majority of voters. The following three principles should be followed when establishing taxes; they are defined as forms of equity, and hence hark back to more or less sophisticated concepts of justice.

(1) *Horizontal equity* ('tax like alike'): this principle states that for a given tax schedule, individuals in similar circumstances should face the same tax burden. The difficulty is in defining 'like circumstances'. Suppose for example that two couples have a similar (high) income. The first chooses not to have children and to travel extensively. The second chooses to have children, spending on the upkeep and education of the children the same amount that the first couple allocates to travel. Should the state provide fiscal support to the second couple or not? In practice, the answer is often positive, but in theory, the issue is debatable.

(2) *Vertical equity* ('tax unlike unlike'): this principle states that individuals in different circumstances should face different tax burdens and, in particular, that taxation should be progressive. In other words, the share of taxes in income should go up as income goes up. If this principle is not adopted, the options are a proportional tax with the share of taxes in income remaining constant as income goes up, or a regressive tax where the share of taxes goes down as income rises - an option generally recognised as unjust. This principle, traditionally linked to a decreasing marginal utility of income, has often been criticised.

(3) *Intergenerational equity*: this is, in the history of public economics, a more recent principle which implies that each generation or age group should bear a tax burden that finances the benefits it receives, and should not finance it by debt to have it paid by a subsequent, younger generation. Debt is, of course, appropriate when the expenditure is a long-lived one, such as infrastructures like bridges and hospitals, which should therefore be financed by more than one generation.

Even if these principles are respected, taxes distort the choices of citizens since they change the structure of relative prices and costs. Common examples are the prices of goods and services (which are affected by a value added tax) or the cost of labour (in the case of payroll and labour income taxes). Such distortions can be minimised by taxing choices that are not easily altered. These are usually called 'inelastic' choices, as opposed to the 'elastic' ones, which are highly responsive to (among other factors) price.

Given the above as well as issues of administration, compliance, avoidance and evasion, the most common tax prescription is to use taxes with a wide base (that is, few if any exclusions) and a low rate.

Financing language policy

Let us now turn to the financing of language policy as a particular case of public policy. Let us think of a country with two language groups, one majority and one minority.

In the following discussion, we assume that both language groups are of a 'viable' size. In this context, 'viable' contains no *a priori* assumption in terms of 'minimal demolinguistic size', a notion which we consider problematic (Grin, 1992); viability implies here that both groups are sufficiently large to be able to provide and use the full gamut of usual state functions, such as education and health services, possibly ranging from primary schools to universities and from health clinics to specialised hospitals respectively[2].

The first situation which may occur is one where the majority language is used in the provision of all public services with no place for the minority language. From a public choice standpoint, this may be considered distributively acceptable if this is the choice of a majority of minority voters, who may see their best interest served by assimilation into the majority. Such a choice, however, is not a common one, and there is ample evidence that minority communities set great store by having their identity acknowledged and their language used in the public provision of goods and services. Rather, such a situation usually results from a choice by a majority of voters belonging to the majority language group. That this situation be viewed as unfair is a *value* judgement, on which economics has just about nothing to say. Even in terms of culturally and politically determined value judgements, there is a wide range for interpretation and disagreement, exemplified by the many distinctions encountered precisely in those types of discourse that rest solely on normativity, such as international legal instruments on minority rights. In such texts, a distinction is routinely made between indigenous and immigrant minorities; this reflects a pure value judgement.

From an economic standpoint, such a distinction is open for discussion, and could be criticised on the principle that, just like there should be 'no taxation without representation', there should be 'no taxation without language recognition' (Grin & Vaillancourt, 1998). Arguments for differential treatment could, however, be sought in theoretical approaches to the value of linguistic diversity, where the operative concept is not the distributive, but the allocative dimension of language policies.

Given a certain language policy goal, how much should be spent on it? Let us take the case of a set of measures for the provision of minority language services. This is a case where the user group is clearly identifiable, and thus, *a priori*, the amount of services should be equal to what can be financed from the taxes paid by the group for these services. This theoretical rule, however, will yield an appropriate amount of minority language services only if both language groups have similar resources without subsidisation. Given that linguistic minorities often find themselves in a socioeconomically underprivileged situation, the rule often does not apply.

If the minority group is significantly poorer than the majority group, should the latter subsidise the policy in favour of the language of the former? In our opinion, while equalisation payments from the richer to the poorer group are appropriate,

---

[2] By putting aside certain asymmetries between groups, this assumption allows us to focus on the distribution issue proper.

subsidisation of the policy itself (which would amount to earmarked transfers that lower the cost of carrying out activities in the minority language) is problematic. The reason is that direct subsidisation of minority language policies may well result in an artificial increase in its vitality; the policy may imply expenditure not corresponding to what members of the minority community themselves would be willing to spend on their language. By the same token, direct subsidisation may also fall short of the amount of resources they would be ready to devote to this end - if they had them.

In other words, the distribution-based rationale for subsidising minority language policies is exposed to criticism because of its allocative implications. Hence, distributive considerations can fail to justify direct subsidisation of minority language policies themselves (as *distinct* from equalisation payments to redress economic inequality). More precisely, 'justice' may turn out to be a weak argument, not just because social actors can (and most usually do) have widely diverging views on what is 'just', but also because implementing a 'just solution' carries allocative effects that can be seen as detrimental in efficiency terms. Logically stronger arguments in favour of direct policy support for minority languages can, however, be sought by going straight for justifications on allocative grounds: chief among the latter is the notion that linguistic diversity is valuable, just like an unspoilt natural environment, and that because of the unusual features of language as a commodity, we are in presence of a case of 'market failure' justifying government intervention. In short, supporting minority languages may often turn out to be more defensible not because it is (distributively) *fair*, but because it is (allocatively) *efficient*.

One should note, however, that the allocative issue of the selection of the best policy among several possibly policies (that is, the one yielding a higher net value than any other, where 'net value' is defined as 'advantages minus drawbacks' or, using more restrictive concepts, 'benefits minus costs') may look quite different from a 'world' than from a country or regional perspective. Consider for example the case of a language L, spoken in countries A and B. L is used as a first language by a large language community (the majority or a sizeable minority) in country A, while it is used as a first language only by a small minority in country B. However, language L is spoken practically nowhere else (e.g., not in neighbouring country C) and is typically not acquired by non-native speakers as a language of wider communication. From a global perspective, the preservation of diversity as an intrinsic source of welfare may require policy measures in favour of language L in international contexts such as a supra-national organisation to which countries A, B and C are party. However, depending (among other factors) on the linguistic make-up of country B, the best policy may be one that does *not* include particular protection or promotion measures for language L. This may be the case if the other languages in country B are in a threatened position, or if there is, in country B, a delicate ethnolinguistic balance which preferential measures in favour of L would upset - at great market and/or non-market cost. One general rule of thumb is that *within any given framework of analysis*, the preservation of diversity generally requires the weak to be protected and promoted against the strong.

Notwithstanding the issue of the level (local, regional, international or other) at which the analysis is carried out, there is one exception to the notion that direct subsidisation of minority language policies may be justified on allocative grounds, but is, paradoxically, more difficult to justify on distributive (or 'equity') grounds. This is when the imperilled position of the minority language is the result of earlier (or, of course, current) oppression - usually at the hand of the holders of power in the majority community. In this case, it cannot be argued that the minority language finds itself in a threatened position just because the community that carries the language has lost interest in it, and direct support for the minority language cannot be dismissed on the grounds that it would distort the structure of signals such as prices and costs[3].

In the case of a self-financing minority language group that can raise its own tax revenue as a subnational entity such as a province, region, member state of a federation, etc., revenues should be raised and used to provide minority language services in the usual fashion. In this case, levying taxes and spending them on promoting the use of the minority language in business, television broadcasting or the daily press, for example, is appropriate to the extent that it does not imply inter-community transfers that would have to be justified in distributive terms. The subnational authorities should even consider borrowing to finance some language promotion activities that will yield benefits for future generations. All this, of course, holds if the subnational entity is homogeneously populated by members of the community - which, at the national level, constitutes a minority.

When more than one country is involved, where there is interaction across borders and each minority group is part of a larger 'continuum', one particular minority community may or may not represent the largest concentration of minority language speakers in the continuum. What matters from a public policy perspective is that minority language-related activities in one country in the continuum can generate high, low, or no externalities for minority language speakers in another country. Externalities will be high in the case of minority language broadcasting, low in the case of minority language schoolbooks, and nil in the case of minority language municipal services. Joint production agreements (and corresponding cross-border financing) should be implemented wherever such external effects are significant. When sharing the financial burden, both the absolute (demolinguistic) size and the economic status of the various minority communities consuming the services must be taken into account.

---

[3] It is often (and incorrectly) assumed that the *existing* arrangement is the preferable option. This is tantamount to arguing in favour of the status quo, and neglects the question of *how* this arrangement has come about historically.

Summary and conclusion

The financing of language policies raises distributive, as distinct from allocative questions. After reviewing some basic concepts, this paper examines their application to language policies aiming at the maintenance or promotion of minority languages.

Basic economic theory speaks in favour of a user-pay approach to financing, meaning that, in the case of minority language policies, members of the minority members themselves should pay for them, in the same way as they pay for privately provided services. This however, presupposes a high degree of socio-economic equality between the majority and the minority. In the absence of such equality, direct monetary transfers from the former to the latter can be required to establish or restore it. This solution is, in principle, preferable to the direct financing of minority language policies out of the public coffers, because direct financing amounts to a manipulation of the structure of prices and costs, and hence may needlessly tamper with actors' actual preferences and concerns. Hence, distributive considerations may justify transfer payments from the majority to the minority, but not necessarily the direct financing of policy measures. There is an exception to this general result when there has been, through earlier or current oppression, what amounts to a forcible transfer of resources from the minority to the majority and, by implication, between their respective languages.

Nonetheless, one somewhat surprising result from this brief foray into the distributive dimension of language policies is that invoking 'justice' is not the strongest argument to use in favour of minority language policies - if one intends to interpret justice also in economic terms and hence make reference to the issue of distribution. Stronger arguments can be found in terms not of resource distribution, but resource allocation, by showing that *if* linguistic diversity is recognised as a source of welfare, just like environmental quality, then it is perfectly sensible, even necessary for the efficient allocation of resources, to use tax money for the maintenance and promotion of minority languages.

More generally, it is far from certain that notions of equity and justice are the most effective tools for those wishing to advance the cause of minorities and minority languages. The almost exclusive reliance on such arguments, not just in militant discourse but also in the academic-political commentary surrounding international legal documents such as the Council of Europe's *Framework Convention for the Rights of National Minorities* or the *Charter for Regional or Minority Languages*, apart from its analytical limitations, may have strategic weaknesses. In particular, it may often amount to preaching to the converted. Policies may vastly benefit from including a marketing approach, as practised for example by the *Bwrdd yr Iaith Gymraeg* (Welsh Language Board). More generally, policies in favour of minority languages stand to gain in credibility if, without neglecting the equity issues involved, they are also shown to promote overall allocative efficiency.

Towards More Fairness in International English: Linguistic Rights of Non-native Speakers?

Ulrich Ammon

The paper deals with the disadvantages of non-native speakers as compared to native speakers of English, for instance in international scientific communication. It discusses possibilities of amelioration, in particular the postulate of the non-native speakers' right to linguistic peculiarities. By agreement with the editor of the volume, and in order to exemplify the problem of native speaker norms and privileges presented here, the language has not been 'corrected', apart from items retrieved by a spell check.

Towards a majority of non-native speakers

Following Kachru, Crystal (1997, 53f.) pictures the expansion of English in three concentric circles: The 'inner circle' of countries with English as a 'primary' or native language and the 'outer' and the 'expanding' circles of countries with English 'in non-native settings'. The inner circle comprises 320-380 million speakers while the two 'non-inner' circles comprise 250-1,300 million (the outer 150-300, the expanding 100-1,000 million).

Clearly, the non-native speakers of English are meanwhile more numerous than the native speakers, except for the lowest possibility in the range of estimated figures. Predictions for the 21st century generally project an overwhelming majority of non-native speakers of English (Graddol's 1997, 10, figures comprise 375 million L1 speakers versus 375 L2 + 750 million EFL speakers, i.e. 1,125 million non-native speakers).

The categories used in these distinctions can be seen as prototypical with clear-cut cases on the one hand (L1) and a continuum between categories on the other (L2, EFL). Even numerous speakers within the inner-circle countries are far from mastering their respective standard varieties which are not really their native varieties. They are nevertheless, as a rule, closer to them than are the populations of the non-inner-circle countries, which is reflected in our simplified term 'native-speaker standards (standard varieties)'. In addition, the distinction between the outer and the expanding circle becomes fuzzy in face of the fact that in some of the latter countries there is much more use of English nowadays than in some of the former (cf. Crystal, 1997, 56). Even Kachru's (e.g. 1982, 36ff) basic distinction between the two non-inner circles, the existence of 'institutionalized varieties' with their own 'standard non-native varieties' versus only 'performance varieties', useful as it is for a start, seems questionable as English becomes institutionalized in more and more countries.

Science is a domain for which this development is typical. All around the world, English has come to serve extensively for research, or research related communication (data collection, publishing, correspondence etc.), particularly in science and technology rather than the humanities (Truchot, 1990; Ammon, 1991, 212-281). As a next step, English is being introduced for teaching, especially at the tertiary level, even in countries with a remarkable history of an own language of science (cf. for Germany, Ammon, 1998). Though tertiary institutions of science may not be central in the sense that all members of the society have direct access to them, regular use of English should still result in 'institutionalized varieties.'

Continuation of correctness judgment according to native-speaker or 'inner-circle-country' standards

In spite of the majority of non-native speakers or the non-inner-circle countries, many of whom use the language actively and regularly in institutional frameworks, the native speakers or the inner-circle countries retain the hold to the yardstick of linguistic correctness. The inner-circle countries' population is usually equalized, at least roughly, with the native speakers of the language. That their command of the language be superior to any others' is by and large taken for granted. Even researchers who are aware of the numerical proportions of speaker groups or who deal with the globalization of the language finally stick to this assumption. Crystal (1997, 130-139) or Graddol (1997, 10-11), for instance, go a long way in presenting and justifying the 'New Englishes' of the outer or even the expanding-circle countries and underlining their values, but Graddol is probably right in pointing out that they, inspite of forming 'distinct varieties', often follow an 'underlying model of correctness' of either Britain or the USA (p.11). Graddol also, like Crystal, finally retains traditional correctness judgments - contrary to what he seems to profess in some sections of his book. This is at least how I read some of his remarks. I see nothing wrong with his ranking *fluency* in spoken English from 'native-like' to 'extremely poor' (p. 11). But he also states, when reporting on the production of a book written in English, that '[t]he development and writing of the book require advanced "native-speaker" skills' (p. 42). Advanced non-native speaker skills wouldn't do, one must conclude. Native-speaker norms remain the final basis of correctness judgments.

Correctness judgment along these lines seems to be particularly rigorous with respect to written scientific or scholarly texts. British or US English language standards relate to different aspects of texts: orthography, vocabulary, grammar, pragmatic and discourse features as well as text structure in the narrower sense. Clyne (1987) has shown that English and German academic texts are structured differently in various respects (linearity/digression (Exkurs), symmetry, advance organizers, and hedging) and that English texts written by Germans tend to retain typical German structures which, as a rule, are evaluated negatively by English readers or reviewers (cf. also the literature on comparisons of English and other languages with respect to text structure in Clyne, 1987). The British reviewer of a handbook of German editors found 'some of the English written by non-native speakers so bad (...) as to be almost incomprehensible' (cf. Ammon, 1989, 267). Similarly, a US reviewer of another book of a German editor, in fact myself, complained about 'near unintelligibility', because 'the grammatical mistakes are so severe.' He also did not appreciate that a 'decidedly German substratum peeks through in many of the papers written in English' (Di Pietro, 1990, 301. Cf. for other examples Coulmas, 1987, 106ff.).

In contrast to such criticism of British or US reviewers, I am doubtful whether the texts under scrutiny were really unintelligible, or even especially hard to understand. Generally, I dare to assume that unintelligibility is not the main reason why texts in non-native English are often rejected or judged negatively by native speakers. One indication is that the native speakers who 'corrected' or 'polished' my own English language texts have never had serious difficulty understanding them correctly except in a few instances. Similar experiences were confirmed by about a dozen German colleagues whom I queried. One should also be aware of the fact that texts produced by native speakers can contain unclarities too, especially ambiguities, and as a consequence be unintelligible at some points.

The question of intelligibility of non-native-speaker texts can of course not be answered without comprehensive empirical research. There is evidence with respect to spoken language - and similar results would probably be found with respect to written language - that non-native English is indeed harder to understand for native speakers than is native English (Nelson, 1982). It has, however, also been confirmed that 'speakers with shared cultural and linguistic norms obtain higher degrees of intelligibility in their language interactions' (Nelson, 1982, 60). Non-native speakers of English understand non-native speakers of the same linguistic background better than non-native speakers of another linguistic background. In addition, non-native speakers of English of any linguistic background probably understand native speakers of British or American Standard English better than they do non-native speakers of another linguistic background other than their own. Nevertheless, there are reasons to assume that native speakers' negative evaluations of non-native-speaker texts are not only, or often not even primarily, based on problems with intelligibility. Do they arise from what has been called 'linguicism'? Are they a special type of linguistic prejudice?

Linguicism?

Linguicism has been characterized as using the languages of different groups as defining criteria and as the basis for hierarchization (Skutnabb-Kangas & Phillipson, 1994, 104; 1996a). There are various aspects of such hierarchization, and the delimitation of linguicism is not always easy. A clear case of linguicism, which seems widespread in the scientific community, are quality judgments of texts according to the language in which they are written. Vandenbroucke (1989, 1461) assumes with respect to medical dissertations in the Netherlands: 'By the language a thesis is written in you immediately judge its quality,' meaning that a thesis in English is valued more highly - as to its content! - than a thesis in Dutch. Matched-guise technique with written texts in Scandinavia confirmed the possibility of such judgment. Two different texts, each in two language versions: the national Scandinavian language and English, were presented to referees: 'the majority of different aspects of scientific content was assessed to be better in English than in the national language version for both manuscripts' (Nylenna, Riis & Karlsson, 1994, 151).

It could also be argued that it is linguicism if native speakers of a prestige language are ranked higher socially (in some way) than non-native speakers. Is it, however, still linguicism if texts in line with native-speaker standards are valued more highly than those with 'deviations' from these standards? Calling this linguicism seems to be justified if the native-speaker standards do not guarantee more communicative efficiency. They in fact may not, at least in the future, with the growing number of non-native speakers. Reasonably safe judgement would of course require comprehensive empirical research. Yet even dealing theoretically with this question in a convincing manner is, to my view, beyond the scope of this short paper, which will therefore be limited to some general suggestions.

Any alternative to native-speaker standards would have to specify in which way they should be extended or changed. Doing away with standards altogether would certainly be no viable option, since it would endanger successful communication. Would it be possible to encorporate special features of non-native English - of Indian, Chinese, Japanese, French, Spanish, German or other Englishes - as elements of International English (or World English)? Which elements could that be? Would these elements have to be explicitly defined in some manual (codex) of International English, so that they could be studied by anyone interested? Or would it suffice to appeal to all the participants in international communication to be as tolerant as possible with respect to any linguistic peculiarity, as long as the text remains intelligible? This appeal would of course also imply very serious attempts at comprehension. Perhaps, new international standards, different from native-speaker standards, would gradually develop on the basis of such a new culture of communication and could finally be codified. There is a bulk of publications dealing with related questions which should be scrutinized for ideas and evidence, like for instance the literature on modified (mostly simplified) English for international communication or on EFL teaching objectives (closeness to native-speaker competence). Hartmut Heberland proposed some of these ideas in a much earlier article, in which he suggested to develop a 'new, independent norm of academic English... which would be different from US or British English to the degree that speakers of those dialects would have to learn it, if they want to write it or speak it properly...' and which 'would serve the purposes of its community of speakers better than any existing standard of English would, since it would be far less culture-bound and ethnocentric than all the other Englishes we can choose between today' (Haberland, 1989, 936-7).

Language rights?

Those difficult questions will finally have to be answered if any postulate of 'the non-native speakers' right to linguistic peculiarities' (cf. Ammon, 1998, 278-282) is to be taken seriously, i.e. put into practice. Obviously, not all linguistic peculiarities are acceptable if communication is to function. It might be for these difficulties, why Skutnabb-Kangas and Phillipson (1994) mention no such 'linguistic human right.' It even seems hard to place any non-native speakers' right to linguistic peculiarities into their system. Rather, such a right straddles across their 'necessary' and their 'enrichment-oriented rights' (ibid., 102), depending on the function of English as a non-native language, but doesn't really fit into either. The deeper reason might be that their system of linguistic rights is itself based on the ideal of native-speaker standards or norms.

It seems to me, however, that systematic provision for such a right should seriously be considered in face of the disadvantages of the non-native speakers of English, and actually non-native speakers of any prestige language with rigorous standards. Murray and Dingwall (1997, 56) concede that the dominance of English as a language of science 'may give native speakers of English an unfair advantage in the competition to publish results.' When they point out, however, that native speakers of English too need extensive training before they are capable of writing scientific articles, they seem to forget that the Swiss scientists, whose fate they examine, get the equivalent training. It is even a central objective of university courses in Switzerland, particularly seminars. Swiss scientists are therefore, as a rule, very well capable of writing scientific texts - but according to their own and not anglosaxon norms. Disadvantaging such users of English could be called 'discrimination' with respect to the non-native speakers' right to linguistic peculiarities, if we had it, and be criticized accordingly. It would of course be necessary to show functioning alternatives to the present situation.

There have been demands of learners' rights which seem to be related to our suggestions. Thus, Gomes de Matos (1998, 15) postulated for EFL learners '[t]he right (as non-native speakers) to deviate [from native-speaker standards! U.A.] in noncrucial areas that do not affect intelligibility or communication (...)' His ideals remain, however, the native-speaker competence or the standards of the inner-circle countries. In contrast, I would like to challenge the inner-circle countries' exclusive control of the standards of International English. It seems to me that there is no real justification for this kind of control in a world with a growing majority of speakers of the language outside the inner-circle countries. In the case of a planned standard, or set of standards, one could think of a transnational institution, perhaps similar to that for Esperanto, to be put in charge. However, an unplanned, spontaneous development of standards through interaction might be more practical. Changes along the suggested lines probably presuppose long-lasting persistence and growing self-confidence on the side of the non-native speakers with respect to their own use of English.

The non-native speakers' right to linguistic peculiarities remains at the moment a rather helpless postulate. It needs more elaboration as well as integration into an extended system of linguistic human rights. It also needs support through political action. It should become part of the agenda of linguistic and other scholarly or scientific associations, or their conferences, and be presented to political parties or institutions, for instance of the European Union. - For a start, the non-native speakers of English could as a minimum try to raise awareness of their problems (cf. Ammon, 1990) and demand more linguistic tolerance from the language's native speakers. They should use their growing number as their argument, among others. In face of these numbers, rigorous enforcement of native-speaker standards amounts to the suppression of a disadvantaged majority by a privileged minority.

Linguicism in Action: Language and Power in Academic Institutions

Masaki Oda

Linguicism in operation is illustrated through a case study of an undergraduate studying at an academic institution overseas. Focusing on the complex relationships of power which exist in institutions, in particular between teachers and students, and between native-speakers of a language and non-natives, the issue of how language is used as a means of controlling students ideologically is explored. The case confirms that language is playing an increasingly important role as a means of control and domination, as shown by Tove Skutnabb-Kangas (2000).

Linguicism in action

Aki Maeda was an undergraduate at a Japanese university when she participated in a study-abroad programme at a college in the UK. In this programme, students are enrolled in courses in English as a Second Language (ESL) and 'Introduction to British culture' between April and July. Between October and March, they are allowed to take several regular undergraduate courses, depending on their proficiency in English.

A series of incidents started at an ESL class during her first week in the UK in April. In the class she was given a reading passage as an assignment. The students were told by the instructor to read it and prepare a reaction to share with classmates the following day. The passage was about Japanese students in the UK. In the passage there were pejorative descriptions of Japanese students, for example 'Japanese students do not talk in class, because they are generally not interested in studying'. She felt that these statements were offensive.

In the next class Aki expressed her reaction to the passage. By contrast, two of her Japanese-speaking classmates did not express an opinion. Three other classmates (one Spanish, one Italian, one Arabic speaker) had very little to say about it as they had never had any exposure to Japanese students. A week later, the students had to take a quiz in which there were several 'reading comprehension' questions. The students had to answer True or False to statements about the passage, for example 'Japanese students never express their opinions in class'. Of course Aki answered 'False' to this particular question, because she believed that it totally depended on each individual. However the instructor marked it 'Wrong'. Needless to say, Aki got a low grade for the quiz. Though she asked her instructor for an explanation, she was not given a satisfactory one.

A few weeks later, Aki received a written warning from the director of the program. This indicated that she would be on probation, as her academic record as well as her behaviour in class were bad, according to the tutor in charge, since Aki had 'often criticised her lesson'. Aki was not sure what she should do, so she called Mr. Hanada, who was in charge of study-abroad programmes at her home university in Japan, and asked for advice.

Mr. Hanada responded that Aki would have to follow what the people in the British institution say, as Aki was in England. In addition, he warned Aki that she would have to modify her behaviour to meet the expectations of those in the English programme. In the meantime, Mr. Hanada contacted the director of the programme in order to clarify what was going on. The response was that they might have to dismiss Aki as she criticised her instructors so much. Aki recalls:

> The class was generally quiet, so the instructor encouraged us to speak. One day, she said 'Aki, why don't you speak in class. This is England, not Japan. You are supposed to give your opinion in class'. So I expressed my opinion in class with courage. Then I was treated as if I were a criminal. (Interview, translated from Japanese by MO).

Mr. Hanada and Aki's home university took no further action. A month later, Aki was summoned by the director of the programme and required to take part in an 'informal' hearing about her misbehaviour in class. She was given two weeks to prepare a statement, and was allowed to take a friend along with her. However, she was not allowed an interpreter at the hearing.

Three members of staff from the English programme took part in the hearing, while Aki was with her Japanese-speaking friend, and her father, who came all the way from Japan. The director, citing Mr. Hanada's response to Aki's inquiry, said that her home university in Japan considered this incident was Aki's personal problem, and thus the university would not want to be involved in the matter.

Throughout the hearing, the director controlled the agenda and Aki was not sure what to expect next. The director asked Aki several questions regarding the textbook in question. The director accused Aki of telling Mr. Hanada about the problem before making any effort to solve it locally, stating that this was not what students were supposed to do in England. The following is an excerpt from a recording provided by Aki's father.

> **Director**: According to Mr. Hanada, you told him that you had been discriminated. Aki, the word 'discrimination' has a very strong meaning in English. Are you aware of it?

Aki: As I told you, I do not remember what exactly I said. But I am sure that I did not mean to offend anybody.

Director: No matter what you said, you offended someone, and this must be taken seriously. You will be on probation.

Aki: Wait a minute. I believe this is an informal hearing. You are not supposed to make any decision until the hearing has been completed. Besides, how do you know if I had told Mr. Hanada that I had been discriminated as I spoke to him in Japanese?

Director: Aki, this is exactly the problem some of your tutors have pointed out. You always criticise someone. That is unacceptable in this country.

The hearing lasted two hours. Aki never received any notification from the director regarding the outcome of the hearing, as it was an informal process according to her. It should also be pointed out that Aki used the Japanese word 'sabetsu' to tell Mr. Hanada what was going on. An English translation of this word could range from 'distinction' to 'discrimination' and thus it would be very difficult for anyone to figure out how exactly it was used when taken out of context.

Following the meeting, a dozen overseas students filed a petition supporting Aki and demanded that the programme revise the textbook in question, as it was offensive. The director was outraged by the students' action and asked every student to come to her office one by one the following week to clarify 'whether they had really wanted to sign the petition'. The students were required to submit a written statement expressing their view of the issue. After seeing the director, most of the students chose to sign a document saying that they would withdraw from the petition. The director had warned them that they would be subject not only to dismissal from the programme, but also to expulsion from the UK, as they would lose their immigration status if they were kicked out of the programme. This was a strong enough threat for most of the students. Moreover, Aki's classmates began blaming her for causing all the troubles they had to go through.

A month later, one of the instructors filed a formal complaint against Aki for harassment on the grounds that the instructor had experienced a series of incidents 'caused by Aki'. This time the hearing was conducted formally by a college-wide committee. A translator was provided, however. Aki had to prepare another set of documents for the committee to review before the hearing. Although many other students had signed the document, none of them helped her this time. She was alone. The complaint was eventually withdrawn as the committee determined that the evidence was not sufficient.

Aki graduated from her home university a year later, and is now pursuing postgraduate studies. While she thinks she is doing fine, her parents say that she has been going to see a psychiatrist regularly. The year in the UK must have been a nightmare for Aki. Though it has been a while since she came back to Japan, Aki still cannot work out or accept what happened to her in the UK.

> I still do not know why I had to go through all that trouble. I just wanted
> to study in England, and I tried to participate actively in class. Did I do
> anything wrong? (Interview, translated by MO).

In the meantime, Mr. Hanada, the Professor of English who was responsible for the
junior year abroad programme in Aki's university, resigned from the position a year
after Aki came back. He cites that the series of incidents was too stressful for him
and he 'would not want to be involved in study-abroad programmes any more'.
Regarding the particular series of incidents, he says:

> I wished I could have helped Aki. But I did not want to fight a battle
> knowing we were going to lose. It happened in the UK, and we had to
> follow their way of doing things. Who the hell in this university would
> like to fight against native speakers in their language on such a
> complicated issue? (Interview, translated from Japanese by MO).

One question is why Aki and Mr. Hanada had to suffer so much. This was a case
which should not have become a big problem. The formal hearing procedure
resorted to is utilised only when there is no other solution available for a conflict
between a student and an instructor. The initial problem should have been solved by
an informal discussion between Aki and the instructor. In fact, Aki had initially
tried to achieve this.

I have personally contacted several institutions in UK and British Council
officers in Japan to find out if it is often the case that such formal procedures are
actually resorted to in British institutions. The majority responded that it is unlikely.

The ESL class in April described earlier suggests that the instructor must have
had a stereotypical image of Japanese students. In fact this is what triggered off the
series of incidents. She labelled Aki as a 'Japanese' student who was supposed to
follow what is considered 'typical' behaviour, rather than regarding Aki Maeda as
an individual. The instructor was upset about the fact that Aki did not behave as a
'typical' Japanese student was supposed to behave: though the instructor had told
her students to express their opinions, she did not expect Aki to be as explicit as she
was.

Spack argues that labelling is misleading as it is often derived from an
assumption that in ESL and EFL (English as a Foreign Language), the culture of
the target language, i.e. British culture in this case, is regarded as 'the norm from
which students are deviating' (1997, 767). This suggests that the educational
discourse was structurally biassed against the Japanese learner and her culture, who
was disempowered (see also Pennycook, 1998b).

Skutnabb-Kangas (2000) sees power in the contemporary world as being
unfairly distributed between two groups: the A team is a group of people who
exercise power and control over the B team. The director of the English language
programme was on the A team, using her dominance of both position and language
to exercise power over Aki on the B team. Linguicism involves an unequal
relationship of this kind: when languages are allocated resources unfairly, the A
team's being confirmed and validated, the B team's being stigmatized, and when an

ideology of inequality has been internalized as natural and normal, rather than being seen as a matter of unequal acccess to power and resources.

Central to Aki's position was the power relationship expressed through unequal access to language of the native speaker and the non-native speaker of the language in question. Aki had to express her ideas precisely under extreme pressure. This was particularly true as the issue was very critical. In other words, one small mistake would cause a critical problem. In the excerpt quoted earlier, when the director states that 'discrimination has a very strong meaning in English', it is very difficult for a non-native speaker to figure out precisely how strong the word is. S/he therefore has to follow the native speaker's judgement and accept that 'This is the way we say things'. This often inhibits a non-native speaker from arguing over the use of words with a native speaker. This kind of inhibition can also be seen in Mr. Hanada's attitude towards the issue. He was not willing to argue against the programme director in the UK, as the fact that he was a non-native speaker would put him at a disadvantage. This put Aki in a very difficult position.

Secondly, there is a power relationship between a teacher and students. In the classroom, teachers have control over students because they decide what to teach, and how to teach. In addition, supervisory administrators may often control these teachers. In Aki's case, the director set the agenda at the hearing to investigate the 'problem': she decided on the date, the participants, and how the topic should be approached (see van Dijk, 1996 and this volume). The same power relationship characterized the interaction between the director and the students who signed the petition. When asked to explain themselves to the director, they were not in a position to refuse, even though they were busy with other assignments. This was because they knew that the director would be deciding on whether they could move on to advanced courses, which most of them wanted. In fact the director effectively used this strategy to hinder other students from supporting Aki, as stated above.

Linguicism is exercised at educational institutions. As discussed above, it is not simply that one overtly discriminates against the other on the basis of language. In Aki's case, it was not only the power relationship between native and non-native speakers of English which created the A team and B team, but also the relationship between teachers and students. The latter itself is not a linguistic matter, and thus is often overlooked.

It is also important to note that scholars have often not been enthusiastic about reporting incidents of this kind at educational institutions, as many of them are affiliated with the institutions as teachers or researchers. However, it is a responsibility of those connected to the institution to show initiative so as to prevent the recurrence of cases like the one reported above, as they are nothing but inhumane acts. In addition, linguists are responsible for accurately documenting the cases so that the community is better equipped to help to solve the problems.

Equality of Opportunity and Assimilation. Or: We German Left-wing Do–gooders and Minority Language Rights

Antje-Katrin Menk

Skutnabb-Kangas' observations on the German educational scene

After Scandinavian-German conferences on the languages of immigrant workers and their children in Roskilde (1978) and Berlin (1980), Tove Skutnabb-Kangas analyzed the situation of immigrants in Scandinavia and Germany (Skutnabb-Kangas, 1982). She came to the conclusion that due to different immigration policies, different educational strategies would be advisable in the two regions. While in Scandinavia residence rights have always been fairly secure and the greatest danger could be seen in assimilation, in Germany residence was by no means secure and segregated school models existed which were the target of much criticism. There was fairly widespread agreement among scientists that integration into the German school system with German language instruction as a priority was desirable and that demands for the mother tongue should be 'postponed' (Skutnabb-Kangas, 1982, 76).

In a footnote (ibid., 64) Skutnabb-Kangas remarks that a confusing terminological difficulty was noted during the conferences: 'the Germans call *integration* what we in Scandinavia call *assimilation*' . And she wonders whether this might mean that there is no German concept for the Scandinavian version of integration, which she specifies as 'voluntary learning of language and culture of the majority without giving up one's own language and culture of origin.'

A conference at Bielefeld, *Der Beitrag der Wissenschaften zur Konstitution ethnischer Minderheiten* (The contribution of the sciences to the creation of ethnic minorities), in 1987, led to another diagnosis of the German situation by Skutnabb-Kangas. At the time, the question of residence did not arise in the discussions.

Several participants (see contributions to Dittrich & Radtke, eds., 1990) queried use of the concepts ethnicity and cultural identity, and the claim was made 'that the focus on language and culture diverts people from the real (i.e. economic and political) problems' (ibid., 340). Skutnabb-Kangas' contribution led to considerable controversy, as she pleaded for more minority research done by minority researchers and for decisions about languages to be made by the minorities themselves.

She noted a tendency among the researchers she criticized: they ignored the expressive side of ethnicity that related to language, culture and identity, while stressing the instrumental side of economic and political equality.

What the Germans saw as scandalous was inequality – in the seventies there was a danger of a segregated admissions policy that would deny access to schools leading to higher level qualifications. As a consequence, it seemed reasonable to demand equality of opportunity for majority and minority children in the school system, and to concentrate on German as the majority language. The case for the L1 was not in dispute, but it seemed reasonable tactics to postpone demands for it when education in Bavaria legitimized segregation mainly through mother tongue maintenance.

At the Bielefeld conference the main problem for immigrants was seen as their continuing political and economic discrimination. At that time most members of the conference did not consider mother tongue education as relevant. Concepts like ethnicity, culture, and languages of origin were considered to be regressive and irrational (Dittrich & Radtke, 1990, 25). In her critique of plans for the conference Skutnabb-Kangas (1990c, 339) refers to the dilemma of pluralism, which her German colleagues did not seem to understand: how reconcile two equally legitimate claims - cultural identity and difference, with socio-economic equality.

Some possible explanations for our 'German deficits'

1. There seems to be an inherent homogenizing effect in the struggle for equality

Lummis (1996) analyzes the concept of equality in the global economy and shows that in its Greek root, *isos,* it has two components, one of fairness, and one of physical/mathematical equality; but since antiquity this distinction has been confused and they have not been kept apart. On the idea of *equality of opportunity,* which he dates back to the nineteenth-century United States, he comes to the conclusion that it does have some homogenizing effect. 'To accept equality of opportunity is to accept the game and to accept the game is to accept the identity of player. In this way, equality of opportunity incorporates some elements of equality and eliminates others, producing a remarkable paradox, a system which generates homogeneity and economic inequality and pronounces the consequences just' (ibid., 43).

There seems to be a general tendency to require some degree of sameness, homogeneity, as a prerequisite for what are considered to be fair chances. The idea of fair treatment might have implied different things to different people, in our case bilingual education for immigrant children, a conclusion very few scientists were aware of.

Looking back to my own position in the seventies, I know that through being obsessed with equal opportunities I supported an assimilative school policy, although this was not my intended goal, nor that of most other people in the field.

2. Ideas of monolingual scientists about language

The participants discussing language at the Bielefeld conference were German academics who were a mirror image of the socially dominant majority group in the country. Skutnabb-Kangas outlined the dangers of monolingual myopia in her contribution, as she has done elsewhere. Her criticism of the majority group making decisions on language policy for the minorities must be taken seriously.

3. Deficient concepts in the field of ethnicity

Dittrich and Radtke's critique of the concept ethnicity from various angles considers it as primarily irrational. Its closeness to the concept of 'Volkstum' cannot be denied. The idea of 'Volkstum' became important in Germany during the eighteenth and nineteenth centuries in reaction to the universal ideas of the French revolution, and had fatal consequences in the formation of German nationalism. Although the criticism of ideological abuse seems justified, to play down or deny the role of ethnic and cultural factors risks distorting the cultural and ethnic determination of one's own world view.

One way to become aware of such difficulties is to study the various world views of groups which are distant from ours as regards ethnicity, religion, and politics. I learned a lot through Seufert's study (1997) of patterns of interpretation (Deutungsmuster) in the Islamist milieu of Turkey. A comparable study of Turkish immigrants in Germany would be very useful. I would not claim that the findings should enter the content areas of intercultural education; they are irrational, nationalistic, full of myths, and specific to time and place. But by provoking us they might lead us to our own patterns of interpretation – assuming that we, the majority in the educational field, 'have ethnicity' too. We might even have some unanalysed political and cultural assumptions that influence our rational judgements.

As an example of ethnic and worldview blindness I can cite an argument put forward by Lenhardt (1990, 209). He claims that immigrant children in German schools are not subjected to specifically *German* dominance but, like all the pupils in the country's schools, to bureaucratic rules. The curricular content is more or less irrelevant- the length of the Rhine or of the Bosporus (sic!), the biography of Luther or Ataturk as subject knowledge, all this has neither a Turkish nor a German character but reflects a bureaucratic structure. Without critiquing Lenhardt's analysis as a whole, I would like to point to the possibility that content for German and Turkish bureaucracies is defined by their respective world views. For example, Luther would be an ethnic German and Protestant for the Spanish immigrant child, a German Christian for the child from Turkey, and Ataturk an ethnic Turk for the Kurdish child, an unbeliever for the Islamist child - and 'just Turkish' for most of us. Content does make a difference.

4. Blindness to ethnic, national and cultural categories becomes most dangerous in connection with language policy

There are several articles in Dittrich and Radtke (1990) which question the importance of language in the context of identity and ethnicity.

- A minority language is considered as 'regressive', as exemplified in bilinguals reporting that at times of sickness they tend to use their mother tongue or regress to preferences which as healthy people they had outgrown a long time ago (Introduction, footnote 56).
- The article by Kummer (265-276) argues from studies in South America, Africa, and nineteenth-century Austria that language is not a given of ethnic and cultural identity, but the construct of an ethnic intelligentsia in a situation of conflict where language and premodern traditions are used as symbolic representation.
- Lenhardt (209) acknowledges that immigrant children, in contrast to their German peers, grow up as bilinguals. But for the social identity of immigrant children, the only relevance is that they are children of workers and school pupils.
- In analyzing Weber on ethnicity, Brumlik (179-190) comes to the conclusion that anyone who does not believe in and hinders ethnic self-definition also promotes assimilation.

Since ethnicity thus has become suspect, to talk about the relationship between language and ethnicity becomes suspect too. Talking about the expressive and emotional aspects of language becomes ideological. I live in a milieu where, due to being conscious of German history, especially of fascism, no one would claim to have a 'German identity'. I know no-one who would define himself or herself as a German patriot, whereas I know progressive people from several countries who call themselves patriots. We leave German identity to the neo-conservatives. In this context we experience our own language only in its neutral function as the lingua franca of the country. It is not seen in its ethnic function.

Stölting-Richert (1994, 1996) comes to the conclusion that for different reasons left-wing educationalists and neo-conservatives in Germany end up with the same language policy, which aims at public monolingualism, while the languages of origin are the private affair of the immigrants. He also sees a direct line leading from the language policy developed during the French Revolution to left-wing positions on multilingualism. There seems to be a need for more debate on this Weltanschauung.

Science and Policy - When does Science Matter?

Ingegerd Municio-Larsson

The 1970s was a decade of innovation and optimism among researchers and teachers engaged in bilingual education in Sweden. The official state-level policy was still that immigrant and minority pupils should be integrated into school classes where instruction was given in Swedish only. In 1969 state funds had been specifically allocated for the purpose of organising instruction for these pupils in Swedish, as well as instruction in the mother tongue. These funds were intended for use during the period of adjustment, prior to integration into Swedish classes, but they were also used in experiments with bilingual education. With an increase in demands for funds to be made available locally, it became increasingly obvious that state policy would have to change.

Social engineering

The long period of social democrat rule in Sweden was imbued with a *folk* ideology, introduced in 1928 by the then Prime Minister, Per Albin Hansson, and successively elaborated upon by other politicians. According to this ideology, the purpose of social democratic policy was to change society into 'a good home for all citizens'. This idea of a 'folk home' was widely used to bring about the citizens' support for radical change. At a time when society was being redesigned by social reforms, citizens' loyalty towards the state was indispensable.

Support for change was also brought about by the rhetoric of social engineering, according to which decisions on reform are based on scientific knowledge. Consequently, policy-making in Sweden can be characterised as a typical example of social engineering. During the decades following the Second World War public commissions proliferated, attacking every conceivable social problem. Primary education was targeted for exceptional attention and it successively underwent a reform process that ended in 1962 with a nine-year compulsory education system. In spite of this interest in education, the specific issue of bilingual education was largely ignored. Instead, the impetus for change came from another policy arena, namely immigration to Sweden. A commission began work on the topic in 1965 and one of their reports made it obvious that the previous monolingual ideology of the Swedish primary education system was losing ground. This initiated another reform process, one that ended in what was called the Home Language Reform Act of 1976.

The presumption of a close connection between knowledge and policy decisions was illustrated by the reform process in primary education. This process occasioned a number of doctoral theses and quite a few professorships in the field of pedagogy. The lack of interest in introducing bilingual education for minority and immigrant pupils was veiled by arguments which claimed that there was insufficient knowledge. But the Swedish education authorities made no effort to remedy this situation. There was therefore during these decades of intensive educational research no funding allocated for the study of minority or immigrant pupils immersed in monolingual Swedish education.

Bilingual education

As a result the cognitive puzzle presented in the official report leading to the Riksdag (Parliament) Bill on home languages relied upon research financed from other sources. The cornerpieces of this puzzle were taken from Tove Skutnabb-Kangas' 1975 thesis *Om tvåspråkighet och skolframgång'* (*On bilingualism and educational achievement*), published in Finland. In this work she gathered all the available evidence on bilingual pupils and their education and placed it in a new paradigm, which drew on linguistics, psychology, pedagogy, and sociology. This approach came to characterise her research. Her aim was to make sense of concrete evidence by means of interpretation. From the beginning she left behaviourism in favour of understanding, and crossed over the boundaries of her original discipline. Her multidisciplinary understanding of bilingualism and educational success provided the perfect motivational background for the Government's Bill on bilingual education for immigrant and minority pupils.

Consequently the 1976 Home Language Reform Act set bilingualism as the goal for immigrant and minority children within the compulsory education system. State resources were allocated for its implementation. However, this was only the starting point for an intricate implementation process. In theory, decisions at state level are to be implemented in accordance with the policy-makers' intentions and instructions. In practice, local decisions are needed to change educational ideologies and activities. Great efforts were undertaken both by bilingual teachers and researchers, of whom one of the most prominent was Tove Skutnabb-Kangas, to convince reluctant, monolingual politicians, school administrators and teachers that bilingual education was not only pedagogically beneficial but a human right for bilingual pupils.

Policy implementation

Empirical studies have shown that because of lack of implementation the ambitions of the 1976 reform were not met (Municio, 1987, Skutnabb-Kangas, 1997). The reform resulted in a considerable increase in the number of pupils registered as entitled to and participating in mother tongue instruction. However, the majority of these pupils were offered mother tongue instruction for only two hours per week. Only 10% were grouped according to their first language and therefore received transitional bilingual education in forms that resembled those outlined in the reform.

What hindered implementation? The ideological resistance to admitting the necessity of bilingual education has a strong historical tradition within the Swedish educational system. Since the turn of the century monolingual education in Swedish has formed part of a nationalistic state project. From the 1930s onwards, this ideology was reinforced with ideas of social engineering, which imply a subordination of individual rights to state interests.

In this respect, the reform of 1976 did not imply an ideological change of direction. The ideology of bilingual education embraced by the reform only reached a small number of teachers, principals, and school administrators. That these new ideas were never accepted by the majority of educators that were involved at the primary level was decisive for their lack of implementation. As can be seen in developments in the 1990s, and visible in the dismantling of the system of mother tongue instruction, there has never been much understanding of or sympathy for these ideas.

Reform context

Instead, the changes related to the reform that actually occurred were induced by other means. First, there was an increase in the total number of pupils enrolled in primary education during the 1970s. Second, the reform provided ear-marked state funds for mother tongue instruction as well as for Swedish language instruction for immigrant pupils. The fact that all school districts experienced an increase in the number of pupils made the organising of special classes as well as the employment of bilingual teachers possible. Furthermore, the way state funding was allocated implied that such reorganising resulted in additional funds to the district.

During the 1980s a development in the opposite direction occurred. In 1985 the number of pupils enrolled in primary education was lower than that of 1971. It became increasingly obvious that mother tongue instruction was threatened. When school districts faced decreasing enrollment rates, it became necessary to make decisions on whether priority was to be given to instruction by a bilingual teacher or by monolingual Swedish teachers.

The quest for scientific truth

In 1984, a research project entitled 'The Education of the Finnish-Speaking Minority in Sweden' was initiated by Kettil Bruun, then a Professor of Sociology at the University of Stockholm, together with Tove Skutnabb-Kangas, Markku Peura, and other researchers. When a heart attack tragically ended Kettil's life on 15 December 1985, Tove and Pertti Toukomaa took over at the helm and the project proceeded as planned.

A few months earlier I had taken part with Kettil in a seminar where we presented the project for researchers, politicians, and administrators. One of the politicians present, himself a member of the School Board of Stockholm, made an interesting remark regarding his expectations from our project's research results. He assured us that if he and other politicians just knew what the best way of organising instruction for immigrant pupils was, then they would not hesitate in implementing it. Their only problem was that they had no conclusive results regarding the possible advantages of bilingual instruction. This revelation demonstrated his strong faith in science as a means to attain correct political decisions. He very probably spoke for many other politicians in School Boards in municipalities with large immigrant populations.

Evidence of bilingualism

In one of the sub-projects, Tove Skutnabb-Kangas studied 'Communication strategies of Finnish youngsters in Sweden'. This project included extensive language proficiency tests. During long discussions in the project group, she revealed her theoretical, as well as ethical, objections against testing. In spite of this she had decided to carry out testing in an attempt to chart the linguistic abilities of pupils in bilingual classes. The need to live up to the demands of scientific evidence, which parents and teachers advocating bilingual education constantly came up against, could not be ignored.

Evidence from this project has been presented in various reports. The tests of the Swedish and Finnish competence of pupils in bilingual education were compared to control groups of native Swedish-speakers and native Finnish-speakers in Finland. Tove Skutnabb-Kangas' conclusion was that these pupils were bilingual to a very high degree. Just as in her 1975 thesis, she presented these results in a wider context of understanding. This included the interpretation of empirical evidence referring to experiences, sentiments, and hopes of both first and second generation immigrants. An example of this is her 1987 report 'Are the Finns in Sweden an Ethnic Minority? Finnish Parents Talk about Finland and Sweden'.

Entering a new decade

Scientific evidence was now available to support the noble goal of active bilingualism as stated in the Home Language Reform of 1976. In spite of this, a rapid decrease in mother tongue instruction has occurred. In 1990 the hours of teacher time spent on home language instruction were 85,700. This fell to 35,600 in 1997. So far as pupils with Finnish as a mother tongue is concerned, the number registered dropped from 24,528 to 15,228, and the numbers of those actually participating from 15,284 to 6,989 during the same period. This last figure includes pupils in the nine independent Swedish-Finnish schools that were established in various municipalities over the same years.

To understand this rapid dismantling of mother tongue instruction we have to look closely at the context. Two important decisions were made at the end of the 1980s. The first related to terms of employment for teachers. Until then, teachers had been employed by the state. This responsibility was now transferred to the municipalities. The second decision changed the system of state funding. When the state was responsible for teacher salaries, the guiding principle for state funding was that state regulations were accompanied by state resources. This system was now replaced by a general state grant to the educational sector of each municipality. As from 1992, the state grants to the municipalities were no longer specified for definite sectors.

These two reforms radically changed conditions within the school sector. When the municipalities became the teachers' employers, the costs of educators became comparable with other education costs. This made it possible to include cuts in teacher-time within decisions on budget priorities. In the relevant negotiations, bilingual teachers fared badly. In addition, as the state no longer paid directly for every specific educational activity, the financial incentives for organising special education, including instruction for minority and immigrant pupils, disappeared.

Scientific knowledge or economic reasons

Have all the efforts to provide scientific knowledge on bilingual education been in vain? A more accurate conclusion seems to be that changes in educational activities generally depend more on other circumstances than scientific evidence. The difference between the 1990s and previous decades is that during times of economic expansion the rhetoric of change is worded in terms borrowed from a variety of professional discourses, whereas when expansion comes to an end, terms from of an economics discourse predominate. Today, at a decision-making level, scientific 'truths' are often subordinated to economic 'truths'.

However, in educational practice scientific knowledge on teaching and learning, language and identity is still required. Thus we do have knowledge of the advantages of bilingual education as practised in the bilingual instruction of the independent schools of today, where they are gaining renewed validity (see Peura, this volume).

From Historical Shame to Present Struggle

Jarmo Lainio

A historical sketch of Finnish in Sweden[1]

When minority language speakers have realized the need to take the future into their own hands, irrespective of what the surrounding society is or is not willing to do to assist them, individuals, historical events, and key groups of people will play crucial roles in the process of the awakening and revitalization of the language, thereby increasing the self-confidence of its speakers. For one of the more recent groups of Finnish-speakers in Sweden, the Sweden Finns, living in most parts of Sweden but concentrated in urban areas, the big cities, and the industrial towns of central Sweden, events, individuals as well as organisations have been of crucial importance (Lainio, 1996, Tarkiainen, 1993). One should of course add that the changes in our basic concepts and ideologies are a fundamental cause of such changes, nevertheless the mediation of these takes place through the deeds of individual actors.

Finnish is a language that has been used in Sweden at least since medieval times. It is also the language that has experienced the most widespread processes of language shift, at both individual and group level. The use of Finnish has been attested in the capital of Sweden since the 13th century, and there has been a Finnish parish for 470 years. Finnish has predominantly been the language of 'simple' people, such as peasants, servants in towns, and wine-carriers, in most Baltic coastal, northern, and central parts of Sweden. Finnish has faced language shift in all these areas, and among all social groups, due to the long-term, implicitly assimilationist policy of Sweden, and support for it at all levels of society. Over the

---

[1] This chapter draws on an interview with Tove Skutnabb-Kangas in 1994, which served for a portrait of her in Part 3 of the History of Finns in Sweden (Lainio, 1996).

centuries the minority group members have overtaken the negative expectations and attitudes concerning the minority and adopted the implicit and at times explicit idea of the superiority of the Swedish-speaking majority. All this has changed radically during the last three decades.

Two groups resisted language and cultural shift for centuries. Except for the isolated 'forest Finns', living in distant areas in several counties, especially Värmland, from the 16th century to the 1970s, there has only been one other group that has survived for more than two centuries with intergenerational transmission of the language, the 'Tornedalians'. These settled in a few border municipalities in northern Sweden in the 11th century, and due to both their geographical position and their links with relatives and neighbours in Finland, they managed to resist assimilation. The Torne Valley was for centuries the route taken by Finns migrating to Sweden, and despite pervasive attempts at assimilation, the area has managed to survive linguistically, unlike most other Finnish-speaking areas in Sweden (Winsa, 1998).

Both the Tornedalians and the Sweden Finns have embraced ideas of ethnolinguistic vitalization since the 1970s. It is probably correct to say that the revitalization process started earlier among the Sweden Finns, not only because of their numerical superiority, but also due to access to ideas put forward by some researchers and proponents of minority empowerment working among and for the Sweden Finns. One of the key people in this respect was Tove Skutnabb-Kangas. Her ideas also linked up to the Tornedalians, since Skutnabb-Kangas and her colleague Pertti Toukomaa referred to semilingualism, which originated in studies by the former professor of Sámi, Nils-Erik Hansegård (see Skutnabb-Kangas, 1984a). He claimed that the Tornedalians, due to the harsh oppression of Finnish by the Swedish authorities and their inadequate acquisition of Swedish, were semilingual. The notion of semilingualism became a winning argument in the struggle for support for the mother tongue and thus bilingual education for the Sweden Finns. This process in turn later reinforced attempts to revitalize Tornedal Finnish as well.

One of Skutnabb-Kangas' problems was that her ideas and methods, not least the threshold ideas of bilingual development and competence, which she and Toukomaa developed with Jim Cummins, were ahead of her time. Few in Sweden then believed in the positive effects of bilingualism. Likewise few understood the importance of external social factors for bilingual development. Skutnabb-Kangas had been working with Einar Haugen at Harvard University in the US, where she was also influenced by the civil rights and women's liberation movements, and her understanding of bilingualism developed in fruitful interaction with North American researchers. While there is generally a tendency for ideas from North America to reach Sweden a decade or more later, Skutnabb-Kangas was in a position to mediate and influence research in the two contexts. In Sweden the stunned audience of laypeople and professional politicians, educationalists, linguists, etc., were deeply conservative, and not ready for the new conceptual framework, which was resisted fiercely. Later on, lip-service was paid to its validity, though the position of 'home languages' and bilingual education is still uncertain (see Municio-Larsson, Peura, Huss, this volume). The early debates were significant for minorities struggling for the right to the mother tongue: semilingualism was one of the few concepts in the bilingual education field that were comprehensible to the layperson.

Another problem Skutnabb-Kangas faced was the fact that Sweden was not a homogeneous society, as was generally claimed, and the majority population resented the older and newer minorities. This was a paradox for someone who had grown up in a bilingual Finland-Swedish environment. Sweden is, after a decade and a half of openness, now back in the assimilationist mould. In the 1990s the new concept is 'perfect Swedish', which contains a hidden argument for the assimilation of minorities and migrants, and thus hinders the development of public bilingual education (see Wingstedt, 1998). As in the period before the debate about semilingualism, knowledge of two languages is seen as a factor hindering the development of Swedish.

The ups and downs of this development have been described and evaluated in various scholarly studies (Hyltenstam & Tuomela, 1996, Lainio, 1997, Janulf, 1998). The issues have also been vividly portrayed by creative writers. The most famous Sweden-Finnish author, who has himself experienced language shift, or linguicide at the individual level, is Antti Jalava. His writings show what the forces of assimilation do to a growing child trying to find a place in society and forge a stable ethnic, adult identity. He has claimed that the feelings are so deep, so emotional, that only art can fully express them (see Jalava, 1988).

What follows is an attempt to give voice to the processes that reflect the results of ethnolinguistic assimilation, shame of a mother tongue, stubborn but silent resistance, awakening and insight, and empowered struggle. The snapshots of history given below parallel the long-term scientific and activist efforts of Skutnabb-Kangas, Toukomaa and others in the Sweden-Finn community. When the home-language debate was at its hottest, the Swedish National Board of Education attempted to muzzle Skutnabb-Kangas (a ban on official reference to her, 'Berufsverbot'). She also worked at the grass-roots level, inter alia with a group of mothers/women in the Rinkeby area, on the outskirts of Stockholm, where school strikes were used as a tool to achieve instruction in Finnish beyond the first six years of schooling. Though the short 'epic' below is seen through the eyes of a boy growing up during the 1960s, the experiences and emotions are doubtless partly collective in kind.

The Sweden Finnish story as a developmental process in the eyes of an assimilated Sweden Finn[2]

I am one of those who did not want to leave, but who had to, had to go west, to the land of milk and honey, to buy a Volvo on credit; I was four years old

I am one of those who did not understand what the teacher said up front, what the other children chanted; I still understood what was beyond the words, the meanness to be found, but also comfort in the tone

I am one of those who were yelled at with all the nasty nicknames for Finns, not once or twice, but seventy times seventy times

I AM ONE OF THOSE

I am one of those who tightened his cold little fist in his pocket and swore silently, in the language that I could still understand, that I *defended*, and which *defended me*

I am one of those who became the class orderly, wanting to show that I am good enough, that I can cope. So I did, even if only with my grades, I showed them all, at school, my relatives in Finland

I am one of those who was never allowed to join my best friend at their summer cottage, the real Swedish countryside

I WAS ALONE

I am one of those who in the first

Olen yksi heistä, jotka eivät halunneet, mutta joiden oli pakko lähteä, loikata länteen, kultamaahan, makean leivän perään, Volvon vähittäisostoon; olin neljä vuotta

Olen yksi heistä, jotka eivät ymmärtäneet, mitä opettaja siellä edessä sanoi, mitä muut lapset hokivat; ymmärsin kuitenkin sanojen takaa, niiden ohitse - sieltä löytyi ilkeyksiä mutta myös lohduttavaa sävyä

Jag är en av dom som blev finnpajsare och finnkoling och Pekka, inte en eller två gånger, utan sjuttio gånger sjuttio gånger

OLEN YKSI HEISTÄ

Olen yksi heistä, joka puristi pientä kylmää nyrkkiään taskussa ja kiroili hiljaa, kielellä, jota vielä ymmärsin, jota *puolustin,* ja joka *puolusti minua*

Olen yksi heistä, joista tuli ordningsman i klassen, joka halusi näyttää, että minäkin kelpaan, pystyn. Ja niin pystyinkin, vaikka vain todistuksillani, näyttämään heille, kaikille, koulussa, Suomen sukulaisilleni

Jag är en av dom som aldrig fick följa med min bästa kompis på landet, det svenska 'landet'

OLIN YKSIN

Jag är en av dom som första veckan i

---

[2] Original (Jarmo Lainio) in Finnish and Swedish; translation by Robert Phillipson and Tove Skutnabb-Kangas. The code-switching in the original text, and in the English translation, is marked through use of Times New Roman for Finnish, and Helvetica for Swedish.

week of July was crammed into the Opel with three siblings, four weeks of clean clothing, copious presents for the relatives, and 48 weeks of pent-up expectations

I AM PART OF THEM

I am one of those who dozed on the ferry, on the wall-to-wall carpet in the restaurant, in the coffee shop, with the coarse bawling of the returnees as an accompaniment, as a lullaby

I AM ONE OF THOSE

I am one of those who remembers the sun-warmed steps of my grandmother's terrace, her roughly cut lawn in the yard, the chilly dew under my feet, the bats flapping in the darkness, the frightening path to the outdoor loo behind the woodshed, the morning fog on the neighbour's field

I am one of those who remembers the scent of the tender birch leaves in June, the sizzling of the sauna, the lemon squash, the dried scales of fish petrified on my fingers, the smell of seaweed, the soughing in the aspen trees, the immense sun that was swallowed night after night by the glittering sea

I am one of those who wasn't able to talk to my cousins the sixth summer, the seventh I stayed away

I WAS ALONE

I am one of those who played soccer and handball and had to explain to my uncle that handball is not the same as volleyball

I AM ONE OF THOSE

I am one of those who said, *I* am Swedish, but *my parents* are from Finland

I WAS ALONE

I am one of those who went to great lengths to avoid the Finns congregating outside the supermarkets, but then who didn't ... They were so close, and yet so

juli packades in i Opeln med tre syskon, fyra veckors rena kläder, mångfaldiga gåvor till släkten, och 48 veckors uppdämd förväntan

OLEN HEITÄ

Jag är en av dom som halvsovit på båten, på filtmattan i salongen, i kafeterian, med hemvändarnas hesa skrål som ackompanje-mang, som vaggvisa

OLEN YKSI HEISTÄ

Olen yksi heistä, jotka muistavat auringon lämmittämät kuistin rappuset, isoäidin karkearuohoisen pihan, jalan alla yön viileän kosteuden, pimeydessä lepattelevat lepakot, pelottavan vessapolun liiterin takana, aamu-usvan naapurin pellolla

Olen yksi heistä, jotka muistavat kesäkuun hennon koivun tuoksun, saunan sihinän, sitruunalemonaadin, kuivat ja kovettuneet kalan suomukset sormissani, merilevän hajun, leppärannan kohinan, valtavan auringon, jonka kimalteleva meri söi ilta illan jälkeen

Jag är en av dom som den sjätte sommaren inte kunde tala med mina kusiner, den sjunde kom jag inte

OLIN YKSIN

Jag är en av dom som spelade fotboll och handboll och som fick förklara för morbror, att handboll inte var lentopallo

OLEN YKSI HEISTÄ

Jag är en av dom som sade, *jag* är svensk, men *mina föräldrar* kommer från Finland

OLIN YKSIN

Jag är en av dom som tog omvägar runt finnarna utanför Domus och Epa, men vem gjorde inte det ... De var så nära, men ändå så avlägsna distant

I AM ONE OF THOSE

I am one of those who was confirmed wearing my elder brother's much too short trousers; the holy words were in Swedish

I AM ONE OF THOSE

I am one of those who heard 'bloody Finn' seventy times seven times, all with the best of intentions, often guiltily followed by: well, you are OK, you are our buddy

I WAS ALONE

I am one of those who felt at home in a gang, in the refreshing wind from the open window of the Volvo, my father's 'Finn Mercedes', surrounded by the rock and protest of youth

I AM ONE OF THOSE

I am one of those who finally had my uncle come over to Sweden; I sang about the happy school-leaver of the future; my uncle sang about the Rose of Kotka until the neighbour above us hit the floor with a broomstick; the inscription of the date in my school graduation ring was written in Swedish

I AM PART OF THEM

I am one of those who sweated at the metal works, swore at the crude metal surfaces that cut into my flesh, I was hammering out hinges for three crowns an hour on piece work; again I tightened my fist in my pocket; I could still spit out swear words in Finnish, that's where my fury was released, how else could it have been worked off

I AM ONE OF THOSE

I am one of those whose mother worked at three jobs: night and day in the home with all the children, days in the nickle plating section of the factory, nights in the office as a cleaning woman

OLEN YKSI HEISTÄ

Jag är en av dom som konfirmerades i storebrors alltför korta byxor; gudsorden var på svenska

OLEN YKSI HEISTÄ

Jag är en av dom som hörde finndjävel, sjuttio gånger sju gånger, i all välmening, ofta med ett skyldigt tillägg: ja du är sjyst, du är ju vår kompis

OLIN YKSIN

Jag är en av dom som kände mig hemma i gänget, i den svalkande vinden från Amazonens helöppna fönster, i farsans finnmersa, omsluten av ungdomsrevolt och rock

OLEN YKSI HEISTÄ

Jag är en av dom som slutligen fick över morbror till Sverige; jag sjöng om studenten, till och med om lyckliga dar; - eno lauloi Kotkan ruusua, kunnes naapurit koputtelivat kattoa luudan päällä; klackringens inskription av studentens datum var på svenska

OLEN HEITÄ

Jag är en av dom som svettades i verkstadshallen, svor över graderna i den grovbehandlade metallen som bet sig fast i skinnet, jag slog gångjärn på ackord för tre kronor i timmen; åter knöt jag näven i fickan; vielä pystyin kiroilemaan ärrä-päät, siinä kiukkuni purkautui, minne muuten se olisi kulunut

OLEN YKSI HEISTÄ

Jag är en av dom vars mor arbetade trefalt, dygnet runt i det barnrika hemmet, dagen på förnicklingsavdelningen på verkstan, kvällen på kontoret som städerska

I AM ONE OF THOSE

I am one of those who wanted to get on, away and beyond the stench of oil, the sound of metal hitting metal, away from the sweat; towards insecurity, towards academia; my father said: - you borrow, you repay, I never borrowed anything!

I AM ONE OF THOSE

I am one of those who paid up, working by candlelight, in the shadow of all possibilities. In tune with my studies, out of tune with myself

I AM ONE OF THOSE

I am one of those who found his way back, past the swearing, to my grandmother's language; I returned to the warmth, through the one who had seen everything, understood all, and who directed me to the original feelings; I started raising my voice, my power has grown year by year. But the laughter, the witty repartee and the jovial banter, characteristics of my family, were peeled off during the journey. I ought to know

I AM PART OF THEM

I am one of those who still hears 'bloody Finn', now only seven times seven times, and with the best of intentions, from 'Sweden's future'; 'the happy school-leavers'. Waiting for lectures to begin, there is plenty of time for many a 'bloody Finn'

I WAS STILL ALONE

I am one of those whose father wanted to be laid to rest in his home church, alongside his father, at his mother's breast; so be it

I am one of those whose mother sacrificed her health for our security, her back carried us, but doesn't carry its own carrier, the carrier of our burdens

I am one of those who has gradually become - **one of us**

I am one of those who is no longer heard, who is no longer seen, who is no more. I

OLEN YKSI HEISTÄ

Jag är en av dom som ville vidare, från oljeoset, ljudet av metall mot metall, från svetten; mot osäkerheten, mot lärdomen; pappa sa': -sää lainaat, sää maksat kans, mää en olk koskaa lainannu!

OLEN YKSI HEISTÄ

Jag är en av dom som betalade, i lampans sken, i skuggan av möjligheterna. I takt med studierna, men i otakt med mig själv

OLEN YKSI HEISTÄ

Jag är en av dom som fann min väg tillbaka, förbi svordomarna, till mormors språk; palasin lämpöön, kaiken nähneen, ymmärtäväisen ihmisen tuella alkuperäisiin tunteisiin; rupesin kohottamaan ääntäni, voima on vuosi vuodelta kasvanut. Mutta hymy, huulenheitto ja rattoisa suunsoitto, sukuni ominaispiirteet, siinä tien varrella karisivat pois. Totta totisesti

OLEN HEITÄ

Jag är en av dom som ännu, senare, fått höra finndjävel, nu bara sju gånger sju gånger, och i all välmening, från Sveriges framtid; 'sjung om studentens lyckliga dar'. På en akademisk kvart hinner man med många finndjävel

OLIN VIELÄ YKSIN

Olen yksi heistä, jonka isä halusi viimeiseen lepoon, kotikirkolle, isänsä viereen, äitinsä helmaan; näin tapahtui

Olen yksi heistä, joiden äiti maksoi turvallisuutemme terveydellään, selkä kantoi meidät, vaan ei kanna omaa kantajaansa enää

Olen yksi heistä, joista on vähitellen tullut - en av oss

Olen yksi heistä, jotka enää eivät kuulu, jotka enää eivät näy, joita enää ei ole.

am one of *those* who have been forgotten, and when they no longer exist, they don't need to be remembered, we are all, after all, *Swedes*... with the best of intentions

I AM NO LONGER ALONE THOUGH

I am one of those who have become one of them, but I have found my way back to a familiar path through my language

I am one of those who has found the double road, and who tells those coming after me: don't try to become one of *us*, or one of *them,* become *yourselves, be your own selves*

I BELONG TO THOSE

I am one of those, who has become one of them, and I have coped. But still I am not too content

I DO NOT ONLY BELONG TO THOSE.

Jag är en av *dom* som glömts bort, och när dom inte finns, behöver dom ju inte bli ihågkomna, vi är ju alla en av oss, *svenskar,* ...i all välmening

EN ENÄÄ SILTI OLE YKSIN

Olen yksi niistä, joista on tullut yksi heistä, mutta olen löytänyt tieni takaisin, tutummalle polulle, kieleni kautta

Jag är en av dom som sökt och funnit den tvåfaldiga vägen, och som säger till dom som kommit efter mig: -försök inte bli inte en av *oss* eller en av *dom,* bli *er själva - olkaa oma itsenne*

OLEN HEITÄ

Olen yksi niistä, joista on tullut yksi heistä, ja olen pärjännyt. Mutta, en ole täysin tyytyväinen

EN OLE YKSIN HEITÄ.

Which Contacts Breed Conflicts?

Miklós Kontra

During the last half century a formidable amount of scholarly research into language contact has been accumulated and we now know a great deal more about the social and linguistic aspects of bilingualism and bilingual speakers than our predecessors. Yet several puzzles remain. For instance, although one of the best studied areas is lexical borrowing, we do not yet know why it occurs in one community and not in a totally similar other community. As Sarah G. Thomason pointed out in a lecture,[1] the speakers of the Native American Salish language which she studies do not seem to have borrowed a single English loanword - they have coined their own word even for *automobile*. Most non-English-speaking peoples in the USA have borrowed *automobile*, but the Salish have not. In what follows I will attempt to tease out another mystery: why some language contacts breed social conflicts but others do not.

Language, education, and human rights are interwoven in multiple and intricate ways but the exact nature of the interaction among these fields in various societies today is not yet sufficiently understood. In the last decade or so a fourth factor, minority rights, has reemerged as a focus of international politics as well.

According to Peter Nelde's hypothesis, language contact breeds language conflict, or more precisely, social conflict, because 'In essence, conflicts cannot occur between languages, they only occur between the speakers of those languages. Thus, the idea of language conflict is a misnomer' (Baker & Jones, 1998, 334). But not all contacts breed conflicts. For instance, Dutch speakers in the USA, Canada, Australia and New Zealand have lived without conflicts (de Bot, 1997), or the autochthonous Hungarians in Austria have no conflicts today. Other autochthonous Hungarians, those in Transylvania, Rumania had a tragic conflict in March 1990, when interethnic violence erupted over the issue of Hungarian-language schools in Tirgu Mureş/Marosvásárhely. The violence, which left at least six dead, was sparked off by a shopkeeper putting up a notice ('Chemist') in Hungarian.

---

[1] The lecture was titled 'Contact-induced typological change' and was delivered at the Linguistics Institute of the Hungarian Academy of Sciences, Budapest, 1 March, 1999.

In what follows I will propose a tentative taxonomy of contact situations with an attempt to predict where conflicts are likely to occur and where they are not.

Let us start with the fundamental difference between autochthonous minorities and immigrant minorities, and some consequences which are often said to follow from this difference (Table 1).

Table 1. A basic distinction

Historical status	Autochthonous minority	Immigrant minority
Citizenship	given	to be obtained
Educational goals	maintenance of language and culture	transitional education
Legal status and language rights	more	less

One example to illustrate these differences is the autochthonous Mexicans in today's New Mexico and the recent undocumented Mexican immigrants in California. The former were conquered in their own land by Americans in 1848, and as such fit the left-hand column of Table 1. The latter fit the right-hand column. In much of the current discourse on English Only in the United States, immigrant minorities are the focus of almost all discussion while autochthonous minorities often tend to be hushed up as if they didn't even exist. Another well-known example is the Swedish-speaking Finns in Finland, who have excellent legal protection, and the Finnish-speaking immigrants (labor migrants) in Sweden, who have almost no linguistic rights (see Skutnabb-Kangas, 1996). But the historical status of minorities is not enough to explain or predict conflicts: they may or may not occur with autochthonous and immigrant minorities alike. I propose that it is the goals of educational and economic-structural policies, combined with the historical status, which may offer better predictions.

Bilingual educational programs have various linguistic goals (dominance in L1, dominance in L2, bilingualism) and societal goals such as apartheid, repatriation, equity and integration, perpetuation of social stratification, assimilation, and linguistic and cultural enrichment (Skutnabb-Kangas, 1990a, 18). As Skutnabb-Kangas (1977) suggested earlier, there are two main aspects of acculturation: *cultural* and *economic-structural incorporation*. She says (1977, 191-2):

> Certain immigrant and minority groups may wish to assimilate culturally in the mainstream society, to give up their distinctive cultural features, their language and religion, but in general *minorities do not want cultural assimilation.* On the other hand, most groups want access to goods and services [...] In particular, if emphasis is laid on social security, economic and occupational life, political participation and opportunities for a good education for the children on an equal basis with the majority, most *minorities want structural incorporation.*

The goals of communities and educational and economic-structural policy-makers in multiethnic and multilingual states can be many. One way to categorize them is into the goals of the (policy-makers of the) majority nation vs. those of the minority or minorities. Line 3 of Table 1 then needs refinement, possibly along the lines of Table 2:

Table 2. The cultural-educational and economic-structural goals of majority and minority communities for autochthonous and immigrant minorities.

Autochthonous minorities	**Immigrant minorities**
Majority goals	
a) maintain	**a)** maintain
(for Swedish-speakers in Finland)	?
b) assimilate	**b)** assimilate
(for Hungarians in Slovakia)	(for Cuban-Americans in Florida)
Minority goals	
a) maintain	**a)** maintain
(Hungarians in Slovakia)	(Cuban-Americans in Florida)
b) assimilate	**b)** assimilate
(Hungarians in Austria)	(Hungarian-Americans)

Among the states with autochthonous minorities, in Finland the Swedish-speaking minority can carry out maintenance policy in agreement with the Finnish-speaking majority (see Skutnabb-Kangas & Phillipson, 1994, 80). On the other hand, the goal of Slovaks in Slovakia, at least until the fall of Vladimír Mečiar's government in 1998, was to assimilate the Hungarian minority in that country (see Kontra, 1995/1996).

The minorities' goals can also be of two kinds: for instance, the Hungarian minority in Slovakia aims to maintain their language and culture, whereas it could be claimed with considerable certainty that the autochthonous Hungarians' goal in Burgenland, Austria is to assimilate to the majority German-speaking population (see Gal, 1979).

The question arises why Hungarians in Slovakia differ from those in Austria. I propose that the difference lies in the balance between the educational-cultural goal and the economic-structural goal of a community. In Burgenland, Austria, after World War II, the economic benefits of incorporation into the dominant Austrian society far outweighed the gains of maintaining the Hungarian language. For instance, Gal (1978) described how Hungarian peasant men could not get Hungarian wives, because Hungarian women would rather marry German-speaking men since they were placed much higher on the socioeconomic ladder than the Hungarian subsistence farmers. However, in communist and postcommunist

Slovakia, the economic benefits of incorporation have been much smaller, consequently the gap between the benefits of cultural-linguistic maintenance versus economic-structural incorporation is also much smaller. This is shown, for instance, by the fact that currently about 80% of Hungarian children go to Hungarian-language schools, despite the social and economic disadvantages which result from education through the medium of a minority language in Slovakia.

As regards states with immigrant minorities, I have yet to find a convincing example of a state where the majority population's goal is to maintain the immigrants' language and culture (if they are different from those of the majority). However, there are many examples of majorities whose aim is to assimilate immigrant minorities; the textbook example of such a country is the United States, where non-Hispanic whites aim to assimilate immigrants. As for the minorities' goals, it can be claimed that the Cuban-Americans' goal in Florida is to maintain their language and culture (see, e.g., Castro, 1992), whereas the goal of the Hungarian-Americans is, by and large, linguistic and social assimilation to mainstream America.

The difference between Cuban-Americans and Hungarian-Americans seems to be similar to that between Hungarians in Slovakia and those in Austria. Cuban-Americans in Florida are economically successful and as such can maintain their language and culture (Castro, 1992). The old-timer Hungarian-Americans, the ones who immigrated between about 1880 and 1925, were economically rather unsuccessful and, consequently, their children and grandchildren were happy to move out of the poor industrial neighborhoods where Hungarian was still spoken. They moved into a more affluent but English-speaking America.

I must admit that the short explanations of the above examples are selective and do not do justice to the multicausality involved in each case. Nevertheless, I would venture the following generalization: Conflicts occur when the majority population's aims clash with those of the minority. We would anticipate little conflict between majority Finns and minority Swedish-speakers in Finland, between German-speaking Austrians and autochthonous Hungarians in Austria, or non-Hispanic whites and Hungarian-Americans in the USA. But severe interethnic conflict can be anticipated between the Slovak majority and the Hungarian minority in Slovakia[2], or perhaps the Cuban-Americans and the non-Hispanic white English-speakers in Florida.

One of the most important battlegrounds where such conflicts are played out is education or language-in-education rights, a research field whose vital importance in social conflict prevention has been championed by Tove Skutnabb-Kangas.

---

[2] In September 1998 a new Slovak government came to power. How it will change the Slovak-Hungarian conflict in Slovakia remains to be seen. As of this writing in April 1999, there are signs of improvement.

Exclusion as Discursive Practice and the Politics of Identity

Mustafa Hussain

The exclusion and marginalisation of new ethnic minorities in post-war Europe, and new forms of racism and xenophobia, can be approached by looking at the politics of identity construction in contemporary Danish society. Identity is a concept that is largely dependent on social validation and institutional power relations, hence it carries different social meanings in different social and sociopolitical contexts. That identity is fluid does not mean that we cannot grasp the mechanisms and processes that objectivise it through the discursive production of symbolic meaning in the societal production of culture. The main thrust of my argument is that the exclusion of minority ethnic communities from the social, economic, and cultural spheres has a great deal to do with the politics of identity construction by institutional discourse. This exclusion needs serious analysis not of immigrant cultures but of the symbolic production of meaning by dominant societal institutions.

Exclusion and the rhetoric of integration

In Denmark over the last 15 years or so, ethnic marginalisation and the concomitant cultural and social exclusion have increased almost in parallel with greater funding for measures and policies that were intended for the integration of ethnic minorities or to combat widespread xenophobic tendencies. It is ironic that following the European Year Against Racism, 1997, public polls conducted by a reputable university, a private firm, and the Commission of the European Union demonstrated that Danish public opinion about minority ethnic communities had degenerated. I am not suggesting any direct causal link between public spending on anti-racism measures and increased distancing tendencies in inter-ethnic relations, discernable in popular attitudes and behaviour, but the ways in which we have been combating xenophobia and racism have had no impact on the (re)production of racial or ethnic prejudice that provides legitimacy for overt racist ideologies and subtle discriminatory practices (see, for example, van Dijk, 1997). Danish integration policies have ignored the cultural processes through which racial prejudice is produced, reproduced, and diffused in late modern societies. The whole domain of ethnic relations in Denmark (as in other parts of Europe) has been characterised by administrative ad hocism. Due to European Union measures, it has been juxtaposed to drug-control, international terrorism, and illegal immigration. Political debate has therefore focused on tightening administrative control, and legislative restrictions on immigration.

The rhetoric of the integration of minorities into Danish society is thus premised on arguments that ignore power relations in minority-majority interaction. Paradoxically, minority identities are regarded as objects for change and transformation, whereas majority identity is considered permanent in the main scenario of knowledge production by powerful societal institutions. This exemplifies an inherent contradiction within mainstream discourse: it simultaneously constructs the culture of immigrants as an essential category, with an emphasis on tradition and religion, whereas Danish culture is defined as modern, progressive, and dynamic. Yet it is the minorities who are expected to change so as to integrate into Danish society. In fact Danish cultural identity has been in constant flux, particularly in recent centuries, and long before immigrants of non-European origin arrived. Even citizenship is not a very old concept.

There is thus arbitrariness in the understanding of the ethnic identity of both majority and minority. It is not essential to the group, but is used as a tag for identification of 'the Other'. The cognitive frames through which we make distinctions between 'us' and 'them' are provided discursively in a cultural process of the politics of identity, embedded in institutional practices. The power to define 'the Other' always lies with the majority. Despite considerable public spending on several political and legislative measures, inter-ethnic relations in Denmark have been going downhill for several years. Without the current upswing in the economy, the employment rate of the minority ethnic community would be much worse than current statistics indicate. There are very clear signs of the large-scale social exclusion of ethnic minority groups, marginalisation and an almost total lack of psychological contact with the surrounding society.

This whole problematic relates to the ontological question of what Danish culture and identity is to be in the growing global village, in a late modern age characterised by de-traditionalisation and greater individualisation (Giddens, 1990) on the one hand, and by increased intercultural and intracultural diversity and what postmodernists call the fragmentation of identities on the other. These affect social cohesion and solidarity.

Institutional analysis

To understand the question as to why and how the social exclusion of ethnic minorities continues despite the apparently good intentions of the liberal and intellectual elite of Danish society, it is imperative to undertake an institutional analysis of present-day Danish society, both in its local and its global contexts. Debate, and a number of social indicators and recent attitude surveys, suggest that the Danish population exhibits one of the highest levels in European Union countries of negative attitudes and fear of minorities of non-European origin. When theorising about this phenomenon, a number of factors are referred to: unemployment, traditional culture and Islam, ethnic crime and violence, the influx of refugees from very alien cultures, and so forth. This is the usual way in which the ethnic reality is explained in elite discourse and public debate. I would however claim that this production and diffusion of knowledge about the minority population is due to an intensified ethnification of the minorities, which the politics of identity requires for the maintenance of a unique Danish identity. A process which in its turn keeps the migrants and their descendants out of the collectivity. There is also support for this claim in the major debates about Danish membership of the European Union in the 1980s.

Seen from the perspective of social theory, this kind of knowledge production privileges structure over agency: the minority subjects are constituted by their culture and are without agency, the majority are free subjects and actors. Thus to have a racist stance (racism here including culturally based discrimination) towards minorities is not a societal phenomenon, an outcome of the reproduction of culture, but is largely explained as a matter of individual attitude, causally linked to cultural and behavioural characteristics among the minority ethnic communities themselves.

Ethnic relations and cultural discrimination cannot be explained by such a simplistic, static model of causal relationships. For instance it is widely believed that the Danish anti-immigrant 'Folkeparti' did well in the 1998 parliamentary elections because of the party leader's rhetoric. But such rhetorical strategies do not operate in a vacuum. They presuppose shared cognitive frames that are already present in the dominant discourse and in the institutional practices of cultural reproduction. What made the party's rhetoric workable and comprehensible was the prevailing discourses on ethnicity over a period of years, and long before an ethnic myth could be exploited politically (Schierup, 1993).

My point is that we should reconsider the rationale behind explanations of the hostility towards minorities. We should not rely blindly on attitude surveys. These can very well complement the analysis but are unable to uncover the rhetorical strategies used in public discourse. One widely canvassed hypothesis about Danish hostility to minorities is the view that ethnic minorities are more prone to crime and violence by virtue of their culture and ethnicity. One might then ask whether there could be anything in human nature or biology that differentiates the Danes from other human groups, nations, tribes, 'races' or people. I know that it sounds quite absurd to formulate a question in this way in the contemporary world, but the view that all Danes (a collectivity bounded by territorial boundaries) have monolithic and unified cultural traits is continuously communicated by the press unreflectively as common-sense reality. Consider the apparently innocent question which the newsreader on Danish public service TV put to another journalist when Somali refugees were complaining of racist discrimination:

Are we Danes really racists?
The answer of course lies in the question. The journalist being interviewed, himself a member of an ethnic minority, replies with a definite 'No'.
Now imagine that the question had been formulated like this:
Is there racism in Denmark?
I am certain that the reply would have been 'Yes'. But that would have changed the way the whole story was framed and many viewers' understanding of race relations. Another example, not from a tabloid but on prime time TV news:
More and more immigrants are undergoing plastic surgery to look like us.
Implicit in this story is the view that there exists a certain physical Danish identity which only the Danes have in common. All the 'Other' members of the society, immigrants, are a homogenous class of species that do not share the same phenotypical characteristics. Note also that the newsreader is not addressing the entire population of Denmark, as is required by the policy guidelines for a public service TV station. The immigrant population is excluded from the national audience.

Media exclusionary practices do not occur in isolation

In democratic societies, power is exercised more by persuasion than coercion. The mechanisms behind the production of ethnic boundaries or identities, legitimising ethnic inclusion and exclusion, require scrutiny in ways that relate them to societal power. Such analysis enables us to see policies such as those of the Minister of the Interior, when reducing financial allowances for political refugees, as not being the work of a single agent, but as the product of the discourse on ethnic minorities articulated by the *collective agency* of societal institutions, politicians, administrators, the intellectual elite, academia, and the mass media. Even in the most explicit anti-racist ideologies, and in liberal multiculturalist discourse that advocates diversity, we are, I fear, talking, classifying, attributing, categorising, measuring, and describing ethnic realities through the filter of the dominant discourse on ethnicity.
Public consensus at any moment of time is a result and a reflection of institutional power and practices. This might sound as if I am committing the same mistake as anti-racists or social analysts who privilege structure and system over agency. Such a perspective ultimately results in considering the Danish people as cultural dupes. This, however, is not the case in the approach followed here, the discursive construction of identity by institutional practices. We need to keep in mind that in modern democratic societies there are always competing discourses. Systemic determinism is therefore not absolute, deviation from the general consensus is possible, but not without consequences. Despite the predominance of an ethnocentric perspective on ethnic identity and culture in academic research,

governmental enquiries, political debate, and the media, resistance to the ideological production of ethnic reality is not altogether absent.

But such resistance remains peripheral. I have personally experienced how very competent scholars on ethnicity and race relations have been marginalized. Tove Skutnabb-Kangas has produced some of the most original research on multilingual education, her work is widely used at home and abroad, but she has herself been marginalized in Danish academia and research. In contemporary Denmark, every career-oriented academic or journalist - like political parties seeking popularity - knows which path to follow on ethnic issues. I know of several researchers of minority background who have become so disillusioned that they have left the country for good.

There is detailed empirically-based analysis of how the Danish press disseminates distorted ethnic images, and serves to exclude minorities from any ontological identification with the country in which they may even have been born, schooled and grown up (Hussain et al., 1997). These media discourses position them in a spectrum of multiple identities according to context. When implicated in crime, they are assigned tags of identity pertaining to their ethnicity, nationality, religion and culture, and such generic terms as 'second generation immigrants'. If they are victims of crime or discrimination, they are identified by their social roles, gender, or other generalised identities. Despite the relative autonomy of the press, such media practices could not occur without linkages to the discursive practices of the wider society.

The increasing ethnification of minority identities, the chalking out of immutable cultural boundaries in institutional discourse, and an unreflective rhetoric of integration by the political, administrative, academic, and media elites serve to socially exclude minorities of non-European origin. Thus is 'normality' constituted in Danish social formation in late modernity. Whether modernity and its discontents would require a post-modernisation of social theory itself (Rattansi & Westwood, 1994), or we should simply surrender to the idea of a post-modern society in which 'anything goes', is a matter of academic choice and perception. This, however, gives little comfort to those who are marginalized and excluded, in Denmark and throughout Europe.

Part IV. Power: Policies for Multilingualism

One of the most important A team strategies, used in all –isms, is to socially construct the A team's own resources, especially their non-material resources, so that only *these* are seen as The Resources, to be learned or acquired also by others. This is done by *glorifying the A team resources*, socially constructing the dominant languages (and their speakers) and cultures as Us, as the self-evident norms, the mainstream, valuable resources. Thus *A team resources are validated as convertible* to positions of structural power.

At the same time, the *B team resources*, especially their non-material resources, the linguistic and cultural capital embodied in the languages and cultures of the dominated, are *invalidated through the stigmatisation process*. Their resources (and the minorities/dominated groups themselves) are socially constructed as Other, and treated as handicaps, deficiencies, rather than resources, as something to be got rid of rather than to cherish. They are *constructed as invisible non-resources* which through this invalidation become *non-convertible* to other resources and to positions of structural power.

Tove Skutnabb-Kangas, 2000, 405.

Paradoxes of Plurilingualism. For better? For worse? And Beyond?[1]

Angéline Martel

Turina keessatt killen millaan adeemti
By persevering the egg walks on legs
Oromo Proverb (Ethiopia)

Prologue

Are these the best of times for plurilingualism?
Are these the worst of times for linguistic diversity?
Let us postulate that answering these questions would be uninteresting: attempts to provide closure. Of greater importance are questions and paradoxes as efforts to understand the roots of discourses and events.

Squarely formulated, these two questions point to the deep, and often opacified, convictions that ground language research, policy, and activism. These convictions rest on (often unformulated) notions of 'the Good', in the name of plurilingualism and linguistic diversity.

At the macrohistorical level, the questions also announce a global paradigmatic shift: one that has a profound impact on what is seen as 'better' or 'worse' conditions for speakers and/of languages of the world.

[1] Gratefulness for inspiration from Tove, Monique, Myriam, Marie-Louise, Dora, Geneviève, Estelle; Jean-Claude, Robert, Tedsuo, Daniel, Charles, Kungelica, Frank ... .

The global socio-political context: Shifting axes

Though unequally positioned, socio-political clusters of ideologies interact globally today: opposing, interpenetrating, inter-influencing each other. In the process, they articulate new relationships between individuals and collectivities, relationships that do not place either in a dominant position, relationships that place them as necessary complements to each other.

> *Njobvu ziumaninyana, udzu umabuutika*
> *When elephants fight, it is the grass that suffers*
> *Chichiwa proverb (Malawi)*

On a hierarchical (vertical) axis, dominant ideologies cluster around relations of competition. And the current globalization of market economies and societies under the leadership of Western civilisation intensifies competition into competitiveness[2]. These ideologies rest on (at least) four poles on a Darwinian conclusion, inspired by natural and primitive survival conditions in the physical and animal world, that the *strongest* survives better; on the notion of *freedom* as a privileged instrument of human development; on the idea that *profit*, as an extension of the economic framework, is a legitimate and desirable reward (the Good) for human activities; and on the thought that *money,* as an instrument of universality, governs the need for positioning and can provide a desired 'object'. Privileged positioning in power struggles is provided by profits. Action has instrumental ends. Technique and reason are effective means for impersonal objectives.

Numerous experiences can attest to the strength of these ideologies. The most obvious is the generalised pricing and merchandising of words, languages, ideas, cultures, individuals, nature, objects, etc.

Competitiveness has profound effects on socio-political structures, changing the West, changing other civilisations. States, whose conduct is determined by power and wealth, align their objectives on market logic and position themselves against each other, form strategic alliances against other large blocks. Mafia organisations rival each other and dominate societies and governments. Cultures are colonised, namely through the influence of Western (primarily American) media and entertainment industry. Millions of children and women work in semi-slavery conditions when multinationals seek to reduce production costs. New privileged classes are rising: 'info-rich' who have access to Internet and communication technologies; 'Triadians' who live in the three richest regions of the world (North America, Western Europe and Japan); 'jet setters' who work for multinationals, etc. Ecosytems essential to life (soils, oceans, animals, genomes, etc.) are exploited to

---

[2] 'Competitiveness' indicates that competition, which can be at times a source of creativity, is intensified and becomes an end in itself rather than a means to another end.

depletion. Small, autochthonous, minority languages are disappearing at a rate faster than ever in history, to the benefit of international and/or dominant languages. In short, competitiveness reinforces conditions of oppression / submission / conflict / rivalry / control / authority / imperialism / centralisation / monopoly in capital-oriented actions.

> *Ayudándose tres, para peso de seis*
> *Three helping each other are as good as six*
> *Spanish proverb*

On an egalitarian (horizontal) axis, clusters of ideologies based on solidarity and complementarity are attempting to deflect the power axis, seeking to resist, and counteract, parasitic and predatory socio-political organisations favoured by competitiveness. They too are a product of globalization through intercultural communication and intercivilizational exchanges. They also rest on (at least) four poles; on a challenge to the Darwinian notion of survival of the fittest substituting the notion of *responsibility* of the stronger towards the weaker; on *complementarity with 'Other/s'* as a privileged instrument of human development; on constant *resistance* to (absolute) power, authority and domination through new actors who share the podium: individuals (activists, intellectuals), non-profit organisations, gender, ethnic, and linguistic communities; on qualitative goals (the Good) of *individual wellness* through collective development as support. It is a people to people, a person to person movement through horizontal networks. Of importance are lived identities and personal logic (vs. rationality). And exchange is valued to replace parasitic symbiosis and predatory behaviour. This cluster legitimates and values diversity, be it linguistic, cultural, racial, sexual, geographical, etc. In so doing, it accords equality to peoples, communities and individuals and favours a non-violent ethos in revolutionary politics and social interactions. Diversity then is not marginal to the centre. On the contrary, diversity is a community of individuals. The notion of 'interactant' could be used to name the actors in this paradigm.

Enlarging this cluster of ideologies could be called the 'true progress of humanity'.

Although successes are mitigated by the domination of oppressive power structures, forces attest to the widening radiation of solidarity ideologies. Democracies, although not actually providing free and democratic life chances, are on the rise, particularly since the 1970s, defining themselves as structures of emancipation from totalitarianisms (and not only in opposition to communism). Paradoxically, it is under the leadership of the West, whose efforts to contain its own violence attempt to establish principles of coexistence, that national constitutional dispositions and international covenants for the protection of the weaker communities and individuals are increasingly promulgated. Numerous non-governmental associations, be they community-based, national or international, are founded in defence of, solidarity with, help for the weak / poor / less powerful. Social and civil movements are bonding through activism and critical resistance.

Dictators are beginning to be held accountable for their crimes. Minorities are increasingly given the means to develop their community and their language, in particular through education. The words of people at the margins of power, at the margins of cultures are being published and made accessible worldwide. In short, complementarity / solidarity reinforces individual and collective actions of emancipation / empowerment / liberation / negotiation / autonomy / independence / self-determination / decentralisation / self-management.

> *Okwahlul' amadoda kuyabikwa*
> *What beats men must be reported*
> *Zulu proverb*

And there is a sense today that ideas, institutions, and political structures resting on the vertical axis represent a deficit model of human organisation. Largely products and constructs of the Western world and of its political culture, like the Nation-State, products exported with Western Europe's historical world-wide displacement of its internal competitions and wars, they are not adapted to meet the budding axial shift. They are not structures based on peace and sharing. On the contrary, they are based on competition and even warfare.

Languages, as markers of civilisations and communities, as instruments of communications, as processes of understanding are tributary and makers of ideologies. The impact of the vertical-hierarchical-competitiveness axis on languages and communities has been documented. But explorations of the horizontal-solidarity axis are still in their infancy.

Paradox 1: Plurilingualism and the pecking order of nations

On the axis of competitiveness, powerful actors are merging and becoming more powerful. Their language becomes, *de facto* by structure, a *lingua franca*. A movement of resistance calls for policies based on plurilingualism.

> *Revealed at Usu Point*[3]
> *One who fails to share will be punished*
> *Palauan proverb*

---

[3] This proverb, incomprehensible to us, condenses the story of an avaricious woman who lived in Falelatai. She used to hide her food, so the story goes, rather than share it with her relatives. When the truth became known to the villagers, they cut off one of her fingers, buried it at Usu Point and erected a little mount as a warning to others.

Discourses and policies in favour of plurilingualism partake of both clusters of ideologies; a budding vision has to rest its infancy on ancient grounds. The prefix 'pluri' is a term of equalization and the aim of advocates of plurilingualism is to establish collaboration and solidarity in order to create spaces for many languages. But this solidarity actually only makes sense in a structure of competition, in power struggles. States, mostly Western European, attempt to entrench a construct that calls for a new paradigm of complementarity and solidarity while resting on the ancient power struggle of competition. Paradoxical? Yes.

> *Only when all contribute their firewood*
> *can they build up a strong fire*
> *Chinese proverb*

On the other hand, the construct of 'diversity', also inspired by Charles Darwin, is descriptive of human geography. The global revolts and manifestations of the sixties, legitimizing resistance to conformity and uniformity, gave a new perspective to the word (Jucquois, 1996). Today, the term 'linguistic diversity' is closer to the solidarity/complementarity ideologies. But interestingly, this resistance, when used by State policy makers is transformed into calls for 'diversification': a re-entry into the competition ideologies to sustain plurilingualism.

The more profound paradox is then that linguistic competition, itself based on differences, seeks to favour the coexistence of languages in a paradigm that values rivalry and leads to the overpowering and disintegrating of differences.

Differences then? How?

Paradox 2: Minority status as valuable

> *Galu wamfumu ndi mfumu ya agalu*
> *The King's dog is the king of dogs*
> *Chichiwa proverb (Malawi)*

With globalization, with the construction of supra-State entities, large and powerful States, even ex-colonising Nations, are learning about the condition of a minority position. The paradox is that the powerful of yesterday are confronted with the power structures and the language policies that they helped consolidate.

Many 'official' language policy actions, while valuably preserving a 'majority' language, have given advantages to their speakers and reduced linguistic diversity: globally, the number of States is infinitesimal compared to the number of languages. Official language policies lead to normalisation (choosing one language variety as official): another factor in decreasing diversity of usage. Furthermore, a logic of hierarchisation of languages, applied to State and supra-State entities in the name of communications, can only further reduce linguistic diversity.

Therefore, as an alternative to majority prerogatives, there is a need to deconstruct the power paradigm behind the concept of minority. Members of majorities, in becoming members of minorities, could become attuned to the power inequalities that they themselves reject. In so doing, they should be reminded that, if they lack power in regard to a larger and more powerful block, they have that power in regard to the less powerful than themselves, the minorities within States. There is then a most valuable lesson to be learnt from the minority condition, a most valuable knowledge of negotiation, of solidarity, of complementarity that should be valued, one that could lead to the axial shift referred to in the introduction. Paradoxical? Yes.

Another sociolinguistic concept, diglossia, although not marked as descriptive of power relations by Charles Ferguson (quite the contrary, it referred to a complementarity of two languages) has become descriptive of inequalities and domination. In view of the leading role of concepts in the advancement of ideologies, how do we now pose concepts that are descriptive of the harmony and the complementarity of languages? Can we develop such forward-looking concepts as polyglossia? Can we describe the conditions of complementarity of languages of the Amazonian Indians? The conditions of complementarity of languages in exogamous families? Can we value marginalized languages so that people do not learn to speak the dominant language out loud and their community language silently, as Tove Skutnabb-Kangas puts it?...

The crucial question is then not one of power. Instead, it is a question of 'Why power?'

Paradox 3: (De/Re)Construction of linguistic identities

Iso lilodw' aliphumeleli
One eye does not succeed
Zulu proverb

The construction of life, of institutions and politics around cultural and collective identities is a historical rule and not an exception. The exception is the forging of identities within Nation-States. The exception is the use of politics to define identities (Castells, 1998); States *have* used languages to construct allegiances and loyalties.

In the politics of competition, (re)affirmed identities request political recognition (Taylor, 1998) as a necessary token of structural security. And the politicisation of identities within competition polarises their plurality, focalises on a few dimensions, establishes a dynamic of good and evil, of anticipated (or real) threat from Other/s.

The paradox is that the current (re)birth of cultural and linguistic identities, above and below the nation-State, reappears when these socio-political structures are contested as too powerful or powerless. The movement could then be an effort to shake away from allegiance in competition and to reconstitute identity in solidarities[4].

In an era of communication, people construct their own identities, from experiences, from communities, from cultural and civilisation codes, increasingly in non-State spaces. Amongst these, linguistic identities are pluralistic: interaction in different languages is multiplying, understandings from different world visions are available.

Linguistic bridges. How can linguistic identities be built on solidarity, equality, and inclusion?

Paradox 4: Structures of power, power of structures

Àìgbó 'fà l'à ńwòkè, ifá kan kò sí ní párá
When you cannot interpret the riddle of the oracle, you keep
gazing up at the rafters, but you won't find the answer there
Yoruba proverb

All advances in the human condition have involved challenging institutions and practices that were treated as necessary and inevitable (Falk, 1995).

A paradox here is that we of Western civilisations call for a neutralising of our own (Eurocentric) concepts and structures based on competition. At the same time, we attempt to build structures on solidarity/complementarity modes that are inclusive of the voices, the languages and experiences of Other/s, including other civilisations and communities.

We need to realise that in competition, all individuals are not supported by protective environments. Instead, the system serves the powerful few and disadvantages most whose interests are marginalized (Touraine, 1997). For interactants, there is an order of solidity of languages: transnational and multinational, national and official, regional and community. Linguistic diversity does not seem particularly favoured by this order of solidity if it is left to the law of the strongest.

To construct structures that demystify power towards 'power to power', in solidarity, two avenues should continue to be explored.

Beyond the self-legitimating discourse of the importance of the rule of law lies the pedagogical role of its principles. The law, linguistic human rights, constitutional rights, reveal power structures and are more and more oriented

---

[4] Interestingly, the plural word 'solidarities' does not exist in English.

toward protection of the weak/poor/marginalised. The pedagogy of the Universal Declaration of Human Rights is a witness to this. Although most, if not all, of the States of the world do not entrench and live by the letter of its law, the principles are widely accepted and adopted. Violations are denounced, at least by opposing-aligned States. And researchers can play a role in documenting and describing oppression and the processes of liberation of minority linguistic communities through the pedagogy of constitutional dispositions.

The caveat today, however, is that the West can no longer claim a monopoly on the principles of law. A conversation must be established between civilisations to articulate conditions of solidarity/complementarity, as they are lived each in their own way, in particular spheres (family, friendships, community solidarities, etc), across communities of the world.

But the construction of a new solidarity paradigm can only be possible through a shift to modes of human interaction based on exchange. Education has here a large role to play for it must teach a re-equilibration of human relations: from parasitic relations, when one takes all and gives not, to exchange relations and reciprocity. Education can serve to make us become actors of exchange, detaching us from our primordial mores of parasites.

Most will object that we cannot today achieve human organisations based on solidarity and complementarity. That competition will always prevail. That competition is a basic mode of human relations. Based on the past of humanity, it is quite true that examples of harmonious cohabitation are few. But history is not cyclical. It is pyramidal. And for an axial shift to occur, we must call for it, in our visions, in our actions. We must become interactants with a vision.

Do we not need an international, intercivilizational pact on complementarity, of languages, of customs, of laws?

> *Vision without action is a daydream.*
> *Action without vision is a nightmare*
> *Japanese proverb*

Conclusion

Are these the best of times for plurilingualism?
Are these the worst of times for linguistic diversity?

We could answer: 'Yes *and* No'. All is not well, nor just, nor equitable; numerous actions are undertaken in the name of plurilingualism and linguistic diversity; a tremendous amount of words are spoken and written in plea or description. Few unmask competitive bases when they occur.

But concurrently, and also consequently, profound changes are occurring towards solidarity and complementarity.

But again, dominating forces are intensifying.

The West, as locus of polarisation of the better and the worse of clusters of ideologies now has a moral responsibility to decentre itself, to bring the margins to the centre, to listen more, to speak less.

Beyond? Together?

> *A journey of a thousand miles begins with a single step*
> *Chinese proverb*

Promoting Multilingualism and Linguistic Human Rights in the Era of Economic Rationalism and Globalization[1]

Michael Clyne

Meeting Tove

It is 28 years since Einar and Eva Haugen introduced me to Tove in the restaurant of the University of Copenhagen during the 1972 AILA (Association Internationale de Linguistique Appliquée) Conference. We subsequently met at numerous conferences, remained in contact through correspondence and email, and in 1994 to our delight, she and Robert spent several months in our department as visiting scholars. Right from the first encounter, I realized that we had a great deal in common in that we were both bilinguals. This in itself is hardly anything special since, as we all know, more than half of the world's population is bilingual. But we both regarded bilinguals as a special category of people who bear a responsibility for the welfare and rights of other bilinguals. Exactly what that entailed was probably what we didn't agree on entirely but had many opportunities to discuss on various occasions. I certainly learned from Tove that our obligation to other bilinguals extended to political activism in support of minority rights and not just the dissemination of research results as part of advocacy.

Within a few months of that first encounter in Copenhagen, many opportunities for such activism presented themselves. On my return from nine months overseas, I found myself in a radically changed Australia. A new government had replaced the unsatisfactory assimilation policy with multiculturalism. This was based on a new national identity, social equity, and cultural democracy. A broad coalition of ethnic communities, trades unions, teachers, and professional linguists lobbied for the teaching of what came to be known as 'community languages' in primary and secondary schools and universities and for the provision of services in community

---

[1] I thank Sandra Kipp for helpful comments.

languages, including radio, TV, library holdings, interpreting and professional workers. Although politicking was time consuming, it was incredibly successful. In the 1980s, the same exercise was repeated in the development of a national policy on languages, first through a government inquiry into language policy needs, then through planning at the state level, and finally with the real thing (Lo Bianco, 1987) and its implementation.

Are social and economic agendas compatible?

By the time Tove and Robert visited Australia in 1994, things had started to deteriorate. The balance between social equity, cultural enrichment, and economic strategies as motivations for the promotion of multilingualism (Lo Bianco, 1987) and in all other public issues had shifted towards short term economic objectives. In terms of multilingualism, there was an increasingly prevalent argument which assumed a key position within the Productive Diversity policy promulgated in 1992 by the then Prime Minister Paul Keating, namely that Australia needs to utilize the talents and resources of the multicultural population to make the nation more economically viable as it takes its place in the global economy and within an integrated Asia-Pacific region. This actually had the potential to strengthen other goals related to multilingualism - social equity and cultural enrichment. If someone has a background in a community language which has also become a commodity, that person may be regarded as an asset to the nation and their social position and economic opportunities enhanced by their personal possession of the asset. In addition, other Australians acquiring that language for economic purposes would learn to understand and appreciate the relevant culture for that is an integral part of even the most instrumentally oriented language program. In fact, at least in some parts of Australia, the economic argument has led to an unprecedented participation in language programs and to policies requiring all children to take a language other than English for as many as 11 years of schooling.

However, there are a number of serious problems with the value of the economic argument for the status of community languages. One is that it introduces a distinction between 'important' and 'unimportant' languages. Up to 1973, young people with a background in a certain language (e.g. German, Italian, Russian) could study it at school and university and count it as an examination subject whereas others with a background in another language (e.g. Arabic, Polish, Turkish) could not study it to an advanced level or gain credit for it. This was changed in 1973, with the progressive introduction of all community languages for which there was an expressed demand as examination subjects. Students were now taught at classes at state secondary schools opened on Saturdays to offer languages not available at their regular school. Thus there was no longer a dividing line between 'important' and 'unimportant' languages, for in a multicultural society all languages were important. The availability of programs and examinations in a wide range of languages continues, and transmissions in almost all community languages are available on radio and TV. However, in some states the economic criterion is applied in decisions concerning priority languages for schools and that is not healthy for a multicultural society. Another problem concerning Productive Diversity is that not all companies were convinced about the value of language study (see Kipp et al., 1995) and while some bilinguals were helped professionally through the emphasis on instrumental value (among other things, language loadings are paid to bi- or multilingual public servants), this has not happened in every respect. Another new assumption was that Asian languages were more important languages than other languages because of their significance for trade and tourism. That the sources of Australia's future wealth cannot be predicted is borne out by the Asian currency crisis. Economic developments and catastrophes can occur very rapidly and economic decisions are made far from where they can be discussed and questioned.

Another matter which accompanied the commoditization of education was in sharp contrast to the above-mentioned possible social spin-offs of productive diversity. It was the *majority group* claiming for itself school-based learning of languages of economic benefit, reverting to examination assessment policies of the 1950s and early 60s where students were discriminated against if they were believed to have an advantage. This practice was (re)introduced in particular for languages considered 'difficult' and/or which had a recent immigration population (e.g. Chinese, Korean, Indonesian, Spanish). In different states, the practice involved the setting of separate examinations for 'first' and 'second' language learners, different standardization of marks or differential eligibility for the bonus some universities give for those who have matriculated in a language other than English. Some states acknowledge the difficulties of those with not very high proficiency in English, the language of assessment in non-language subjects, and trade that in against the potentially good result in the background language. However, what makes these practices undesirable is the way they disadvantage the second and third generation bilinguals who through their efforts and those of their parents have maintained the language, for there is a wide diversity among the 'background speakers' - 1st, 2nd, 3rd generation, active, passive home users, dialect speakers, those with both parents or only one parent or only grandparents employing the language now, those who have lived or been to school in a country where the language is spoken. (The basis of categorization is a form to be completed by all examination candidates. No such form exists for any other subject area where an advantage could be perceived, e.g. theatre studies, music, computer studies, Clyne et al., 1997).

The effects of economic rationalism are felt very dramatically in universities, which have been struck by financial cuts, including the obligation to pay from their declining operating grants salary increases for which government is not prepared to provide funding. Programs in languages with small enrolments, such as Dutch, Hindi, Khmer, Russian, Thai, and Vietnamese, have been closed down, and other languages are being forced to cut teaching hours, with the Web being regarded as a panacea which can save teaching hours and therefore facilitate cost cutting.

Inadequate language teaching at university will affect further the quality of teachers available at primary and secondary level.

Like Joshua Fishman (1991), Robert and Tove have demonstrated a healthy scepticism as to whether good intentions will really translate into quality bilingualism and language maintenance in Australia, in Robert and Tove's case because the necessary quality programs do not exist in schools (Phillipson & Skutnabb-Kangas, 1997). These days we have to be sceptical about policies that are measured in terms of budgets and kids on seats. However, it must be considered what the alternative might be (e.g. badly intentioned monolingualism). A problem with 'mainstreaming' multiculturalism is that it has an upside and a downside. On the one hand, it is desirable because if everyone were to accept multiculturalism as a reality, its survival would be ensured. On the other hand, if all mainstream activities are downsized and subjected to market forces, then this will also apply to multiculturalism. And this, rather than the targeting of multiculturalism for marginalization, is what has been afflicting Australia.

The question might be asked - What can be done to maintain a socially motivated language policy in the days of globalization and economic rationalism? I believe it is the principle that Australia's identity is a multicultural one in which bilinguals and biculturals (with dual identities) have a vital role to play and are not considered to 'belong' less than English monolinguals and monoculturals. This idea of national cohesion can leave open the door to further advances in multiculturalism in better times. It protects minorities from the kind of discriminatory behaviour (e.g. in Slovakia, see Lanstyak, this volume) against which we protested together in 1996. It does not, however, offer protection against such examples of political opportunism as one Australian premier changing the name of the Macedonian language to 'Macedonian (Slavonic)' under pressure from diplomatic representatives of another country and community representatives of another ethnic group.

In the era of globalization and economic rationalism, perhaps more than at other times, keeping open the multicultural/multilingual agenda, including its principles and at least some infrastructure, is essential so that an easy path back can be traced in better times. My Utopia is not to be found in some faraway country - it is Australia in the 1970s and early 1980s, when almost everything was possible.

Language Resilience and Educational Empowerment: Philippines and Australia

Jerzy J. Smolicz and Margaret J. Secombe

In the context of globalisation, Tove Skutnabb-Kangas' life-long research on the place of languages in multilingual societies has acquired new and urgent relevance. Her work on minority education and linguistic human rights can now be judged as providing authoritative answers to the burning social issues that must be resolved if multilingual societies are to avoid fragmentation through internal implosion or revolutionary explosion.

One of the main thrusts of Tove Skutnabb-Kangas' research has been to question the assumption of the benefits to be derived from the concept of a monolingual nation-state. For long this European construct has enjoyed a positive image as harbinger of modernity and democracy, with the homogeneity of language and culture ensuring political liberty and equal access to educational and social achievement for all citizens. This image is still alive and propagated as a cure for ethnic conflict in the countries of Asia and Africa, only recently freed from colonial domination, with these same colonial powers being presented as exemplars of linguistic and ethnic harmony and stability.

The dangers of state-imposed monolingualism are forcefully highlighted in post-colonial contexts where there has been little liberty and equality and much cultural and linguistic suppression in the name of stability through uniformity. In this connection Tombiah's (1996, 126) comments on the lack of evidence for the transferability of a Western theoretical construct to post-colonial societies seem pertinent. He notes that it would be 'a fundamental fallacy (...) to impose a historical construction such as a nation-state, achieved on a distinctive soil, on a dependent world, as if its realisation is a necessary state in *universal* history', especially since even within Europe, 'its claim was questioned and contested'. It would be a sad inversion of the European model if the 'inferiorisation' of languages and cultures by former colonial powers were to be continued by post-colonial independent states in relation to their own indigenous non-dominant linguistic groups.

Post-colonial threads in Australia and the Philippines

The comparison of multilingual countries, such as Australia and the Philippines, suggests a number of important questions. Why is it that some minority linguistic groups appear to have internalised hegemonic domination by others as normal and natural, so that they submit passively to discrimination of their language and culture, while others struggle for their linguistic human rights? Why is it that some linguistic communities, denied the resource of their own school system, or indeed any kind of educational support, manage to maintain their language through the informal domain of home and marketplace, while others, provided with at least some opportunity to acquire literacy in their home language, lose that language in no more than three generations following dislocation from their original homeland? This brief chapter can only attempt to highlight some problems and suggest some degree of explication with special reference to the Philippines and some comparative material from Australia.

Despite their differences, both countries have common threads running through their histories, as well as their present circumstances. Both were invaded, occupied, and had settlements established by leading European powers - Great Britain and Spain respectively. In the case of the Philippines, there was a second dose of colonialism from a former European colony, the United States of America. In both instances, the indigenous population consisted of small local, rural, pastoral, or nomadic communities which could not present viable resistance to the conquerors. Both countries were named by the Europeans and the names given to their inhabitants - Australian and Filipino - were originally reserved for the European settlers.

The numerically small Aboriginal population of Australia (under 2%) is divided into a number of linguistic groups. Despite current efforts to save those languages that remain, most 'languages of Australia' are moving along the path towards extinction, reflecting the world-wide shrinking of linguistic diversity at a rate that is relatively even faster than the disappearance of biological diversity (Skutnabb-Kangas & Phillipson, 1998). In contrast, the major indigenous languages of the Philippines have survived, and one of them - in its 'intellectualised' form renamed Filipino - has acquired the functions of both official and national language. The two countries also share the impact of an English linguistic heritage, with over four fifths of the Australian population in 1996 using English as their only home language, and some two thirds of the Filipinos declaring an ability to speak English by 1980 (Gonzales, 1996a, 42).

Despite the dominance of English in all the official spheres of life, both countries are multilingual and have adopted national language policies that take note of this, but in a very different manner. While in Australia the dominance of English is taken for granted, so that it is not mentioned as either an official or national language in the constitution, in the Philippines, by contrast, national and official languages were included formally in the 1973 Constitution, with English fulfilling the role of an official language alongside Filipino, and Spanish finally losing its official status in the Constitution of 1987. The multilingualism of the Philippines is, however, much more ramified and deeply embedded in the community than could be inferred from the widely reported rivalry between English and Filipino. The emergence of Tagalog as 'Filipino' and its imposition as the only 'national' language, to the exclusion of Philippine languages other than Tagalog (PLOT) from schools, are complex issues which are still not fully resolved (Gonzales, 1996b, 231).

Fragility of Australian linguistic pluralism

Although the existence of the plurality of languages in Australia is now probably more accepted than at any time in the history of the English language dominance of the country since the period of *laissez faire* pluralism in the mid-nineteenth century, toleration of languages is less firmly entrenched in the Australian ethos than religious pluralism. Minority languages remain vulnerable and it is difficult to assess the extent to which schools have contributed to stabilising the country's linguistic pluralism. For practical purposes, English dominates the scene, even when minority community languages are taught as school subjects in the mainstream or independent schools.

The weakness of Australian bilingualism lies in the fact that despite the great range of languages which are being offered as fully fledged end-of-the-school examination subjects that can count for university entrance, some of these languages have very small enrollments and are taught in very few of the schools, which have often been rather grudging and vacillating in their support. Languages (other than English) remain an unpopular option at senior secondary school level with no more than 10-20% of students taking them as matriculation subjects. Linguistic erosion at community level (as revealed by census data 1976-1996) is best demonstrated by the shift away from the use of community languages towards English only in the home of the second generation, particularly for children of exogamous marriage. Despite, therefore, the significant multicultural reforms in Australian schools, the multilingualism of the country from the perspective of community languages appears to be transitional, although this to some extent is being counter-balanced by the growing popularity of Asian languages such as Japanese, Chinese and Indonesian, that are being increasingly taught as 'foreign' languages.

Multilingualism and schooling in the Philippines

The Philippines present a contrasting picture to the Australian scene, with recent studies confirming the vitality of indigenous languages in the everyday usage of the population, including even those languages which have been excluded from the school curriculum.

Our own study on patterns of language use among non-Tagalog background students showed that those respondents who had reached the senior high school stage accepted the current state of triglossia in their communities, with the three languages (English, Filipino, and the regional PLOT, labelled as 'vernacular') activated in various domains of the students' lives, but with very clear differentiation in patterns of usage (Smolicz & Nical, 1997). In the formal school domain, the preponderant usage of English (for science and mathematics) and Filipino (for other subjects), excludes the 'vernacular' from the curriculum and even from most student-teacher interaction. Comments from the students' personal statements indicated that the use of the 'vernacular' by a student to the teacher could at times be interpreted as a sign of rudeness and lack of the proper respect due to the teacher.

The situation is much more dramatic for the children of the rural poor from non-Tagalog provinces who begin schooling in what are virtually two new languages: English and Filipino. Even after completing this kind of elementary education, the rural children (as opposed to the city students in our high school study) often speak only halting English, or are too shy to speak English at all. For such young people the Filipino language also remains basic and insufficiently internalised, preventing them from acquiring adequate literacy in any language, including their mother tongue (Gonzales, 1996a, 43).

In contrast to the situation in Australia, where most immigrant groups of European or Asian origin could be regarded initially as fragments of nations with a long history of the literary development of their languages, many of the linguistic dilemmas that currently face the Philippines are the product of the double dose of colonial domination which has delayed the literary development of all the eight major indigenous languages of the country.

The Spanish clergy used the indigenous languages in their missionary work, which succeeded in making the Philippines one of the most Christian countries of Asia, while almost inadvertently helping those tongues to acquire their first written records. Literary development was, however, stunted by the restriction of literacy to a very small elite, with literature confined to religious subjects that excluded many aspects of native culture as pagan and with no chance given to the development of an indigenous literature based on people's own experiences. Until the educational reforms of 1863, the education of the indigenous peoples was confined to elementary schooling, and only the children of Spaniards were allowed to receive higher education.

While the American policy, which propagated compulsory education in English for all Filipinos, was initially directed mainly against Spanish, it was almost equally hostile to the indigenous languages of the country, with penalties imposed upon pupils using their home languages on the school premises.

Independence was conceptualised in terms of the European model of the monolingual nation-state. When the search for one national language through the fusion of eight major Filipino languages failed, the adoption of one of them was perceived as the only way to prevent total domination by the colonial language, English. This move was interpreted by the native Tagalog speakers as an advantageous outcome, while elite members of other language groups were prepared to accept such a compromise, provided English remained dominant in government, universities, and business life. The resulting education policies (built on Filipino/Tagalog and English bilingualism) have continued the subordination of all the other languages of the Philippines. In this way, the centuries-old submission to Spanish religion and English language was compounded by an additional subordination to the new 'national' tongue 'Filipino' - with all other languages relegated to the home and marketplace.

The non-Tagalog Filipinos' acquiescence to the virtual elimination of their tongues from education may need an explanation when compared with the Australian immigrant groups which, although scattered across the continent and without any territorial base, have been able to win a level of recognition at school that still eludes their Filipino minority counterparts. One explanation is that among the more influential and wealthy sections of the population in all the regions of the country, English is often used at home, so that children have a background knowledge of it when they start school at six, or even earlier, if they have their formal introduction to English in a fee-paying pre-school. Private schools have often been able to increase the time allocated to English without incurring too much trouble with the directives on Filipino language in the Bilingual Education Policy.

Another interpretation for the lack of teaching of vernaculars was provided by respondents in our high school study who explained that it was due to their insufficient confidence in the maturity of their home tongue as a literary language and their sense of its inadequacy in the learning situation (Smolicz & Nical, 1997). Such diffidence among speakers of the various Filipino vernaculars is quite understandable in view of some four centuries of colonial rule. In contrast, Australian minority group members were in a much more favourable position, mostly originating from countries with linguistic core values fully crystallised, often following their successful defence against foreign suppression, as in the case of the Baltic, Polish, and Greek languages. Since 1946, the policy of filipinisation through the imposition of Tagalog has further undermined non-Tagalog Filipinos' faith in the validity of their own languages as possible media for education and broader intellectual development. Such policies, unless reversed, represent the threat of ultimate linguicism.

Proponents of the 'Bilingual Policy', with Filipino/Tagalog as the only indigenous language in the curriculum, fail to recognise such a threat and are under the illusion that, by eliminating PLOT from all education and official functions and relegating their speakers to illiteracy in their home tongue, they are preventing English from completely dominating the life of the country. In fact, by their policies they are producing the opposite effect. Denied the opportunity to study and advance in their own languages, educated young people, especially in the Visayan provinces, are turning to English in preference to Filipino, which they perceive as the core values of other people, and of very much less use than English in their quest for education and work outside of the Philippines (Smolicz & Nical, 1997). In this way, advocates of Tagalog/Filipino as the only worthy partner alongside English, are in fact furthering the interest of those forces within their country and outside of it, which already acknowledge English, the global language, as sufficient on its own for all the needs of the Philippines. In consequence, the country, is now being subjected to linguistic imperialism which, as Phillipson (1998, 104) points out, is a 'sub-type of cultural imperialism, along with media, educational and scientific imperialism'. The continued hold of English on upper and middle strata of Filipino society and its spread as the language of science and mathematics in schools and of all higher education, business, and finance, promotes 'one-way learning' and perpetuates 'structural and cultural inequalities' which strike hardest against the least powerful in society.

The struggle for survival and development of minority languages in education elsewhere in the world suggests, however, that acceptance of such inequalities may not last forever. If the Philippines' authorities feel impelled to continue following the less than fortunate European tradition that presumes that each state should possess a single and exclusive national language, it may be only a matter of time before dissenting voices appear among the non-Tagalog provinces of the Philippines. This has already occurred in the Islamic part of the Southern Philippines where the population, with its quite distinct culture and religion, has long been in standing rebellion against the current government authorities and has already been successful in winning a special status for Arabic, as well as a degree of local autonomy.

From a comparative perspective the achievement of Australia lies in the extent to which it has been able to reshape itself as a multicultural country. It has demonstrated that tolerance of diversity and gradually emerging pluralist policies in language education are a better guarantee of stability than forced assimilation to one dominant language and culture. The fragility of its linguistic pluralism can be attributed in part to the lack of a regional/territorial base for all immigrant community languages, except English, and a lack of domains, other than the home, where they can be activated. Even those young people who complete school and tertiary studies of their home language, ultimately find their minority language domain restricted to their families and a scattering of fellow group members in ethnic organisations, with very limited opportunities for using their linguistic skills in the Anglo-dominated 'mainstream' society.

Within their home-community territorial base, the languages of the Philippines other than Tagalog (PLOT) have succeeded in surviving, but their literary development remains precarious under the present policies. Recent signs of regional awakening have been apparent in the advocacy of Cebuano, the largest PLOT, to replace Tagalog-Filipino for official purposes in the Cebuano-speaking provinces. Such early signs of awakening language consciousness point to the need for an eventual recognition that the stability of the country, as well as the equitable distribution of education and social opportunities, requires acceptance of the bilingual principles advocated by Tove Skutnabb-Kangas, which in the case of the Philippines mean that it is possible for Filipinos to be literate in their mother tongue and still be fluent in Filipino, as the national language of the country.

Language Policy and Planning in South Africa: Some Insights

Neville Alexander

The relationship between English and what we shall call simply the African languages is the crux of the language question in South Africa. Until recently, the spotlight was always put on the relationship between English and Afrikaans, a fact which reflects the colonial history of the country. Now that the democratic transformation has begun, the central issues in respect of which the majority of the people will put their imprint on this society are beginning to emerge clearly. Of these, there can be no doubt, the language dispensation is among the most important for the long-term development and stability of the country. It ought also to be said that even though people only learn from history in very special circumstances, South Africa's intelligentsia is very conscious of the trajectories which were followed by other African countries in the period after the retreat of the imperialist powers, especially Britain, France and Belgium. There is, thus, just the slightest of possibilities that some of the more devastating policy mistakes that were made in most of those countries under their neo-colonial governments will be avoided in the case of South Africa.

In what follows, I want to draw attention to a few of the most significant insights arrived at by language activists, scholars, and professionals in South Africa during the past forty years or so, i.e., during the period when the official policy of apartheid informed all state practice. The few issues I highlight here, I believe, were understood in terms similar to, and in some cases were directly informed by, the views of Tove Skutnabb-Kangas and her intellectual milieu.

The first of these insights is the fact that unless linguistic human rights and the equality of status and usage of the African languages were translated into practice, the democratisation of South Africa, i.e., the real empowerment of the oppressed black people of this country, would remain in the realm of mere rhetoric. It became clear to those of us who, since the mid-1950s, have waged the struggle for the realisation of these fundamental goals, that we are confronted with a daunting task, one which entails overwhelming political struggles. It is clear that the nature of the post-colonial state, the fact that all the institutions and bureaucratic practices of the colonial state are continued in the era of independence without much amendment, predetermines, or at least constrains, language policy as well as most other social policies. For the sake of continuity and 'convenience', the aspiring middle-class elites simply continue the policies of the former colonial overlords. Added to this merely administrative moment is the class moment, which was described so clearly by Pierre Alexandre on the morrow of independence and liberation. Knowledge of English (or French/Portuguese), it is realised even if not acknowledged explicitly by the elites, constitutes cultural capital which demarcates the class boundaries between the tiny upper layer of people who are more or less proficient in these European languages and the vast majority of mainly rural (in South Africa today, increasingly urban) people who either do not know these languages at all or have only a very inadequate grasp of them. One way or the other, it is obvious that the pressures (economic, bureaucratic, and cultural) to perpetuate the status quo ante in respect of the functional domains in which the different languages are used are extremely great. Only very few regimes in post-colonial Africa (notably, Guinea, Somalia, and Tanzania) were able or willing to resist these pressures for longer or shorter periods.

In this regard, the lingua franca status of English, or of other former colonial languages, has to be re-examined. While it is undoubtedly true that in the South African case, it can only redound to the benefit of the majority if they are given ready access to the effective acquisition of English as their first or second additional language, it is equally true that this is by no means the only possible route open to a new government to facilitate effective communication among all the citizens of the country. It is at this point that the fundamental insight regarding the reality of multilingualism in most modern societies and the linking or integrative effects of multilingual proficiency and of a systematic policy of promoting multilingualism become evident. In this connection, the work of Skutnabb-Kangas and Cummins has played an invaluable catalytic and validating role in the South African debate about language policy and planning. Together with the earlier generation of sociologists of language, such as Fishman, Ferguson, Haugen, and others, through their work they helped to shape the parameters within which the whole question was discussed. Their traces are to be found in numerous official documents of the new South Africa. It is especially in the domain of multilingual education that their contributions have been most penetrating. As recently as 1997, Tove suggested that the best way forward for South African education, given the social and cultural strength of English and Afrikaans, might be to let all children entering school be immersed in the relevant African language, depending on the province of South Africa to which the discussion refers. Although this is a suggestion which will definitely not fly in the short to medium term, it is precisely this kind of boldness based on first principles as well as abundant empirical evidence that inspired us to take the plunge, especially in the later 1980s. Our own reality and experience were reinforced by this work and one way or another, the monolingual habitus (Gogolin, 1994) was definitively laid to rest among most of those scholars and professionals who helped to shape post-apartheid language policy.

Eventually, we were to formulate our position more precisely in terms of both multilingual proficiency and (critical) multilingual awareness. In this regard, one of the most devastating insights we arrived at in the course of our work was that South African education for more than three-quarters of the children at school is based on an English as a Third Language system. In other words, while English is used as a language of learning and teaching in most black schools, the teachers who were/are using the language to teach the school subjects, including English itself, were/are in most cases not very proficient second-language or third-language speakers of English. This is the direct result of apartheid education and is, naturally, not the fault of the teachers (see Hartshorne, 1995). If there is one factor that explains the brutal attrition rate in South African schools - in 1997, some 53% of all the students who wrote the Matriculation (school-leaving) examination failed - this is surely the obvious candidate. While we know that a system based on the second language as medium works well if taught by first-language speakers or by proficient second-language speakers, in South Africa we are very many years away from such a situation, quite apart from the consideration that since we have the choice today, it is obviously more appropriate and in the long term, it will be more efficient, to opt for a system based on first- or home-language medium. The corollary to this is that for as long as necessary, we have to promote an additive bilingual approach to schooling, the reason being that all our children should be afforded access to effective acquisition of English while the African languages are being properly equipped for use in all high-status functions of our society.

Any other policy is not only unrealistic and counter-intuitive but would also go against the trend of world history. After all, no people has ever voluntarily given up its language in favour of another. People who have been conquered and especially those who have been enslaved have done so under duress but no free people can be expected to do so, whatever the signs to the contrary at any given moment. The dialectical turn-around against the global hegemony of English can already be observed in all manner of assertive as well as defensive behaviour by peoples who see their languages being marginalised. South Africa will be no different. Indeed, the very technology that is accelerating the growth of English as a global language will serve the local languages as lines of defence and as strategic weapons for enforcing the retreat or repositioning of English in the global constellation.

In this connection, it is important to point to what appears to be the almost insurmountable obstacle of the language attitudes of the African peoples themselves. The social-psychological effects of the hegemony of English in the South African and the broader African context are no less than astonishing. What Ngũgĩ wa Thiong'o called 'the decolonisation of the mind' is the most urgent task facing those of us who realise the degree of cultural and broadly social violation attending the depredations of colonial conquest. There is no doubt that the situation is one of programmed failure, at worst, and mediocrity, at best. The African intelligentsia, generally speaking, have reinforced the empirical reality of the dominance of English and French respectively, to which all African people were/are subjected. They have done so by not sufficiently analysing and countering the deleterious socio-economic and cultural effects of the colonial language dispensation. The electoral rhetoric of self-seeking leaders, with a few notable exceptions, which is reflected also in various policy documents and charters of the

Organisation of African Unity, mockingly confirms the lack of political will on the part of most of these leaders to implement a consequential, consistently democratic language policy, one in which the languages of the people will come into their own and over time begin to challenge and eventually displace the European languages as the languages of power.

The result is the notorious underestimation by most of the peoples of Africa of their own languages. Although their allegiance to the former colonial languages does not transcend the instrumental value of these languages in most cases, their belief that all that is worthwhile can only be accessed through these languages is tantamount to a kind of software that is inhabited by corrupting viruses. Such people cannot tap the wells of creativity or display the initiative and the ingenuity which inhere in all human beings. In Africa, it is sad to say, because of this stubborn fact, the exception proves the rule.

The need to address this self-defeating set of structurally imposed dispositions is obvious to all who work in Africa. Whatever one may think of the particularities of the rhetoric of the 'African Renaissance', it is an obvious, if desperate, attempt to discover the metaphorical universe in and through which the necessary paradigm shift can be effected. Those of us who concentrate on the language question have arrived at a set of objectives which we are attempting to realise within the life span of the next two generations. Of these, the most pressing is the task of training a core of language planners and policy people, professionals who have a crystal-clear understanding of the relationship between the politics of the day and the conceptualisation, formulation, and implementation of language policy. The lack of such a body of people in South Africa, certainly, is one of the main reasons why so few politicians and other policy people have understood the economic, political, and cultural significance of the language question. The concrete task consists of confronting the active and tacit resistance and opportunism of middle-class politicians and to inspire a new generation of African social activists to tackle the real issues of democratic transformation.

It is my view that this task will be accomplished only if the theoretical basis is laid firmly in all social domains. In the domain of language rights, the work of Tove Skutnabb-Kangas and her colleagues constitutes an invaluable part of the arsenal of ideas and experience needed to undertake this historic task.

Mother Tongue Education: The Key to African Language Development? A Conversation with an Imagined South African Audience

Zubeida Desai

The first section of this chapter considers some of the constraints on the development of African languages[1]. The second explores the thesis that the key to African language development is mother tongue education. Through a simulated dialogue with an imagined South African audience, it highlights arguments or assumptions heard on numerous occasions in various parts of South Africa and my response to them. The third section attempts to draw some conclusions from the South African experience.

Constraints on the development of African languages

Despite the fact that many people outside South Africa have hailed our new language policy of eleven official languages as progressive and far-reaching, many South Africans are concerned about the lack of promotion and development of African languages. These people often cite negative attitudes on the part of the speakers of African languages as the major stumbling block in promoting African languages (Alexander, 1999). The negative attitudes are perceived as being immutable and often overwhelm language activists with a sense of hopelessness.

However, the issue is far more complex as is illustrated by the Mazruis (Ali and Alamin) in their very interesting book, *The Power of Babel*. They raise three possible historical reasons for the lack of promotion and development of indigenous languages in Africa. These are, not necessarily in order, the following. The preeminence of the oral tradition in many languages in sub-Saharan Africa. To quote them:

---

[1] An earlier version of this paper was delivered at a seminar organized by the Goedgedacht Forum in Cape Town on 16 July 1999.

> The overwhelming majority of sub-Saharan African languages belonged to the oral tradition until the late nineteenth and early twentieth centuries. There is no ancient literature outside Ethiopia and the Islamized city states of East and West Africa. (Mazrui, A. & A., 1998, 5)

In South Africa, for example, the first book printed in Xhosa was as recently as 1824 by Scottish missionaries (personal communication, Ms. Nomlomo, 11 July 1999).

According to the Mazruis, the written tradition is usually more stabilizing for languages than the oral tradition. In addition, it is through the written form that languages are preserved and developed. But even if there is a written form, without a *culture of writing*, it will be very difficult to use a particular language in higher domains such as government, the courts, and in education.

The second reason provided by them is the absence of linguistic nationalism in Africa south of the Sahara. They define linguistic nationalism as 'that version of nationalism which is concerned about the value of its own language, seeks to defend it against other languages, and *encourages its use and enrichment'* (ibid., 5, my emphasis). They argue that nationalism about African languages is relatively weak as compared with India, the Middle East, or France. Interestingly, the two exceptions they cite are the Somali and the Afrikaners who both regard language as central to their cultural identity.

Linked to the second reason is the third, the question of linguistic diversity and linguistic scale. The authors argue that the difference between, say, sub-Saharan Africa and India is not linguistic diversity but rather linguistic scale. While there are languages spoken by some twenty million people, the overwhelming majority of African languages are spoken by far smaller numbers. The question they pose is whether the scale of the linguistic constituency can influence nationalistic sensitivity. This might not necessarily be the case, as experiences in the Pan South African Language Board (PANSALB), an independent, statutory body set up by the government to promote multilingualism, indicate that minority language speakers of languages such as Tsonga, Ndebele, Swati, and Venda are more keen to assert their language rights than say Zulu or Xhosa speakers. However, the question of linguistic scale does rear its head when economic issues arise. It is cheaper to produce books in bulk.

These are some of the reasons that could be cited, according to the authors, for phenomena such as the fact that, in non-Arabic-speaking Africa, 'a modern surgeon who does not speak a European language is virtually a sociolinguistic impossibility.' (ibid., 64-65) Replace surgeon with any profession.

These introductory remarks serve to provide the broad context within which to locate the debate about the role of indigenous languages in South Africa, a country where citizens have a great deal of constitutional space within which to campaign for the promotion and development of African languages. What then prevents South Africans from doing so?

Experience seems to show that it is often through establishing different *practices* that attitudes change. Negative attitudes towards African languages are not immutable. But somehow, people shy away from advocacy work around promoting African languages. The constant refrain 'Parents want English' is indicative of this. As one can change practices to combat AIDS, likewise one can change practices to combat the intellectual stunting of our young people. Skutnabb-Kangas (1990a) makes the telling point that the criterion used to divide people into groups that have unequal access to power and resources has shifted from biological 'race' and culture to *language*.

It is in the light of this that I would like to highlight, as my main point, that mother tongue education is the key to the development and promotion of African languages, an extremely controversial position to take in South Africa, particularly post-apartheid South Africa. It is for this reason that I propose to present this part of my response in the form of an imagined conversation. It is in fact the kind that actually does happen quite often.

A conversation between Zubeida Desai and an Imagined South African Audience (ISAA) on mother tongue education

ZD: Wouldn't you agree that people learn best in a language that they know best? So why is it that African language speakers, unlike Afrikaans and English speakers, don't study through their mother tongues?

ISAA: Yes, that's true but what's the point. My children won't get a job without English. It's different for Afrikaans and English speakers, their languages are important languages.

ZD: But there are other ways of learning a language. You don't have to use it as a medium of instruction. I learnt Afrikaans as a subject at school and today I can read academic articles in Afrikaans, supervise students writing their theses in Afrikaans, and so on. I acknowledge that English plays an important role in our country today and that people want to learn it, and want their children to learn it. It's not a matter of either African languages or English. One can do both. We can learn a lesson from Afrikaans speakers in this regard. 'Moedertaalonderwys' (mother tongue education) did not mean that Afrikaans speakers did not acquire English.

ISAA: But our languages are not developed. They do not have the technical vocabulary that English has and there aren't many textbooks in African languages beyond the initial years.

ZD: Languages develop through use - the more you use a language the more it is bound to develop. Terminology is not created in a vacuum. And now the PANSALB has been given the task of overseeing the establishment of national lexicography units for the eleven official languages. But these units will only work well if African languages, like English and Afrikaans, are used in domains other than the home. Textbooks in African languages will be published if there is a demand for them, if you assert your language rights. You are entitled to.

ISAA: But that means we have to wait till these textbooks are written and the units are in place before African languages can be used in the classroom. And that will take ages.

ZD: No, it doesn't have to be like that. I think we need to look at the issue in stages. What is possible immediately? What is possible in the medium term? And what is possible in the long term? And then we, including government, need to plan for that systematically.

On the question of a lack of textbooks and materials in African languages - most learners are better in the *receptive skills,* that is, listening and reading, in a second language. *Productive skills*, that is, speaking and writing, are more difficult to acquire in another language. Given this, what prevents schools from allowing learners to respond to assignments and examinations in their own languages, despite the materials being available in English only? Nothing. Yet this is not something that is happening on a regular basis at schools.

ISAA: But what if the teachers do not know our children's mother tongues? That is the case at most of the former white schools.

ZD: I acknowledge that it is a problem, but let us concentrate for the time being on the majority of schools, for these former white schools only accommodate between 8% and 10% of the school-going population. In an area like Khayelitsha, an African township in Cape Town, most teachers would be speakers of the same home language as most learners. The matter becomes more complicated in multilingual areas such as those in Gauteng Province. In such cases, educational authorities and schools would have to consider accommodating particular languages at particular schools, ideally not single language schools. So school A might accommodate say Tswana and Afrikaans speakers, whilst school B might have Zulu, Sotho, and English speakers, to use arbitrary examples. But the point I am making is that such a situation *will have to be planned for.* It cannot happen on an ad hoc basis.

ISAA: But won't this lead to the revival of apartheid, where people were herded into 'homelands' on linguistic grounds and learners were forced into particular language streams to entrench the apartheid design for that area?

ZD: One cannot rule out such a danger, but the context in South Africa is very different today. We have to plan our schools and our activities in such a way that mother tongue education facilitates learning for our children, without 'ghettoising' them into ethnic groups or leading to linguistic apartheid. The school day will have to cater for activities which involve all learners. Some such activities could be cultural, sports-related, or values-related.

On the question of former white, coloured, and Indian schools, these schools are currently integrated at a pupil level, but not at a teacher level. This situation will have to change if we have the interests of learners at heart. We cannot allow a situation where schools have large numbers of African language speakers as pupils, but no African language speakers as teachers.

ISAA: But what about the point raised earlier about textbooks in African languages? When is this likely to happen?

ZD: I would argue that it is only by using African languages in education, as media of instruction, that a culture of writing is going to flourish in these languages. If they are confined to the spoken word and not used for record purposes, they will remain confined to low domains.

By using them in education, which includes creative writing, a real demand will arise for such material. For one cannot ignore market-related issues - publishers are not likely to invest in African languages if the demand is not there. And bulk distribution would obviously reduce the costs of production.

Teachers, and educators in general, have a huge role to play in this regard. There is a lot of space to experiment, to pilot new materials, new ways of doing things. So what is stopping us?

From this conversation it is clear that the reasons cited by the Mazruis for the lack of promotion of African languages still play a part in the current reality of South Africa. However, the single most important reason in my opinion is the lack of written materials in African languages and the absence of a culture of writing and reading in African languages. It is partly for this reason that I raise to pre-eminence the issue of mother tongue education. It is only when languages are used in high domains such as education that they will develop. Extending the use of African languages in education, and this applies to any indigenous language, is the route to linguistic empowerment and personal empowerment for the speakers of these languages - a position that has been consistently championed by Skutnabb-Kangas.

Common Practice and Linguistic Human Rights: A-Team v. B-Team Coercion or the Co-construction of 'Utopia'

Shelley K. Taylor

But how is a young, middle-class, white woman going to recognize what she sees in that setting?

That worried query came from a thesis committee member as I submitted a proposal which outlined how I would (steadfastly) venture into a Canadian setting fraught with racial tension, social inequities, and historic injustices to do data collection. As fate would have it, before entering that setting, I took up a scholarship in Denmark and encountered Tove Skutnabb-Kangas at first hand. While I had 'read' her before meeting her, and was thus not unprepared for her work and attitudes, I did not know how deeply she held her convictions before meeting her. Through discussion and watching Tove in action as she championed minority causes and individuals, I came to appreciate her conviction, to learn from it, and to better 'see' inequities.

The following outlines, first, some key theoretical principles underlying Tove's work (Skutnabb-Kangas, 2000 & 1990a) and how these principles link up with Cummins' (this volume & 1996) work on coercive and collaborative relations of power; second, how these principles were reflected in settings which I investigated (some domestic, some foreign to the participants) and the comparability of the settings from the point of view of linguistic human rights; and third, how understanding them prepared a 'young, middle-class white woman' to tackle the ultimate challenge of 'making the familiar strange' (Navarro, 1997, 456). Concluding remarks address the issue of whether the ideas discussed are 'utopian'.

Theoretical principles

Linguistic human rights

Key theoretical principles of Skutnabb-Kangas' (2000, 1998 and earlier) work include 'linguistic human rights' and 'A-Team v. B-Team approaches.' Skutnabb-Kangas (1998, 23) identifies as necessary conditions of linguistic human rights the right of the individual to:

1. Fully learn, use in most official situations (including schools) and identify with her mother tongue(s)/L1 and have that identification accepted and respected by others;
2. Learn (one of) the official language(s) of the country of residence and thus become bilingual (or trilingual, as the case may be);
3. Not have a change of L1 imposed (which includes knowledge of long-term consequences in the case of a voluntary language shift); and
4. Profit from the state education system, no matter what her L1 is (Skutnabb-Kangas, 1998, 23).

At present, many minority individuals cannot fully learn their L1 (e.g., develop both oracy and literacy) or use their L1 in official settings such as schools. They cannot become balanced bilinguals with the help of the school (those who do, often succeed despite the school). Many cannot derive maximum benefit from state education. And many cannot control whether their L1 will remain a fully known language that they can transfer to their children if they so wish – they are forced to language shift. In short, they do not have linguistic human rights.

One reason why the necessary conditions of linguistic human rights are not met is that minorities often have many characteristics of the B-Team whereas policy-makers often belong to the A-Team. This may make the application of 'coercive power relations' more likely, i.e. 'the exercise of power by a dominant group (or individual or country) to the detriment of a subordinated group (or individual or country' (Cummins, this volume & 1996, 14).

A-Team vs. B-Team approaches

Skutnabb-Kangas (2000, 387) characterizes people with all A-Team characteristics as middle-class, white (male) majority group members with high levels of formal education who reside in Western cities, and full B-Team members as working class and rural (female) minority group members, 'black', 'red', 'brown' or 'yellow', who have little formal education and live in underdeveloped countries. The power relationship between the two groups is coercive (see above) rather than 'collaborative' (i.e. power 'created with others rather than imposed on or exercised over others', Cummins, 1996, 15). The assumptions on which these polar opposite power relations are based are reflected in whether principles of linguistic human rights are respected or not, as is discussed next.

From the theoretical to the personal: Three cases in comparative perspective

The descriptions in this section involve Aliser, an ethnic Kurd schooled in Turkey, Dilan, an ethnic Kurd schooled in Denmark, and Mi'kmaq students schooled in Canada.

Case 1: Aliser - A Kurdish student schooled in Turkey

As there were no schools in Aliser's home village when he began elementary school in Turkey in the 1960s, he had to leave home and live in a residential school. The language of instruction in state institutions in Turkey is Turkish. Therefore, though the L1 of Aliser and his classmates, all ethnic Kurds, was Kurdish, they were schooled in Turkish. Skutnabb-Kangas and Bucak (1994, 355) explain why Kurdish-medium and bilingual (Turkish-Kurdish) education are not options in Turkey, despite viable population variables (see Taylor & Skutnabb-Kangas, 1997 for discussion). Such education is at odds with the Turkish Constitution. It states in Article 42/9: 'No language other than Turkish may be taught as a native language to citizens of Turkey in instructional and educational institutions' (Skutnabb-Kangas & Bucak, 1994, 355). Thus, although Turkey's official language was Aliser's second language, after years away from home at residential school, Turkish-medium schooling, and no opportunity to speak Kurdish, Turkish gradually became his dominant language.

'We couldn't see our parents or other relatives during school breaks. That's part of the assimilation process. If you can't keep up family and cultural links, you're more easily assimilated.

Turkish became my dominant language because I never learned to write in my mother tongue. Not only did I not learn my language, but I'm a loss to others who would like to know it: I'm better educated and could teach them, but I never learned it.'

Today Aliser, political refugee in Canada, 'chooses' to speak mainly English, like the mother, to the son, and Turkish, and only very little Kurdish (Zaza). This is a case of involuntary language shift and a case of lost linguistic human rights.

Case 2: Dilan - A Kurdish student schooled in Denmark

Dilan's parents, ethnic Kurds, emigrated from Turkey to Denmark, where Dilan was born in the 1980s. Though the language of instruction in state education in

Denmark is Danish, Dilan was enrolled in an experimental bilingual/bicultural education program offered in Danish and Turkish. Her ethnolinguistic identity was invisibilized from school authorities by her passport which listed her as a Turk, and by Turkish teachers at the school who did not disclose the fact that Dilan and her Kurdish peers did not know Turkish (see Taylor, 1997). Consequently, she received instruction through the medium of two non-native languages and no instruction in her L1, not even as a subject.

Though Dilan was dominant in Kurdish prior to beginning school, at the time I interviewed her, Dilan could not understand Kurdish very well, could not read it, did not like the language, and did not even like listening to Kurdish music (Taylor, 1996). Her language shift can be attributed to her languages of schooling, especially Turkish, which led her to develop a Turkish-based friendship network and a predilection for Turkish, even at home.

Dilan's use of Turkish in the home was also due to a (historical) language shift. The variant of Kurdish spoken by Dilan's parents featured extensive Kurdish-Turkish codeswitching in the wake of prolonged language contact, namely over the hundred years since the Kurdish population had been relocated to central Turkey (near Sivas) as part of a Turkification program. Thus, Dilan's was a long legacy of involuntary language shift.

Case 3: Mi'kmaq students schooled in Canada

The Mi'kmaq students in the study which I conducted after returning from Denmark were monolingual speakers of English (Taylor, 1993). Most of their grandparents were the products of the (earlier) Canadian residential school system. Although Mi'kmaq was the grandparents' L1, the parent generation had undergone a gradual language shift from Mi'kmaq to English after receiving English-medium schooling in the 1970s. The parents had encountered so much grief being schooled in a language other than their L1 (Mi'kmaq), that they had decided to speak English at home so their children (the present-day immersion cohort) would not encounter the same hardships at school.

The students were enrolled in an early French immersion program. Many of them were also enrolled in pull-out Mi'kmaq instruction for 60 minutes a week. Thus the students were learning Mi'kmaq as a third (though ancestral) language. This proved problematic. First, Mi'kmaq was offered at the same time as Social Studies each year. Originally, school authorities expected Social Studies to be taught in Mi'kmaq, but the students did not have the requisite language proficiency to learn a content subject in that language. Second, the Mi'kmaq instructors were chosen for their language proficiency, not for their L2 teaching background. They were simply some of the few remaining adults with adequate fluency in the language. (This is a common situation for most indigenous peoples – their language has not been part of any training for teaching it as either L1 or L2). The Mi'kmaq parents were aware of these problems and, because of them, many chose not to enroll their children in Mi'kmaq. Thus, while Mi'kmaq students enrolled in French immersion had the option of becoming bilingual in Canada's two official languages, they had little opportunity to regain their ancestral language or become trilingual.

Commonalities and differences

Commonalities and differences between these cases become apparent in Table 1.

Table 1. Are Linguistic Human Rights Principles Respected or Not?

Linguistic human rights principles respected or not	Cases		
	1. Aliser, Kurd in Turkey, national minority	2. Dilan, Kurd in Denmark, immigrant minority	3. Mi'kmaq in Canada, an indigenous people
1. Fully learn (L), use (U) & identify with (I) L1?	L No U No I Yes	L No U No I No	L No U No I Yes
2. Learn official language(s) & become bi-/trilingual?	Official language(s): Yes Bi-/trilingualism: No		
3. Forced language shift?	Yes, for next generation	Yes, for this generation	Yes, for previous generation
4. Profit from state education system, no matter what the students' L1?	No	No	N/A

With one minor exception (Principle 4, Case 3), the commonalities between the three cases summarized in Table 1 are striking. In no case are the three first principles of linguistic human rights fully met.

Principle 1: B-Team students could not fully learn their L1 (in Case 3, the L1 refers to their ancestral language, Mi'kmaq, not to English) or use it in official situations, including the school. Identification with it was prohibited by school in Aliser's case and not supported in the Mi'kmaq case. According to Skutnabb-Kangas (2000), this fits one of the early UN definitions of linguistic genocide: 'Prohibiting the use of the language of the group in daily intercourse and in schools...' (in Article 3a in the final Draft of what in 1948 became the UN

Convention on the Prevention and Punishment of the Crime of Genocide; Article 3 was voted down in the General Assembly).

Principle 2: B-Team students could learn the official language (e.g., Turkish in Turkey, Danish in Denmark - unevenly, English and French in Canada), but without the benefit of a bilingual program which would have taught them their L1 and allowed them to become balanced bi- or trilinguals.

Principle 3: Language shift has occurred or will occur in all cases. Aliser and Dilan became dominant in Turkish, at the expense of Kurdish (a subtractive language learning situation), and the Mi'kmaq students were unable to speak Mi'kmaq fluently. No one is able (and in Dilan's case not willing either) to pass it on to their children. According to Skutnabb-Kangas (2000), this fits one of the UN definitions of genocide: 'forcibly transferring children of one· group to another group' (Article 2e in the UN Convention on the Prevention and Punishment of the Crime of Genocide).

Principle 4: For similar reasons as for Principle 2 (no bilingual education), neither Aliser nor Dilan could profit from the state education system to the same extent as students whose L1 was the language of instruction. Even when some minority students do profit, this often happens despite the school, not because of the way their formal education is organised. The case of the Mi'kmaq children in this category is murkier as they mix A- and B-Team characteristics: While their present 'L1' is an A-Team language (i.e., since English supplanted their ancestral language already in an earlier generation), they are clearly B-Team members whose educational success rate does not match that of their dominant group, A-Team peers (see Cummins, 1997).

Giving A-Team members insight into B-Team worlds

Skutnabb-Kangas' work enabled me to see the comparability between the latter cases, including the Canadian case. Her work has drawn attention to inadequacies of the myth of the level playing field on which all school-children in democratic societies are supposed to be able to succeed equally (see Wink & Wink, this volume). Providing equal opportunities to all (including linguistic human rights) does not mean granting 'special' (or preferential) treatment to minorities. Finally, her work also sheds light on inequities which many *young, middle-class, white* men and women may otherwise not (have) recognize(d) in settings near to or far from home. As such, Skutnabb-Kangas' work has the power and potential to effect change, one step (and one A-Team member) at a time.

In my case, Tove's work prepared me to see through to the sometimes hidden coercive relations of power which underlie familiar practices and common beliefs. It prepared me to hear and situate disabling, deficit theory-based arguments, rationalizations and explanations in the interviews I conducted with the Mi'kmaq children's educators, who were A-Team members one and all. It also gave me the scope to compare phenomena such as coercive A-Team/B-Team relations in international perspective rather than from a North America-centric perspective. In short, it taught me to recognize the differences between the educational experiences of A- and B-Team children and the inequities involved.

Conclusion

In light of the above, one might wonder why the following question arises so frequently: *Aren't coercive relations of power (and the concomitant A-Team vs. B-Team approach) inevitable in today's world?*, as does the patronizing suggestion that it is utopian to think that things might be otherwise. Still, utopian visions exist. Skutnabb-Kangas (1990a), like Cummins (this volume & 1996), describes how things could be, were 'utopia' to be co-constructed by A- and B-Team members[1]: the content of minority schooling could be prioritized[2], as could be B-Team members' academic success rates.

My personal utopia would be for A-Team members to gain enough insight into, understanding of, and empathy for B-Team members' realities so that the former would not only 'see' inequities, but would also develop the will to co-construct better practices with the latter. Since A-Team members are presently power-holders, their goodwill is necessary for significant progress to occur. Skutnabb-Kangas' work is a crucial bridge for them to cross on their path to progress and understanding.

---

[1] This applies even if A-team members only collaborate with B-team members to avert financial losses (see Skutnabb-Kangas, 1990b and Cummins, 1996).

[2] 'School could be restructured so that it reflects the view that minorities actually enrich society. Minorities who so desire could establish mother tongue medium instruction as a legally constituted *right* throughout all of schooling. Then minorities would finally be able to concentrate their energies on discussing the *content* of schooling instead of having to use it to fight for the right to get the *form* they feel is best for their children, namely mother tongue medium classes' (Skutnabb-Kangas 1990b, 139, my translation from Danish).

As for the B-Team members whose cases are described above, their losses are substantial and they have ample will to alter common practice; but, at present, they lack power. They must co-construct 'utopia' even if, to them, the question of how to reinvent the status quo is not utopian. It is a need: the need to gain long overdue language rights, and the right to equity, power, and education.

Creating a Bilingual Family in a 'Monolingual' Country

Leena Huss

Throughout Europe bilingual families face similar problems when trying to raise their children bilingually. Newsletters in several countries[1], tell the same tale, regardless of the official policy vis-à-vis minority languages and regardless of the languages concerned. Other people's negative attitudes towards bilingual upbringing and anxieties about whether it might harm the child seem to overshadow the everyday life of the family. However, some parents stubbornly stick to their aim, link up with other families in a similar situation, gather information about childhood bilingualism, and fight against the prejudices of the surrounding world. Many parents feel that it is a really worth-while effort, and the rewards of family bilingualism are described in bright colours. Parents maintain that the double linguistic heritage belongs to their children, connects the children to past generations, and strengthens their identities. These beliefs are passed on to other families, to give them strength during difficult periods. This is needed especially in countries where monolingualism in the majority language has long been the norm.

When I moved from Finland to Sweden, I went through the metamorphosis that so many emigrants experience: one changes from being a 'normally competent' person into a 'deviant', 'different' human being. Suddenly, one belongs to those who are 'not from here', do not speak in the same way as everybody else, do not have the cultural and social knowledge that is taken for granted in people native to the country. I had the advantage of knowing some Swedish when I arrived, from school and university, but in practice my skills were not nearly adequate. A year or two passed before I could relax and let the words flow freely. After a while I noticed another change: my own mother tongue was beginning to fall away. Suddenly it became difficult to remember words, or to explain something that I had learned in Sweden, in Swedish, and where knowledge of special terminology was needed. At the same time, I worried that I would never learn to speak Swedish as

---

[1] Examples include *The Bilingual Family Newsletter* from England, the bulletin of 'Interessengemeinschaft Mehrsprachiger Familien' in Germany and of 'Föreningen för Flerspråkiga Familjer' in Sweden.

well as I spoke Finnish when I left Finland. Would my fate be 'OK Swedish - OK Finnish', a bit worse than everybody else in both languages? In view of this, I started reading Finnish books again, and later began studying Fenno-Ugric languages at the university - something that had never occurred to me as long as I lived in Finland. Then I had only been interested in foreign languages, and not Finnish.

When my first child was born in 1974, I had just moved to Sweden and the marriage with my Swedish husband - the reason for my immigrating - was still new. I had not yet begun worrying about my Finnish, but I felt clearly handicapped in Swedish, and felt that Finnish was the only language that I could and would speak to my child. My husband, a linguist like myself, agreed, so I did not have to cope with one problem that many immigrant parents encounter: trying to convince an unsympathetic partner of the importance of being able to communicate with one's child in one's own language. I have since met many unsympathetic people, like a physician at the child welfare centre who indirectly discouraged me from speaking anything other than Swedish to my child. I have often wondered how much influence doctors, teachers and other so-called authorities wield. They will, without having the least experience or knowledge of bilingual development, and completely disregarding this fact, 'give advice' and sometimes even orders about how parents in bilingual families should deal with language issues. It is like hiring your car mechanic as a doctor or asking your doctor to repair the car.

In our case, the indirect warning against bilingual upbringing did not really matter because my husband and I had made up our minds. Together we perused everything written about child bilingualism that we came across. In the mid-1970s, the selection was limited, and the scholarly publications[2]) unsuitable for use as parents' guides to bilingual upbringing. However, we found some articles and brochures recommending the one parent - one language principle for a bilingual family. This suited us very well: we felt it was the natural thing to do.

My arrival in Sweden coincided with large scale migration from Finland (see Lainio, this volume) and intense debate about the schooling of immigrant children (see Municio, this volume). Skutnabb-Kangas' view that the mother tongue of immigrant children should be protected created a favourable climate for bilingual families like ours and the founding of 'home language classes' with mother-tongue-medium instruction for several of the larger language groups.

Regardless of the volatility of the debate, our micro-level bilingual programme proceeded as planned. With our first child, Swedish was established as the language between father and son, and Finnish between mother and son. This pattern was well established when our second son was born. We parents always spoke Swedish together, but my husband showed a keen interest in Finnish, and had learned enough to understand what I said to the children. However, the fragile balance of

---

[2] For instance Leopold's huge study *Speech Development of a Bilingual Child: A Linguist's Record* (1939-1949), Ronjat's *Le développement du langage observé chez un enfant bilingue* (1913), Burling's article 'Language development of a Garo and English speaking child' in *Word* 15/1959.

language use at home was soon disturbed by the overwhelming inflow of the majority language from outside. In spite of me working with translation, hence spending a lot of time at home with the children when they were small, I noticed that the boys' Swedish rapidly became stronger than their Finnish. In such an ideologically monolingual society as the Swedish, it was extremely difficult to maintain another language, and especially a somewhat stigmatized language like Finnish. We realized that I had to make a special effort if we really wanted the children to grow up bilingual, and I was determined to do so. I felt that the Finnish language was important for my own sense of well-being in Sweden; it was what made me able to continue being *me*. Swedish had of course also become a part of my identity; it was after all the language used between me and my husband and therefore a 'language of the heart' as well. But without Finnish and the whole of my Finnish history, I was a pale shadow of myself, with an incomplete language - something that I definitely did not want for my children. There was therefore a strong family pressure towards bilingualism, while the surrounding society encouraged monolingualism.

From the mid 1980s, the impact of the 'Don't Forget Swedish!' doctrine (Hyltenstam, 1986), to be followed by 'Do Forget the Home Language!' in the 1990s (Nauclér, 1997), was noticeable in the press. Articles warned against too much emphasis on the mother-tongue of minority children. I had by then met other Finnish parents who were eager to discuss family bilingualism and who found it exceedingly difficult to fight negative attitudes in their surroundings. The Stockholm linguist Ulla-Britt Kotsinas was launching her theory of *rinkebysvenska* ('Rinkeby Swedish'), a grammatically simplified youth variety of Swedish spoken in the Stockholm suburb Rinkeby with a large immigrant population. This variety, sprinkled with foreign borrowings, was, according to Kotsinas, establishing itself as a new dialect of Swedish. Despite her statements that *rinkebysvenska* was by no means a language to be feared, many parents now experienced that they were warned against bilingual upbringing of their children 'lest the children learn *rinkebysvenska*'. A group of us decided to found an association for parents in bi- and multilingual families.[3] Sympathy and support from other parents were needed in many such families and the association was soon busy organizing meetings and information campaigns about bilingualism.

In our family, concerns about meeting prejudice and trying to maintain a balance between the two languages were initially only a matter for the adults. For the boys, the bilingualism of our family was completely natural. Both spoke Finnish with me, sometimes more or less mixed with Swedish, but still Finnish. With my husband, they spoke Swedish without any other elements mixed in. Their friends were Swedish-speaking, as was all of our environment, and discounting a couple of annual visits to Finland and some of my adult Finnish friends, I was the only source of Finnish for the boys during their early years. The linguistic situation changed dramatically when the boys were three and six years old. We moved to Helsinki. In

---

[3] Föreningen för Flerspråkiga Familjer (Association for Multilingual Families), FFF, founded in 1986.

Finland, a country with two national languages, we suddenly faced the choice between Finnish- and Swedish-medium day-care for our children. We were initially attracted to the idea of a Swedish one, but decided to opt for a Finnish one. We wanted the children to retain their 'standard Swedish' accent and thus avoid complications when we moved back to Sweden. We also knew that the boys' Finnish must be strengthened. Our eldest son went to a Finnish school for two years. During our years in Helsinki the boys developed native fluency in Finnish and very soon dropped the Swedish borrowings which had been part of their language in Sweden. The complications of Finnish grammar no longer presented any problems. Their Swedish remained seemingly the same, while my husband felt he was under pressure, as he was the one responsible for minority language development in our home, which implied more Swedish bed-time stories, conversation and free-time activities.

Our third child was born in Helsinki and was only one year old when we moved back to Sweden. By that time, the elder brothers had become accustomed to speaking Finnish with each other and Finnish was their stronger language. We expected that, back in Sweden, Swedish would soon replace Finnish as the dominant language of our sons, and we wanted to postpone this as much as possible. With that in mind, we told the boys, then six and nine, that their little brother would not hear much Finnish in Sweden and therefore it was important that they always speak Finnish to him. Both listened and nodded, and amazing as it may sound, they have spoken Finnish to him ever since that day, even after reverting to speaking Swedish with each other. There are therefore interesting patterns of language choice in our family: Finnish between the children and me and between little brother and the bigger brothers; Swedish between the bigger brothers, between my husband and myself and between my husband and all the children.

In spite of the fact that the boys shared the same home environment and were exposed to the same kind of bilingual upbringing, they responded in different ways. Little brother, who was too young when we returned to Sweden to remember his time in Finland, eventually became the 'most Finnish' of the boys, and would shout: 'Speak Finnish!' when he passed the bigger brothers' room and heard them speak Swedish with each other. That is something which I would never have dared to do myself in order not to make the boys irritated and negatively predisposed toward Finnish. Somehow, this was tolerated by the elder brothers, as an idiosyncracy of the youngest one.

In this way we continued over the years, juggling two languages in monolingual Sweden, and found it stimulating. The bigger brothers retained a relaxed attitude towards bilingualism, speaking two languages but never making a big issue out of it, while little brother held the Finnish flag high and discussed language issues or fought ethnic prejudice outside the home, in school and in his circle of friends. The elder brothers are now young adults, 22 and 25 years old, while little brother is 17. A couple of years ago our eldest son became infatuated by the Chinese language, and came back after a long stay in China with a Chinese wife, who thus became another reinforcement of our family's multilingualism.

What do the boys themselves think about their bilingualism? When asked about it, they all say that it has been a privilege to grow up with two languages. They have all done well both in school and socially, and when somebody has been astonished by their ability to speak Finnish[4] or made a joke about their half-Finnish background, they appear not to have been upset. What I myself want to believe is a result of their bilingualism is their interest in all languages and their curiosity about other cultures. I also tend to believe that they have become somewhat more open-minded than they might have been without their special experience. One of the boys, then maybe twelve, said once, when I asked him whether there were any differences between young Finnish people and young Swedish people, that they were really very alike. They were always so very sure, as he put it, that they knew exactly how things were supposed to be. The Swedes thought everything should be as it was in Sweden, while Finns thought everything should be as it was in Finland. If he pointed out to the Swedes that something was different in Finland but worked equally well, they could not understand it at all. In the same way, the Finns could not believe that the Swedish way was also feasible. He knew himself that both ways worked, and that monolingual and monocultural people could only appreciate their own, singular reality.

I dare not have too high hopes for the future, linguistically speaking. Naturally, I hope that the boys will have enough contact with Finnish so that it will not fade away. I am happy that all three also read books in Finnish, even if not nearly as many as in Swedish or even English. Due to lack of bilingual education, the boys' strongest language by far is Swedish and it is uncertain whether Finnish will live on in their own future families. Finnish may not live on in the next generation. But there is a better chance that bilingualism in some form, at least in Swedish and Chinese, will occur in this generation. The situation in Sweden is also vastly different now from what it was in the 1970s and the 1980s, and although we are definitely still in the 'Do Forget the Home Language!' period, there are some encouraging signs. In the wake of the ethnic revival, many linguistic minorities are continuing and intensifying their efforts to maintain and develop their languages. This tendency is clearly visible among Sweden Finns (Skutnabb-Kangas, 1987; Huss & Lindgren, 1999), the Tornedalians (Huss, 1999) and the Sámi.

A prerequisite for language maintenance and revitalization is the intergenerational transmission of the minority language in families. The minorities mentioned above are all concentrating their efforts on raising the consciousness of young parents on language issues. The level of awareness of the benefits of bilingualism for minority children, whether in the form of individual empowerment or enhanced job prospects, has generally risen. It can also be seen in the sudden explosion of *friskolor* (independent schools, see Peura, this volume), an astonishing

---

[4] While the stigma of Finnish is gradually fading in Sweden, people still tend to be surprised by a person who speaks acccent-free fluent Swedish and who also knows Finnish. Knowledge of Finnish in Sweden has in the eyes of the majority long been associated with low competence in Swedish, as well as with other problems.

development, since specific schooling for different groups, ethnic or otherwise, has traditionally been regarded with suspicion in Sweden (Runblom 1995). Bilingual upbringing in the family also seems to be gaining popularity. In my longitudinal study of 21 bilingual Swedish-Finnish[5] preschool children and their families, and in an on-going follow-up interview study of the same children aged 11 and 12, positive attitudes towards bilingualism on the part of the children, their parents and their surroundings seem to have increased.

The literature on child bilingualism available for parents has grown enormously over the past two decades, in Swedish, Finnish and English. However, easy access to information and research results does not imply that they are utilized by political decision-makers. Policy on mother-tongue instruction or bilingual schooling tends to be based on the personal opinions of key people or on 'common-sense' notions of what is considered to be 'in the best interest of the minority child'. Current debate in the media therefore sometimes reminds one, rather depressingly, of the assimilation period of the 1950s and 1960s. In addition to hoping that Sweden will be influenced by international moves on minority rights and linguistic rights, another positive step would be the full acceptance and promotion of family bilingualism in Swedish society, as well as increased bilingual pre-school and school options for children from these families and for other youngsters as well. Increased cultural and linguistic competence is urgently needed in today's world, while the resources available in Sweden in terms of linguistic and ethnic diversity are still largely untapped.

---

[5] The children all had a mixed-marriage background, the majority having a Finnish mother and a Swedish father.

The Reindeer on the Mountain, the Reindeer in the Mind: On Sámi Yoik Lyrics

Harald Gaski

The most obvious example of the need for a culturally internal interpretation technique in relation to Sámi texts must be yoik poetry. The yoik is the original music of the Sámi, with clearly defined parameters for production, function, and practice. The concept of *juoigat* (to yoik) exists over the entire Sámi region, but yoik itself is called different things in the diverse Sámi languages. It is integral to the Sámi sense of community, making the subject of a yoik a part of the society.

The yoik is a way of remembering - it connects a person with the innermost feelings of the theme of the yoik, and may thus communicate between times, persons, and landscapes - like in the long, old yoik which Nils Mattias Andersson from Tärnaby, Sweden yoiked for the Swedish national radio company when they collected yoiks from different regions of Sapmi (Arnberg, Ruong & Unsgaard 1969: 158-62). Nils Mattias Andersson was born in 1882, and was already an old man when the recordings took place in the mid-1950s. He wanted to tell of his life as a reindeer herder through his yoik, and sat down then and there and dictated one of the most beautiful epic poetic pieces we know within Sámi impressionistic poetry, 'The Reindeer on Oulavuolie'.

The yoik opens with Andersson relating how his wife, Anna, sits in the *lávvu*, the Sámi tent, and blows into the embers to light the fire. But his thoughts are not only for his wife - they shift quickly to the large mountain, Oulavuolie, which has a glacier with a deep fissure in it - a crevice. His reindeer run around on the glacier: 'the reindeer run around, run around, run around.' Suddenly, in his memory children appear. Children who were on a fishing trip in a boat, and who caught a big fish - so big, in fact, that they were nearly frightened by it. Nevertheless they thought, according to the yoik, that 'Oulavuolie's beautiful reindeer are finer / Oulavuolie's tall reindeer are finer.' And so he describes the reindeer, using the Sámi language's special terminology to differentiate the animals according to age, gender, and appearance. The reindeer are beautiful, but Oulavuolie with its glacier is dangerous:

> Oulavuolie's huge ice fissure
> ice fissure, huge ice fissure

has sucked up my beautiful tall ones
my beautiful slender reindeer.

Then the yoiker turns back in his reminiscing to the present: 'But now I have grown old / grown old, grown old / and my tall ones have changed / changed, changed / They are no, are no, are no longer.' He remembers the reindeer with the swaying antlers, the beautiful ones who stood proudly aloof, 'when I was the man on Oulavuolie, the man on Oulavuolie'. At the end, he approaches the tent again, sees the woman who blows into the embers, blows on the fire to get it to ignite. And he finishes the poem with a dual image, age and forgetfulness: 'And it is the two of us / Our memory, memory of us / vanishes, vanishes. / We remember and we have forgotten. / We are both old.'

If 'The reindeer on Oulavuolie' is first and foremost a reminiscing yoik with reindeer as its center, under the surface it is also a deeply philosophical text, which relates something about the Sámi's understanding of themselves as a part of a larger whole. At the same time the text is typical of the attitudes toward the Sámi in the 1950s and 1960s in Scandinavia. It is not only a memory of two single individuals and one man's reindeer herd which disappear - the whole Sámi lifestyle can be seen as something which is disappearing. We find in the text a vulnerability regarding that which no longer exists, one which expresses a greater sorrow for 'the tall ones' which have changed and are no longer vital, than for the fact that 'the memory of us / vanishes. We remember and have forgotten / We are both old.' There is a sense of something given up, a resignation in the text - that which the old have stood for is gone; but at the same time the yoiker finds solace in the memories, and perhaps happiness in the fact that his text is preserved in the recording. In this way Andersson's yoik enters the collective Sámi consciousness, and thus comes to represent something besides the defeatist abandonment of a culture's distinctiveness.

Yet even though yoik is so collective in its essence, it nevertheless demonstrates a distinct concept of ownership. It is not the person who composes a yoik who owns it, but rather that which is yoiked. The producer, in this sense, loses the right to his or her product, while the subject assumes dominion over this same creation. This is the traditional role of art in a culture in which the central focus is on collectivity, not in the sense that the individual owns nothing, but rather in so far as a perceived solidarity is what actually holds the culture together. In such a society, an artist is not simply an individual - she or he is also a representative of the entire culture, one element in the distribution of labor within the whole.

The understanding and interpretation of yoik as artistic expression are not dependent on the verbal field of meaning at all. There are many yoiks, especially personal yoiks, which don't have words at all, in which the yoik melody itself, the *luohti*, transmits the yoik's content to the listeners. Just as any given form of art can be beautiful to observe or experience, a yoik should also be pleasant to listen to, providing one with peace of mind and pride in one's soul on behalf of one's own people.

Not merely text, nor just music

I shall try to trace a contextualized interpretation of a cultural form which, first and foremost, is not *merely* text, nor just music, but both of them and even more than just the sum of lyrics and melody.

As is common in all research, yoik studies often divide the genre into smaller segments, in order to delve deeper into the material through detailed analyses. The most common division among 'outside' researchers examining Sámi yoik has been to split it into musical and literary portions. I am, of course, aware of the problems contained in 'dissecting' the yoik in this way and departing from respect for the yoik's unity by splitting up something which is indivisible. The Sámi scholar, Jon Eldar Einejord opposes this approach in his thesis on yoik: 'This can lead the researcher into an impasse, where yoik is merely seen as a collocation of expressive means, as a musical (and possibly literary) expressive form, and not as a social form of expression [...] One could thus overlook the function yoik has in its entirety.' (1975, 62)

The Sámi yoik and multimedia artist, Nils-Aslak Valkeapää, addressing the primary function of yoik, has stated that, 'there was never an understanding that yoik should be presented as art' (1984, 45). The yoik is social in its function, but on the other hand it is clear that it is also aesthetic in its creation and, as such, can function remarkably well as art. But it is equally important to keep in mind yoik's origins - historical and social - when one evaluates the genre's new uses and contexts for performance.

This raises an interesting dilemma of research principles and ethics: one is allowed to dissect yoik in a disciplined manner, but such an operation is nearly synonymous with committing violence on the tradition. A yoik actually only has meaning as a unified structure whose cultural parameters do not allow for a division into musical and textual parts. The question therefore for researchers is whether one should take heed of these traditional boundaries, or should researchers, like artists, have the right to cross these boundaries at will? On the other hand, however, do these boundary transgressions mean that respect for the tradition diminishes, and that important differences become blurred, or do new eras always require new ways? These are important questions in regard to the preservation of traditional cultural forms not only within minority communities, but as a general issue concerning the esteem of 'old' values in our (post)modernist society. When current Sámi singers are modernizing traditional Sámi yoiks to make them fit into the framework of one or another kind of music, are they violating or renewing tradition - or are they just simply creating something fresh, unique and original?

One can label this problematizing of approaches to the (literary) works of writers and other artists of ethnic minorities (Native Americans, the Scandinavian Sámi, the Australian Aborigines, and others) as 'Indigenous Criticism', which in each case would primarily involve concentrating on the specific reading and understanding of a culture's products. I will still try, without in any way trying to diminish the importance of this kind of criticism, to position myself in between the (more) established methods of criticism and the rather esoteric exposition of each specific culture. In a field of communicative scientific practice I feel it is a matter of real urgency to be able to reach out with one's findings, not only to one's own people, but to cross-cultural boundaries and obstacles. I feel this is also the aim and intention of ethnocriticism. I would like to adapt and adjust ethnocriticism to an indigenous approach to traditional Sámi texts, represented by yoik lyrics. At least in my case, this will be a meeting between two basically congenial ways of reading the texts, but presumably with different emphases concerning the interpretation of the material, and naturally with regard to the self-positioning of each analytical practice (for discussion see Gaski, 1997).

A two-fold approach

Ethnocriticism is to a large extent based on work with Native American literary texts, but in no way represents a master narrative for interpreting this literature the Native American way (Krupat, 1992). On the contrary, one might say, ethnocriticism wants to position itself at the frontier, meaning as a movement on the borders between the 'other cultures' way of construing and representing the world' and the 'West's' - Europe and America's - way of producing criticism, something which is not 'internal' or 'indigenous' in relation to traditional native cultures. Ethnocriticism is concerned with differences rather than oppositions, thus seeking to replace oppositional with dialogical models (ibid., 25-26). This situates, in Krupat's words, 'the would-be practioner of ethnocriticism [...] at the various frontier points where the disciplines of anthropology and literature, literature and history, history and philosophy meet and interact' (ibid., 31-32).

A two-fold approach to Sámi texts involves combining the interpretative methods of comparative literature, with familiarity with the cultural background of the yoik, and linguistic skills in Sámi, to facilitate richer comprehension of the texts. There is, nevertheless, a residue left in the text - something, which is not easily explicated through the methodical exposition of the subject. This something I like to think of as being a more or less culturally internal code or mode which is hard to crack without a deep knowledge of the background and context of the story, song, or myth.

Being aware of this extra potential of the text, and being able to explicate it, is of course the advantage of the 'insider' – as is artistic performance, and understanding of the specific values of each culture, its cultural wealth. In the Sámi case the lengthy oppositional yoik poems transcribed by the Finn, Jacob Fellman, in Tana valley in the early 1800s can exemplify this: a subtle use of double meanings in the yoik poetry made it possible to communicate on two levels at the same time, one type of message was conveyed to a Sámi audience and quite a different one to outsiders. While the Sámi listeners immediately understood the underlying encoded message, representatives of the government present at the performance only grasped the meaning of the yoik at its most superficial level.

Even so, however important these internal matters may be, the really interesting point about this 'internality' is that it only comes into its own when it is made communicable to a larger audience - naturally on the condition that we are talking strictly theoretically here, not in a war-like condition where people's lives and well-being depend on the secrecy of encoded messages. Yet even in a situation such as war, most people would be aware of the importance of codes, and thus the enemy would put all his efforts into breaking the code. In literary interpretations of texts celebrating limited openness, some may only want to emphasize their esoteric potential, while others prefer to try to make them more communicative.

I myself, like the ethnocritics, am more interested in the *meeting place* of different texts or cultures, rather than just seeking and explaining the internal meaning of a text to people who supposedly already know it. The 'translation' of a text into new contexts may be much more interesting than just repeating the already obvious. A combination of a linguistic-poetic translation and a culturally contextualized explanation may open up the text to new audiences as an expression of a specific culture, but, at the same time, every translation is also an interpretation, and nothing can - or should - restrain new readers from associating other things with the text as compared to the reception of what I would call the 'primary intended reader or listener'. The Sámi yoiks should primarily be understood in accordance with and within their cultural context, but can in addition be analyzed as, for example, literary expression, as long as one is aware of the alienation this represents from the original cultural context to which they primarily belong as traditional artistic forms of expression. This is also a matter of artistic perspective and hermeneutics, how differing sets of expectations determine the way in which we interpret cultural expression.

'the thin, dark one untouched by a man's hand'

I will suggest how to read one traditional yoik text within a Sámi frame of understanding. It is important to position oneself in the entire context of the creation and performance of yoik. A total understanding of the yoik requires not just being there at a specific time and probably at a specific performance, but also a thorough knowledge of the yoik's musical and textual content, an intimate acquaintance with the person being yoiked, and often trifling but nonetheless characteristic events affecting the person, as well as a good deal of metaphoric competence, which is often rooted in completely local conditions.

In other words, great demands are made on local knowledge, all the way in to the sphere of the intimate, in order to reach full understanding of a yoik's content. This is virtually unachievable through purely *literary* methods. It is possible to interview the yoiker, the yoiked, the closest family members and friends, and the local milieu. This has sometimes been done, and is quite interesting reading in its own right. Nevertheless the problem remains of how to make such an approach methodical, something more than a 'Gallup'- poll, or literary-historical biography, or registering reception of the yoik so as to produce definitive interpretations.

I will comment on a humorous-ironic yoik about an old bachelor who had his eye on some girls, but who never found a wife. The old bachelor comes up with good excuses to explain the fact that he has not yet made his proposal-journey.

Gumpe borai soagnovuoján	The wolf ate the deer hitched for courting
Sáhpán ciebai gabbabeaskka	The mouse gnawed the white fur coat
Báhcán lei vel muzetsággi	Still left was the thin, dark one
Gean ii oktage lean guoskkahan	untouched by a man's hand

On the surface the text tells us that the man could not make his proposal-journey because his dray reindeer had been eaten by the wolf. In addition the mouse had ruined the white reindeer-fur coat he had planned to wear, and naturally one cannot go out proposing without beautiful clothes. But even though the wolf has devoured the reindeer, there is another reindeer, the dark one, that he could have traveled with. But it was not yet tamed, which the text expresses through the information that it had not yet been touched by human hand. An untamed reindeer is not a good draft animal, especially for a proposal-journey where it is important to arrive in style.

The reindeer images in the text serve a double function; they are intended to depict draft reindeer, but at the same time they also represent portraits of women. *Gabba* is a light-haired reindeer, but it can also be a light-haired woman, while *muzet* means a dark-haired reindeer or woman. *Sággi* tells us furthermore that she is slender. It is generally common in yoik texts to use different reindeer names as metaphors for different types of women.

Interpreting *gabba* and *muzet* as metaphors for a light and a dark woman, and the wolf as the picture of another man, a rival, brings out other aspects of the text. The man still fails to make his proposal-journey, but in this reading it is because another man has run off with the light girl whom the bachelor actually loved most. In the text the rival is represented as a wolf. In the meantime, the deceived man still has a chance with the thin, dark one, and the advantage with her is that she is as yet still untouched. With this the yoik also hints at something about the light girl whom he did not get. Of course it would be possible to interpret the text in an even more abstract way, but my point here is primarily simply to show how yoik texts can play with various terms for reindeer so as to describe people, and through this comment on human relationships.

One could continue in this manner with other yoiks, placing the individual text in context, to bring out the entire spectrum of interpretation from an 'internal' perspective, the frame of reference of the primary addressee. My intention has primarily been to indicate that interpretation can achieve more than a purely literary reading of yoik texts that is limited by cultural differences, or perhaps rather by a scarcity of comparable experience in a different language and culture. In addition to these limitations there is the yoik's special character as something other than, and more than, merely literary expression. It is in the (musical) performance that the cultural peculiarities are underscored, emphasized or subdued. We therefore need an interpretative method that is broad enough and open enough to take into account multiple sides - or rather, all sides - of the yoik's complete richness of expression: An exegesis which opens up for possible interpretations of the yoik that make allowances for its peculiarities *qua* yoik as cultural expression, but which at the same time also give us the opportunity to interpret yoik texts as *literary* forms of expression. If one does not allow for this, the yoik's textual aspect will no longer be as interesting in scholarly research. Possibly such a development can be detected in the process that the modern Sámi yoik tradition is entering, with the aestheticizing of the yoik as primarily a musical genre, where the text is often left out, or quite simply no longer created.

Part V. Education: Affirming Diversity, Confirming Rights

Positive discrimination in our view calls for at least the following from the school: Because thorough learning of the mother tongue is very important to the minority child, *pre-school in the mother tongue* should begin as early as possible. This pre-school should be entirely monolingual. All linguistic groups that are numerically large enough should be taught in their mother tongue, preferably at least throughout comprehensive school. The majority language should be taught as L2 from the third grade on.

Tove Skutnabb-Kangas and
Pertti Toukomaa, 1976, 83.

The Linguistic Human Rights of Sign Language Users

Markku Jokinen

Most of the literature on Deaf children focuses on their education, perhaps the most controversial and most frequently discussed area through the centuries. But in spite of Deaf people's long struggle for equal human rights, particularly educational language rights, there is still little research on how most Deaf children are the victims of linguistic genocide every day, every moment, all over the world. Having a sign language accepted as a mother tongue already from birth is the most important human right for Deaf children because sign language is the only language they can acquire spontaneously and naturally without teaching, provided they have exposure to it. Still it is denied to them all over the world.

It is full mastery of language/s that helps children to express their needs and desires and gives them better tools to protect themselves as human beings, i.e. to exercise their human rights to education, to freedom of thought and expression, to protection from all forms of abuse, neglect, and exploitation. If the child has no proper language/s, the result is difficulties in communication between the child and his/her parents, teachers and all others in the environment. This, in turn, has dramatic influence on overall development, cognitive, social, and psychological. The less capable the child is in using his/her language, the less knowledge, tools and necessary support s/he will have. This, in turn, results in a risk of falling victim to all kinds of exploitation and abuse, unfortunately very common all over the world. The realisation of linguistic human rights is thus closely related to the realisation of other human rights.

Granted that most Deaf children are born to hearing parents, we still know too little about how Deaf children who experience full acceptance of their language/s and their culture/s from birth might develop and what their life chances might be. It is through our sign languages that Deaf children receive the wisdom of their Deaf Community. It is this wisdom through which Deaf children will have the tools to survive and develop their full capacities in society at large. This wisdom and experience has been accumulated by similar people before him/her. It is wisdom about the way we live as visual persons, transmitted by our culture and language from the past. I believe it is the wisdom humankind needs.

This article[1] discusses the linguistic human rights of Deaf children in education. We Deaf have almost always exclusively experienced that other people have decided about Deaf education and tried to rear Deaf children to be something else than they are. Our sign languages are a very rich part of global linguistic and cultural diversity. The total number of languages in the world is doubled if our sign languages are taken into account. It is saddening to discover that our languages are almost always excluded from being considered minority languages, from policy programmes, legislation, and human rights instruments.

But I am also asking what we Deaf adults are doing in order to support our children. Are we aware of the impact of nationalism on the linguistic rights of Deaf communities where one national sign language or a foreign sign language could dominate other sign languages used in same country (see Branson & Miller, this volume)? Do we Deaf ourselves practice this linguistic imperialism on other sign languages? If so, we are also weakening possibilities for Deaf children to have education in the languages of their intimate environment (a local sign language with a local spoken language in written form). We might be participating in denying their right to have education through the medium of their mother tongue.

The Deaf child's right to education

It is estimated that of the 70 million Deaf persons in the world, 80%, including a high proportion of Deaf children, live in developing countries (Kuurojen Liitto, 1998). There are about 625 million primary school age children in developing countries. About 130 million, 21% of them do not attend school; nearly two thirds of these are girls and 55% of the children live in only five countries. Thus 79% of these children do have access to primary education (UNICEF, 1999), whereas an average enrollment rate of Deaf children in developing countries is well below 20 %. Eighty per cent are left without any formal education at all. In one fifth of the target countries surveyed by the World Federation of the Deaf (WFD), states outside of Europe and North America, excluding Australia, Japan, New Zealand, and South Africa, fewer than one deaf child out of five ever gets to school. These figures for educational human rights of Deaf children show that one of the most basic human rights, everyone's right to education, is grossly violated.

It is the responsibility of us, Deaf adults, together with parents of Deaf children, to make sure that all Deaf children have access to formal and informal education all over the world. We must inform UNICEF and UNESCO and other important

---

[1] There is a longer version of the arguments in my keynote presentation in the Human Rights Commission of the World Federation of the Deaf Congress, Brisbane, Australia, August 1999, in which I applied Tove Skutnabb-Kangas's work on linguistic human rights, education, and links between biodiversity and linguistic diversity, to the Deaf situation.

institutions of these violations. We must also be the experts on solutions. Development co-operation run by Nordic National Associations of the Deaf in co-operation with Deaf people in the developing countries has proven very fruitful and could be seen as one of most powerful tools to improve the situation of Deaf people. Success is based on the needs and expertise of Deaf people themselves. In these development co-operation projects Deaf people co-operate with authorities on many levels, from planning to implementation of all kind of services needed. They are not only in participation but also in ownership.

Important values of these projects are worldwide joint responsibility and international solidarity. Multiculturalism is stressed and the cultures of the partner countries are respected. Differences and diversities are seen as resources. When human and linguistic equality is one of the goals, improving the general human rights of Deaf persons is an important part of the projects (Kuurojen Liitto, 1998).

The Deaf child's right to have education in her/his mother tongue: linguistic and cultural genocide in the education of Deaf children

In Article III of the final Draft of what in 1948 became the UN International Convention for the Prevention and Punishment of the Crime of Genocide, linguistic genocide was defined as 'prohibiting the use of language of the group in daily intercourse or in schools, or the printing and circulation of publications in the language of the group'. Even if Article III was voted down in the General Assembly and is not part of the final Convention, the definition can be used (see Skutnabb-Kangas, 2000, chapter 7, for details). Skutnabb-Kangas (2000) shows that linguistic genocide is practised throughout the world, the main direct agents being parts of the consciousness industry: the mass media and formal schooling, along with market and other forces. They are shaping the opportunities for the use of indigenous and minority languages (see also Skutnabb-Kangas & Phillipson, 1998; Terralingua, 1999).

According to Skutnabb-Kangas & Phillipson (1998) the use of indigenous or minority languages can be prohibited overtly and directly (through laws, imprisonment, torture, killings, threats) or covertly, indirectly via ideological or structural means, as in the educational systems of most European and North American countries. Indigenous or minority children in day care centres and schools without bilingual teachers are an example of covert linguistic genocide. The absence of these languages from school timetables makes them invisible. Minority mother tongues are presented as non-resources, as 'handicaps' that 'prevent' the children from acquiring the majority language. Therefore they are told to get rid of them. At the same time minority children are in fact prevented from fully acquiring majority resources, majority languages! Educational structures are disabling children. In these structures, instruction is organised through the medium of majority languages in ways which contradict most scientific evidence on how education for bilingualism should be organised (ibid.).

The features mentioned above are easily found in most schools and day care systems for deaf children throughout the world. As soon as a child has been found to be Deaf, sign language should be used as a foundation for vital language development. Instead, parents are advised not to use sign language, and to use speech which the Deaf child can at best make minimal use of but mostly none at all. Racist attitudes and methods of oppression have been changed from overt to more covert ones. 'Advice' has replaced force.

Even for those Deaf children who do get access to formal education, teaching given through the medium of a sign language is also very rare.

The 8 principles which should be followed if the educational goal if high levels of multilingualism for all children, both minorities and majorities, elaborated by Skutnabb-Kangas (1995, 1996; see also Lanstyak, this volume, for another application of the principles), seem to be valid for Deaf children as well. They can reach high levels of bi- or multilingualism in bilingual deaf programmes. Here I give my own short version of some of the principles and comment on them briefly in relation to Deaf children. I have added the first principle about an early start for the benefit of Deaf children:

- use the child's mother tongue as early as possible in education; parents and children need substantial institutional and other support for Sign language;
- use as the main medium of instruction at least during the first eight school years the language which has less chance to develop up to a high formal level. This is not always the mother tongue (as UNESCO urged in 1953): one should rather focus on the language that needs support. For ethnic minorities this is a mother tongue, for ethnic majorities any minority language. The language of the majority can always develop to the higher level because the surrounding society operates in that majority language. For Deaf children the language that needs support is a Sign language;
- at least initially children should be placed in a group where there are only children using the same language; this 'segregation' is a necessity for Deaf children;
- all children should be in the same position vis-à-vis their competence in the language of instruction. It has to be the mother tongue of all children or none of them. Thus 'integrating' Deaf children with hearing children, with the hearing children's mother tongue as the medium of education, does not work;
- all teachers must be bi- or multilingual. If the teacher is not bilingual, s/he is not able to support the child's metalinguistic awareness nor help the child to take advantage of the common underlying proficiency for the languages. Teachers of Deaf children must thus be competent in Sign languages as well as (the written variety of) majority languages;
- any foreign language should be taught via the mother tongue;
- all children have to study both their mother tongue (i.e. a Sign language) and the second language (an oral language in its written form) as subjects

throughout their formal education. Sign languages should be studied as the mother tongue, and the second language as a second language, not a mother tongue);

- both languages have to be used as languages of instruction at some stage of education, but the progression differs for majority and minority groups. If one wants the minority children to achieve a high level of multilingualism, they should not be taught content in intellectually demanding subjects through the medium of the second language before they have received education in this language as a subject at least for seven years, and been taught in this language in less demanding subjects for at least five years. This means that a Sign language should be the main medium of Deaf children's education at least during the first 8 years of school, and during the whole pre-school period.

Only a very small fraction of Deaf children today have access to bilingual deaf education where their national sign language is both the language of teaching and learning and a mother tongue subject in the curriculum (the Nordic countries, parts of USA, some countries in South America and very few others). They enjoy their education as normal children whose linguistic human rights are respected and protected by law. But most education of Deaf children is still based on a philosophy of oralism where the teaching of an oral language, the language of the majority, in fact speech, is seen as a tool for the individual's integration in society. Here, the human being as a physically 'perfect' person is seen as an ideal model. The concept of human being is similar to the medical view based on norms of sameness, as opposed to the multiple notion of human beings where people are different but have the same value as persons. According to the WFD survey in developing countries mentioned above, a sign language is used in some capacity in approximately 40% of schools, but it is not clear whether it has the status of a mother tongue or is a language of instruction or something else (Joutselainen, 1991).

When we compare Deaf education with theoretical models and concepts used in describing the education of hearing linguistic minorities, we can easily find many similarities (see Skutnabb-Kangas, 1996, 1999b, 2000, for these models and concepts). The bilingual deaf education programmes mentioned above are clearly language shelter or maintenance programmes[2] and not in any way segregation

---

[2] According to Skutnabb-Kangas (2000, 600-610), a *language shelter* or *maintenance programme* is a programme where linguistic minority children with a low-status mother tongue voluntarily choose (among existing alternatives) to be instructed through the medium of their own mother tongue, in classes with minority children with the same mother tongue only, where the teacher is bilingual and where they get good teaching in the majority language as a second/foreign language, also given by a bilingual teacher. In higher grades, after grade 6, a few subjects may be taught through the medium of the majority language.

programmes[3], despite the initial physical segregation. On the other hand, oral programmes for Deaf children are submersion programmes[4]: the children's mother tongue has no official status in the education system, it is excluded by various sanctions, from physical to more hidden and indirect methods. This is a clear example of the linguistic and cultural genocide which oral programmes aim for.

The programmes classified as transitional models[5] use the mother tongue of the child only as a tool for learning the language of the majority, and it is removed as soon as the child has barely learned the basic language skills of that language. The

---

[3] According to Skutnabb-Kangas (2000, 591-592), a *segregation programme* is a programme where linguistic minority children with a low-status mother tongue are forced to accept instruction through the medium of their own mother tongue (or the national language of their country of origin - e.g. Kurdish children from Turkey in Bavaria taught through the medium of Turkish not Kurdish) in classes with minority children (with the same mother tongue) only, where the teacher may be monolingual or bilingual but is often poorly trained, where the class/school has poorer facilities and fewer resources than classes/schools for dominant group children, where the teaching of the dominant language is poor or non-existent and where the dominant language is not used as a medium at all (e.g. South African primary education under apartheid).

[4] According to Skutnabb-Kangas (2000, 582-587) a *submersion* or *sink-or-swim programme* is a programme where linguistic minority children with a low-status mother tongue are forced to accept instruction through the medium of a foreign majority/official language with high status, in classes where some children are native speakers of the language of instruction, where the teacher does not understand the mother tongue of the minority children, and where the majority language constitutes a threat to the minority children's mother tongue (MT), which runs the risk of being displaced or replaced (MT is not being learned properly; MT is 'forgotten'; MT does not develop because the children are forbidden to use it or are made to feel ashamed of it) -a *subtractive* language learning situation. This is the most common - and most disastrous - method in the present world for educating minority children.

[5] According to Skutnabb-Kangas (2000, 592-600) a *transitional programme* is a programme where linguistic minority children with a low-status mother tongue are initially instructed through the medium of their mother tongue for a few years and where their mother tongue has no intrinsic value, only an instrumental value. It is used only in order for the children to learn the majority language better, and so as to give them some subject-matter knowledge while they are learning the majority language. As soon as they can function to some extent in the majority language orally, they are transferred to a majority language medium programme. A transitional programme is a more sophisticated version of submersion programmes, a more 'humane' way of assimilating. These programmes are common in the education of migrant children in some of the more progressive settings (some programmes in Sweden, Holland, USA etc). They are also used in parts of 'Anglophone' Africa.

programmes of Total Communication in the education for the deaf resemble this model. The use of sign language (or, rather, only some signs from sign language) is marginal only and sign language has no official status; it only serves the purpose of teaching the majority language. Again, sign languages are being killed in these programmes.

Technology, 'normalisation' and well-meaning advice as tools of linguistic genocide

Technological instruments are also used as a tool of linguistic genocide. Cochlear implants are the most recent means. The one important human feature that differentiates us from other linguistic minorities is the sensorial difference called deafness or rather our strong natural visual capabilities that have guaranteed the survival of sign languages until today. It has also helped us generate sign languages over the ages. As long as there are Deaf people there will always be sign languages.

But unfortunately Deaf children are today threatened by the ever stronger measures of normalisation practised by medicine. Do disabled and disabling education systems for Deaf children also serve the financial interests of those in power? Are substantial investments in cochlear implants part of the economic exploitation of Deaf children, supported by a monolingual and monocultural 'free market' ideology (more a political dogma than an economic system today, Skutnabb-Kangas, 1999b)? Is this what lies behind these crude measures that are against the spirit of the Convention on the Rights of Child?

I was invited in July 1999 as a speaker at the Congress of FEPAL (The Spanish Association of Teachers Specialised in Audiotechnics and Language) to give a paper about bilingual deaf education. The programme consisted mostly of speeches about cochlear implants: their impact on learning speech (oral language), optimal time of implanting, etc. The implants were believed to solve almost all problems of learning an oral language and to help profoundly deaf children to attain the goals of education previously thought unattainable. The belief of the experts in the power of technology was very strong and raised unrealistic expectations during the Congress. The experts seemed to experience the opinions and suspicions of and comments by the Deaf participants as very hostile and insulting. Once more, as many times before in history, monolingual and monocultural views as a way of solving the problems of minority groups prevailed very strongly. And everyone forgot the linguistic human rights of Deaf children, especially their right to have their mother tongue, sign language, as the medium of instruction and as a subject.

It is these 'well-meaning' actions of those in power that are very hard to fight against. It is these formal education systems run by people from the majority groups and medical counselling and child care that are advising parents not to use sign language with their infants that have tried to kill our sign languages over the centuries. Perhaps this has been one of the most intensive and protracted linguistic genocides in history. It is our duty as Deaf adults to tell people more about this, document it, and demand a stop to the violation of the human rights of Deaf children. If we stay silent with this genocide happening all the time, we become partners with other killing agents and allow this unequal power relationship to continue.

Linguistic human rights and the Deaf

The present binding linguistic human rights in education clauses are completely insufficient for protecting and maintaining linguistic diversity (Skutnabb-Kangas, 2000). Even according to the OSCE's *The Hague Recommendations Regarding the Education Rights of National Minorities & Explanatory Note* (1996[6]) 'the international human rights instruments that make reference to minority language education remain somewhat vague and general. They make no specific reference to degrees of access nor do they stipulate which levels of mother tongue education should be made available to minorities and by what means'. The weakness of the international human instruments is one of the reasons for linguistic genocide. The UN Standard Rules on Equalisation of Opportunities stress that sign language should be used *in families*, in education and in the communities of the Deaf child (my emphasis). The mass media, especially television, should serve sign language users. The education of Deaf children may be most suitably conducted in special schools where sign language is used.

But Deaf children also encounter other problems, only a few of which can be enumerated. According to Krausneker's research (1999), in the EU minority language policies generally exclude sign languages. This may be mostly because of misconceptions about sign languages. There are still many people all over the world who do not see sign languages as true and fully-fledged languages. The other 'natural' reason is that deaf issues are generally dealt with within the area of disabilities. This ignores the important linguistic question of the status and rights of sign languages. Sign languages are legally recognised in only 17 countries in the world. In four of them sign language is mentioned in the Constitution: Finland, Portugal, South Africa, and Uganda. The draft Universal Declaration of Linguistic Rights, submitted to UNESCO in June 1996, the first attempt at formulating a universal document about language rights exclusively, unfortunately does not relate to sign language users either (Skutnabb-Kangas & Phillipson 1998, 7).

Because sign languages are seldom seen as mother tongues/first languages of Deaf children, the children are not regarded as members of linguistic minorities. They are seen exclusively as disabled children who have special needs. It is

---

[6] See Skutnabb-Kangas 1999b, chapter 7, on the general protection in human rights instruments of linguistic human rights in education. See also de Varennes, this volume.

therefore very important to start thinking about using other terms in addition to the term 'Deaf'. In my country, Finland, we have discussed the term 'sign language user'/'sign language using person', because it has more positive connotations than the term 'Deaf' for the general public (note that we have a long experience of two national languages). Our Constitution (in force since 1995) states that 'the rights of those who use sign language ... shall be guaranteed by an Act of Parliament'. Among those who use sign languages are also hearing people (one of) whose mother tongue(s) is a sign language, and their rights are protected too. We should not forget the rights of hearing sign language users (whose parents or elder sister/brother are Deaf); they are part of a sign language using community.

Parents have the right/freedom to choose a school for their child (e.g. according to the *International Covenant on Economic, Social and Cultural Rights*), and, according to Article 18 of the *Convention on the Rights of the Child* 'parents have the primary responsibility for the upbringing and development of the child. The best interests of the child will be their basic concern'. But how will parents find out what are 'the best interests of the child', especially, when the parents differ from their Deaf children, as hearing parents do? Are they offered all the relevant information to help them make the right choices for their Deaf child? Do medical experts understand the crucial importance of sign language for the development of a Deaf child? Human rights conventions are silent on this in relation to both Deaf and hearing children, which raises fundamental philosophical and ethical issues.

Branson and Miller (1998) have dealt eminently with the issue of hierarchies between sign languages. Most countries probably have more than one sign language. One should then carefully consider how to promote and seek recognition of these sign languages. Naming just one sign language as a national language may create a minority status for other sign languages and thus weaken the possibility for the Deaf child to be educated in her/his community sign language. There is therefore a need for the selection of natural and culturally relevant sign languages as vehicles for the development of bilingual deaf education. It is then possible for students to move naturally between on the one hand their local sign language (acquired fully) and the selected natural 'national' sign language, and on the other from their local spoken language in its written form to other spoken languages in their written forms.

Sign languages have been the victims of another kind of nationalism when artificial sign systems have been created all over the world. Signs have been forcibly replaced or modified to represent spoken national languages. This kind of nationalism is unfortunately still very common, depriving Deaf children of the use and development of proper sign language. Attempts by Western experts to change local sign languages, or replace them with national sign languages from their own countries, are also crude examples of international neo-colonial processes. The Deaf themselves, unfortunately, have practised this linguistic imperialism in other countries. It is the responsibility of national associations to avoid this insult to the linguistic human rights of Deaf children and adults, especially in developing countries. I think most of us would not like to make the same mistakes as those majority language advocates leading us to monolingual stupidity and naivety, where monolingualism is seen as normal, inevitable, desirable, and sufficient, a position that is not supported by any scientific evidence (Skutnabb-Kangas, 2000). On the contrary, it is normal to be multilingual and multicultural, and it is normal that we are striving for this in our attempts to fight for linguistic human rights for Deaf children. It is through linguistic and cultural diversity that we reach the unity of humankind.

Responsibilities of national associations of the Deaf and members of the World Federation of the Deaf

A common feature in political demands and efforts of the Deaf worldwide has been a demand for linguistic rights, essential to the cultural and personal identities of Deaf children and adults, a cornerstone of human rights protection, tolerance, and conflict prevention. The judgement from an international hearing on violations of language rights, as these are formulated in the People's Communication Charter, states that respect for communication and language rights contributes to peaceful, democratic societies and entails dialogue between state authorities and minority language groups[7].

Control of a language is often a tool for power over the lives of other people. We have always been victims of this use of power, and are against it. We, as Deaf adults, with experience of life as Deaf, are responsible for defending the linguistic human rights of Deaf children; we have some power ourselves to do something for them, and they often do not. Deaf children cannot wait any longer. It is therefore important to examine the goals of our own activities, also in preparation for the dialogue with others:

- Do the human rights of the Deaf children have top priority? There are so many abused, exploited, neglected, forgotten, and killed Deaf children all over the world. All Deaf associations aim for equal citizenship in our societies, but how much thought has been given to the situation of Deaf children?
- Are Deaf associations for Deaf children too? I have visited many local deaf clubs in different parts of the world but seldom seen organised activities for Deaf children and their parents. Have we given the responsibility for Deaf children to others, medical personnel, institutions, and parents?
- We demand that our sign languages be used in the education of Deaf children, but how about infants living at home with their parents? Do parents receive

---

[7] The judgement is published for The World Association for Christian Communication and the People's Communication Charter as *Linguicide. The Death of Language.* London & Amsterdam, 1999. It is also available at <http://www.wacc.org.uk> and <http://www.waag.org/pcc>; see also Hamelink, this volume.

free sign language training? Do we ensure that all Deaf children have a chance to use their own sign languages from birth?

The Finnish Association of the Deaf in its motion to the WFD General Assembly in Brisbane, 1999, asked WFD, as part of a general survey of human rights, to carry out a global survey of the linguistic rights of the Deaf, with special attention to whether Deaf rights have been considered in human rights instruments, whether and how they are being implemented, and what measures should be taken to ensure them. The emphasis should be on Deaf children's right to their own language, and the results would form the basis of an action plan to improve the linguistic human rights of the Deaf worldwide.

We should be more actively fighting for linguistic human rights in education for Deaf children together with other minority language groups, experts, activists, language-related institutions and organisations worldwide. It is no longer enough to demand rights only as Deaf persons. We as sign language users achieve our goals more constructively if we work together with others. It is children who keep our languages alive. It is children, Deaf and hearing, who enrich the linguistic and cultural diversity in the world.

The Linguistic Problem Child has Many Names

Pertti Toukomaa

It is a commonplace that the beloved child has many names. The problem child also has many names. The problem child of language development is disturbed bilingualism to which many emotional, personality, and cognitive function disorders are connected. Scandinavian research and debate on minorities has referred to this type of development, where the child learns neither language at a monolingual level, despite living in an environment where this is required for school achievement, jobs, and the like, as semilingualism.

This is an old notion, even if the names for it have changed. It was for instance observed at the beginning of the 20th century in North American settings, where Indians were reported as forgetting their mother tongues faster than they learned English (Bloomfield, 1927). These children were not at the same level as monolingual native speakers, as they were in the position of not knowing any language properly.

Subtractive bilingualism

The Canadian social psychologist Wallace E. Lambert (1979) describes subtractive bilingual development as where a second language overpowers the position of the mother tongue without the mother tongue having the opportunity to develop. Children in this type of situation generally belong to minority families who have little formal education and low socio-economic status. Their education takes place through the medium of the majority language.

As an example of subtractive bilingual development, Lambert cites Latin American migrants whose children attended English-speaking schools in the USA. The oppression of their mother tongue not only involves disturbance in their language development but can also lead to learning difficulties, behavioural disturbances, and delay in the learning of concepts.

By contrast, to develop in a bilingual environment means richness and extra stimulation when the mother tongue is not threatened and has the possibility to develop simultaneously while the child is learning the other language. According to Lambert, this type of situation is additive, and enriching for the development of both languages. This may occur with the child who belongs to a language minority if education is given through the medium of the mother tongue. It may also occur with the child belonging to the majority language group, for example in language immersion programmes.

Linguistic researchers oriented toward social psychology also speak of the contrasting pair 'elite' and 'common' bilingualism. 'Common' refers to a population with a fairly low level of formal schooling and socio-economic status. Bilingualism or multilingualism has never been a problem for the migrant families of diplomats, visiting university lecturers or experts. These homes have been able to give the stimulation and support necessary to maintain the mother tongue and its development while the foreign tongue is being learned.

Parents of families with little formal education and low social status may often have neither the time nor the energy to support the development of the children's mother tongue enough. Meanwhile, the foreign-tongued school and other surroundings may easily lead the limited language development into a vicious circle of subtractive bilingualism. The division into 'elite' and 'common' bilingualism explains why the educational policy-maker who has become bilingual through formal education has difficulty in understanding the problems which children of migrants with relatively little formal education confront when attending a school offering education in a foreign language.

Semilingualism

The debate on semilingualism began in Scandinavia with the publication of Nils-Erik Hansegård´s book *Tvåspråkighet eller halvspråkighet?* (Bilingualism or semilingualism?) in 1968. The book dealt with language and developmental problems that arose in Northern Sweden's Finnish minority families because of the language at school being Swedish and the educational aim being assimilation into the Swedish language (see Lainio, this volume).

Hansegård lists the characteristics of semilingualism as an insufficiency in both languages in any of the following categories: a) size of repertoire of words and phrases; b) linguistic correctness; c) degree of automatism; d) ability to neologize; e) mastery of cognitive functions of language; and f) richness of meanings. In a later publication (1990), semilingualism is regarded as meaning 'insufficient compound linguistic competence'.

Semilingualism, where one is not fully competent in the mother tongue and fails to learn the deeper meanings of concepts in another language, reflects those unfavourable linguistic and psychological consequences which have come about through the suppression of mother tongue development. There are many other contributory factors connected to the issue other than purely linguistic ones.

Semilingualism is more a pedagogical, sociocultural, and political phenomenon than a purely linguistic one. It is manifested in, among other things, a lack of development in language-linked emotional expression when the move to another language has occurred too early and at the expense of the development of the mother tongue. Insufficient or ineffective teaching of the new language is partially responsible for the fact that this language is not learnt as well as modern society requires.

After a number of paediatricians campaigned for assistance to be directed to the 'lost generation' of migrant youth, the debate in Sweden about semilingualism expanded to include the school situation of migrant children. Doctors viewed the assimilatory school instruction as producing language oppression in those belonging to this group, who suffered from psychological problems, behavioural disturbances, and school difficulties.

As a researcher into the position of minorities in Sweden in the 1970s, I took part with Tove Skutnabb-Kangas in the debate about semilingualism. This discussion and the research which figured prominently in it (e.g. Skutnabb-Kangas & Toukomaa, 1976) seem to have partially influenced Swedish law, so that in 1979 Sweden adjusted its home language law so as to guarantee at least two hours a week of mother tongue lessons for all children belonging to families speaking a foreign language. Although a framework of two hours of lessons a week could not accomplish the achievement of the basic aim of functional bilingualism, home language instruction does however seem to function in practice as a kind of 'first aid' serving to counteract the most catastrophic 'lost generation' consequences among the second and third generation of Finnish immigrants.

Lingual homelessness

At approximately the same time as the semilingualism debate in Sweden was at its peak, a discussion about 'lingual homelessness' (sprachliche Heimatlosigkeit) arose in one region of Germany. It was significantly influenced by the research of Els Oksaar of Hamburg University, whose studies (1978) of bilingualism showed that monolingual children belonging to a linguistic minority who are restricted to education in the majority language may sooner or later end up in a situation where they no longer receive sufficient stimuli in the mother tongue to maintain it. The mother tongue skills of these children are weaker than those of children of the same age who have received mother tongue teaching.

However, their command of the majority language may not be at a comparable level to that of native speakers of the language. Skills in the majority language do not develop sufficiently because the concepts are not mastered in the mother tongue. When one is not able to think or express oneself sufficiently in either language, this signifies lingual homelessness. A lingually homeless person may also be subject to personality disorders. A person in this situation, especially a young one, is often also culturally homeless and rootless. In general, cultural alienation and problems of identity development may also be linked to lingual homelessness.

Alexithymia

Irma Moilanen, a Professor of Child Psychiatry at the University of Oulu, formed cross-disciplinary work groups for researching the problems of the children of migrants returning from Sweden to Finland, and found a combination of symptoms which seemed to have similarities with the psychiatric state alexithymia (1995). This involves the verbal inability to express one's emotions, which can lead to non-verbal expressions of stress, e.g. psychosomatic symptoms.

The term can be understood as implying types of vocabulary defect or linguistic emotional disturbance. It is a combination of symptoms in child psychiatry where there is insufficient learning of the mother tongue and, above all, an incompleteness of the emotional meanings of words. The scarcity of vocabulary and concepts may be partially reflected in overall intellectual development and emotional well-being. The kind of disturbances associated with alexithymia are comparable to those seen in earlier research into semilingualism and lingual homelessness.

Additional evidence in favour of maintaining minority children's mother tongue can be seen in Olli Kuure's doctoral dissertation (1997), which dealt with comprehensive school children's bilingualism in Finland and Sweden. According to Kuure, the teaching of the mother tongue to Finnish migrant children in Sweden for the entire duration of their comprehensive schooling leads to a high level of bilingualism and bicultural identity. By contrast, lack of continuity of the medium (language) of education in the educational provision can endanger a child's mental development, leading to scholarly under-achievement and behavioural and emotional disorders.

The 'at risk' group consisted of students who had insufficient skills to express their feelings in either language. This led, according to Kuure's and Moilanen's studies, to psychiatric symptoms, psychosomatic illnesses, behavioural disorders, and feelings of inferiority as well as poor school achievement. The stable and successful group consisted of students who had used their Finnish mother tongue at home and school, and had used both languages outside the home with friends.

Clinically disfluent or 'non-non'

In the School District of Southern California, the Spanish-speaking students who allegedly do not know English, Spanish, or any other language at native level are labelled 'clinically disfluent' (according to Valadez et al., 1997). In Los Angeles the minority children who have a low level in both languages are called 'non-nons'.

These low achieving bilinguals are considered synonymous with semilinguals by Valadez et al. (1997).

Hallahan and Kauffman (1991, 230) acknowledge that all normal speech 'is characterised by some interruptions in speech flow'. A disorder may be suspected, according to them, only when a speaker's efforts are so intense or the interruptions in the flow of speech are so frequent or pervasive that they keep him or her from being understood or draw extraordinary attention'. In my experience as a school psychologist in Sweden, this kind of situation was typical of Finnish immigrant children who had conceptual difficulties in both languages (see also Skutnabb-Kangas & Toukomaa, 1976).

The phenomenon of the bilingual developmental disorder, with its many names, will not disappear through attempts to sweep it under the carpet or to deny its existence, as certain linguists in Scandinavia and elsewhere have tried to do with semilingualism. On the contrary, the issue must be emphasised and discussed profusely so that the educational disadvantages linked to the misguided education of minority language children disappear. Swedish debates on semilingualism in the 1970s led to many improvements for Finnish migrant children's school conditions and language tuition: teaching of the home language, mother tongue classes, etc. This is how research and the use of it as a tool for minority language policy can function in an emancipatory manner, its objective being to remove grievances.

Creating a Successful Minority School

Markku Peura

Swedish minority policy: assimilation

Sweden-Finns are a young minority which emerged as a result of large-scale immigration after the second world war. Most of the Finns moved to Sweden during the 1950s and 1960s. If the 'second generation' is also counted, the number may now be around 400,000. It is also important to remember that Finnish language and culture have been present in Sweden for 1000 years (see Lainio, this volume), mostly because Finland was a Swedish colony for 650 years (see Lindgren, this volume). Swedish policy towards ethnic minorities has been assimilationist, as has typically been the case in European nation states.

This policy was also practised in relation to immigrants. In the middle of the 1970s there was a shift in rhetoric: assimilation was rejected in official documents, and it was claimed that a policy of assimilation had never existed! Among immigrants and other ethnic minorities the shift towards multiculturalism and multilingualism gave rise to high expectations for change.

In my view, this shift has so far been mostly rhetorical. Sweden has had great trouble in accepting, for instance, language rights for minorities, and basic linguistic human rights have not been implemented. An illustrative example: the government still (1999) vacillates over ratifying the *European Charter for Regional or Minority Languages*, even with respect to the indigenous Sámi languages. Most other European countries have already signed. The state is thus ambivalent: it endorses a 'multicultural society' in the abstract, but fails to put a minority policy into effect.

The Sweden-Finnish experience may be of interest not only to migrant and minority groups in Sweden but to any minorities who are struggling for the right to learn their mother tongue and for positive acceptance of their culture and identity. Our experience involves the minority organising its own institutions, such as day-care centres and schools, so as to guarantee that children can learn their mother tongue and develop strong self-confidence and identity.

From an assimilation model to a bilingual model

When Finnish-speaking children started school in the 1950s, there were no alternatives to the ordinary classes with all instruction in Swedish, and no mother tongue teaching, not even as a subject. Thinking about minority languages and education was influenced by the controversy surrounding semilingualism and inappropriate schooling in northern Sweden (see Lainio, and Toukomaa, this volume) and by research showing that bilingual children can succeed in school just as well as monolinguals.

Immigration from Finland was at its peak during the final years of the 1960s. Teachers found it difficult to cope with classes with a strong representation of Finnish children who initially did not speak a word of Swedish. To handle the pedagogical problem several different strategies were experimented with. In some schools the children were put in classes below their age level so that they would have time to learn Swedish. In some schools pupils were grouped together in 'language clinics', to be 'cured' of not knowing Swedish. In other schools Finnish children were gathered into a class of their own, and a teacher from Finland was recruited to teach them through the medium of the Finnish language.

This gave rise to totally new thinking within the Swedish school system, and started something like an ethnic movement among the Finns. Finnish parents noticed very soon that this model (with Finnish as the medium of instruction) was very good for their children. The parents began to organise so as to prevent the Swedish authorities from abolishing these classes and to demand the right to have them continue throughout compulsory school.

Swedish principals and teachers appreciated that this model worked well, but they saw it as a temporary one which would not be needed when the pupils had 'learned Swedish'. Sweden-Finns started studying the language question, in order to be able to negotiate with politicians, administrators, principals and others. In the 1970s the most useful information, theoretical and empirical, came from Tove Skutnabb-Kangas and Pertti Toukomaa, who published some important reports for UNESCO and who travelled throughout Sweden to lecture at meetings organised by parents or Finnish associations.

The Swedish National Board of Education was against these classes, which have had many names: officially they were called 'home language classes'; Sweden-Finns used the name 'mother tongue classes'; a more neutral and correct name, 'bilingual classes', is now in use (the classes teach through the medium of two languages). In 1979 the Board of Education changed its position: it wrote a circular to schools presenting three possible ways of organising 'the education of immigrant pupils'. The first was the 'ordinary Swedish class', but with 'home language' lessons (usually 1-2 lessons per week); the second was a fifty-fifty model (50% Swedish pupils, 50% from one immigrant language group), and the third was the 'home language' class. The first was a submersion model, the second an early-exit transitional model, and the third a late-exit transitional model.

From the mid-1970s to the late 1980s there was a struggle over the third model proposed by the Board, bilingual classes. By that time there was a strong conviction among both parents and minority organisations that this model was far superior to the others. The Sweden-Finns organised on a large scale, held meetings and demonstrations, studied, wrote articles, and organised about 15 school strikes. The Sweden-Finnish school issue was even discussed at inter-governmental level.

A major research project, 'The Sweden-Finnish school issue', was undertaken between 1986 and 1989 in several towns which had bilingual classes, and which Tove Skutnabb-Kangas and three contributors to this volume (Municio, Toukomaa, and myself) were involved in. A mass of evidence on factors influencing successful school achievement was produced (see Skutnabb-Kangas & Peura, eds., 1994). One significant practical result was the realisation that if the Sweden-Finns did not start their own schools, they would lose the battle for bilingual education. In 1987 the largest Sweden-Finnish organisation, the National Union of Sweden-Finnish Associations, took the decision to start their own schools.

'Free schools'

A working group was charged with starting a school in Stockholm and after three years (and almost a year of delay caused by government officials) the first Sweden-Finnish school opened in August 1990. In 1999 there are 9 schools (Stockholm, Gothenburg, Malmö, Eskilstuna, Motala, Botkyrka, Järva, Örebro and Upplands Väsby). These schools are called 'friskolor' ('free schools', the earlier name was 'private schools').

A new Swedish law in 1991-92 gave parents the right to choose the type of school they wished for their children, with state funding following the pupil. One goal of these reforms was that schools should compete with each other, and have different profiles (such as strength in maths or music). Another goal was to make it easier to start private schools. Both reforms were important in extending democracy by giving more power to parents. Earlier, children were obliged to go to the school in their home area. The other democratic change was that it became possible for anyone wishing to establish a school to attempt to do so, without special educational insight or a large income from fees being a requirement. Legislation now forbids fees because free schools get the same resources as all other schools.

The Sweden-Finnish schools are bilingual schools. The main aim is to develop the pupils' bilingualism in Finnish and Swedish, their competence in Finnish and Swedish cultures, and a strong bilingual, bicultural identity. The 9 schools cooperate at several levels: the principals meet 4–5 times a year; there are joint courses for the teachers; the schools have joint projects to develop methods of work; they co-ordinate their approaches to the Swedish school authorities, and so on. The schools are far from identical. There are differences regarding:

1. how both languages are treated;
2. how many hours a week Finnish and Swedish are used as the medium of instruction;
3. to what extent the teachers are bilingual or monolingual.

Many other variations are due to local factors and the number of pupils. Some of the schools are very small, not yet covering all grades. Altogether the 9 schools have in 1999 about 1,000 pupils.

The Sweden-Finnish school in Upplands Väsby

The Sweden-Finnish school in Upplands Väsby (20 kilometres outside Stockholm) was started by the Finnish-speaking parent association in 1993. About 16 % of the population of Upplands Väsby are of Finnish origin. Initially the school had the first six grades of compulsory school, and by 1996 all nine. The parents decided from the start that the school should also have a day-care centre for 1-5-year-old children and a pre-school class for 6-year-olds. The school also has an after-school centre for children in the pre-school class and in grades 1-4. This centre opens at 7 in the morning and closes at 5.30 p.m. All this means that the school has a long span of time (in many cases 13-14 years) and a great opportunity to influence the children's overall development and especially their bilingualism and biculturalism because many of them begin as toddlers at the day-care centre and only leave at the age of sixteen.

The main goal of the school is high levels of bilingualism in Finnish and Swedish and a strong bicultural identity. Both languages are used as media of instruction according to a careful plan where the time allocated to each varies according to the age of the pupil.

Finnish is the only language used by the staff in the *day-care centre*, to develop the mother tongue. Some children speak Swedish better than Finnish when they arrive. The bilingual staff understand it, and the children are free to use Swedish if they feel more at ease in Swedish. Some children are bilingual from the beginning because they come from bilingual families. But most children come from families where both parents are Finnish-speakers. The *pre-school* class also works through the *medium* of *Finnish*. Swedish is introduced by steps (Figure 1).

Figure 1. Model of bilingual education

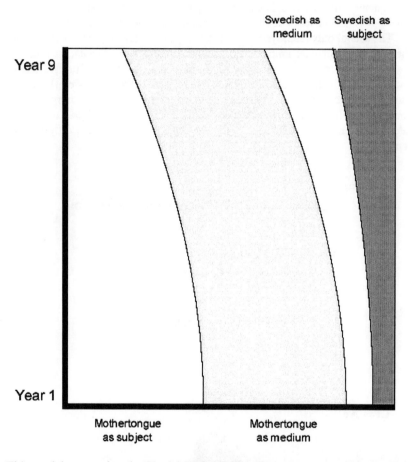

Swedish as medium   Swedish as subject

Year 9

Year 1

Mothertongue as subject   Mothertongue as medium

This model means that the Finnish and Swedish languages are used in parallel. In the lower grades, *Finnish* dominates as the *medium* of instruction. During the higher grades the proportion in *Finnish* and *Swedish* (as *media)* is about 50-50. *Finnish* is taught as a *subject* throughout all 9 years. Learning to read and write is taught through the medium of Finnish.

Swedish is taught as a *subject* from the third grade. It is used from the first grade in some context-embedded subjects as the *medium* of instruction, e.g. sports and handicraft, taught by teachers who are ethnic Swedes. These subjects are taught through Swedish through all nine grades. The idea behind this is that the school makes it possible for the pupils always to speak Swedish in a natural way with certain persons (one person – one language) and that these teachers are native speakers of Swedish. Since these teachers are in a bilingual school, they also learn Finnish, at least to a certain extent.

There are many benefits connected with this bilingual model. One is that mathematics, for instance, is taught through Finnish but the textbooks are Swedish. This is because the teachers found these books educationally sounder.

The school only employs trained teachers, most with Swedish qualifications. Of the 35 people in total employed by the school, 28 are bilingual in Finnish and Swedish, 6 are 'monolingual' in Swedish, and 1 is multilingual (Turkish, Bulgarian, Swedish). The majority of the children are bilingual (Finnish, Swedish), many are monolingual in Finnish (for instance because they have recently immigrated) and some are multilingual (for instance with Romany, Spanish, Farsi or Turkish in addition to Finnish and Swedish, often because the parents have different mother tongues).

The vision of the Sweden-Finnish school

MAIN GOALS – THE VISION:

BILINGUALISM – BICULTURALISM

Creative   **Tolerant**

Strong selfconfidence   **Curious**

When the school started, a common vision was discussed and created together by the parents and the staff. One very important aspect in our vision is 'strong self-confidence'. This relates to Finnish history, to Finland being dominated by Sweden for such a long time: Swedish language and culture (laws, administration, education) dominated Finnish society, not only during the colonial time, but also during the Russian period, and still exerts some influence on how people see each other. Many Swedes seem to more or less automatically feel superior when meeting a Finn and many Finns feel inferior when meeting a Swede. Especially among Finnish immigrants this supported the development of various kinds of 'strategies' for how to cope with the prejudice and discrimination they met. One was to try to become 'a Swede' (often more 'Swedish' than ethnic Swedes themselves; assimilation). The opposite strategy was to isolate themselves from Swedes (self-segregation). If a Finn does not open her mouth with Swedes, nobody knows that she is a Finn (because the physical features of Finns and Swedes are similar). The first generation of Finnish immigrants was often ashamed of being Finnish. The idea of strong self-confidence means that the Sweden-Finnish school tries to work in a way that empowers the pupils, making them proud of their bilingualism and biculturalism.

At the same time the Sweden-Finnish schools feel that there is a need to develop new methods of work. Creativity and curiosity are encouraged, a lot of time, effort, and resources go into the use of drama and music to give children the chance to express themselves and to dare to show who they are and what they know and can do. Tolerance is one of the most important aspects of our vision. The Finns were met by prejudice when they came as immigrants to Sweden. Later, many other groups immigrated to Sweden and met even more prejudice and racism. It is especially important for an ethnic minority school to make children aware of these phenomena and to learn from history.

Conclusion

There is still a fear of what Swedes call 'ethnic schools' in Sweden. It is as if 'big brother' were afraid of losing control if all children do not attend the standard Swedish school which Swedish politicians often call 'the best school in the world'.

Today other minority groups want to have their own schools too. Several Arabic-medium schools are in operation. In the autumn of 1999 a Russian free school started up, and schools in other languages are planned. At the same time there are numerous reports of immigrant children not doing well in the Swedish school, not getting qualifications for upper secondary school, not learning Swedish well, and dropping (or being pushed) out of school.

The Sweden-Finnish school experience is clear. In a school which is administered by the minority itself the children do not experience failure because:
a. they understand the language of instruction;

b.   they are accepted for what they are (not being inferior);
c.   the parents have chosen the school and actively participate in the work of the
     school;
d.   most teachers belong to the same ethnic group as the children and parents;
e.   relations between parents and school are totally unlike those in official schools.
     The parents have, for instance, the power to take their children out if they are
     not satisfied, they demand that their voice is heard, and they actively influence
     the work done in school, week by week.

These factors contribute to over 90% of the pupils in Sweden-Finnish school
attaining the qualifications for continuing in the upper secondary school. In general
they appear to reach the goals in our vision for the school.

Our experience in Sweden very obviously confirms what representatives of
many indigenous peoples and ethnic minorities as well as many researchers have
claimed, namely that learning, using, and identifying with the mother tongue is a
human right and provides a basis for a harmonious and well-rounded personality.

Bilingual versus Bilingual Education: The Case of Slovakia

Istvan Lanstyak

> One of the most successful means of destroying or retarding languages
> has been, and remains, education. (Skutnabb-Kangas, 1990b, 6)

The problem

While throughout the world the bulk of academics engaged in questions of minority education are enthusiastic proponents of bilingual education, most members of the Hungarian minority in Slovakia are fiercely opposed to the type of bilingual education proposed by the authorities under the misleading label 'alternative' education.[1] Not only parents and the students themselves reject the idea of teaching some subjects in Slovak while advocating the retention of schools with Hungarian as the language of instruction, but also the social elite, including politicians legally elected to represent the minority.

This opposition is not new, it has an almost forty-year-old tradition: the first attempt to transform mother tongue medium education into bilingual education was made in 1961; since then a number of proposals have been submitted (in 1977, 1978, 1980-1981, 1983, 1995). None of them has been successful, however, because of the strong opposition of parents, which in the era of communist dictatorship (1948-1989) can only be counted as a miracle.

To understand the reason for this 'unusual' behaviour of Hungarians we must first specify the concept bilingual education.

---

[1] I want to thank Juliet Langman from the University of Texas at San Antonio for a linguistic revision of the text and for her helpful comments.

Monolingual - bilingual education

Though the primary and secondary educational institutions which about three quarters of Hungarians attend[2] are called 'schools with Hungarian language instruction', they are not really monolingual, for at least two reasons. Firstly: one of the aims of the education in these schools is to produce functional bilinguals. Secondly: though in primary and grammar schools (gimnázium) the mother tongue is almost the only medium of instruction (with the exception of physical training, which is supposed to be instructed bilingually), the second language (Slovak) plays an important role in the curriculum:

- it is taught as a subject for five lessons per week in primary nine-year schools from grade 1 and three lessons per week in secondary schools (with teaching beginning in kindergarten, at the age of 3);
- from grade 5 on, the specialized terminology of the natural sciences is taught bilingually;
- from grade 7 on, each natural science lesson should end with a recapitulation in Slovak;
- students at primary schools may choose Slovak conversation and/or Slovak specialized conversation (i.e. talking about maths, physics, chemistry, or biology) as an optional subject; at secondary schools specialized conversation in one of these subjects is compulsory;
- final examinations at the secondary schools tend to be bilingual in a number of schools.[3]

From this follows that what has been presented as debates between proponents of monolingual and bilingual education focuses in fact on two different types of bilingual education. Since all research data show some degree of Hungarian dominance in most native speakers of Hungarian, we may still ask: what is the reason for rejecting the possibility of acquiring better Slovak via using it as a medium of instruction? To answer this question we have to cast a glance at the history and present day situation of Hungarians in Slovakia, including their demographic characteristics.

---

[2] The rest of Hungarians attend Slovak schools, i.e. schools where Hungarian is not taught even as a subject.

[3] Furthermore the prevalence of Hungarian as the language of instruction is true mostly of primary schools and grammar schools; in most of the secondary technical schools and especially vocational schools, science and technical subjects are usually taught in Slovak.

Hungarians and their language in Slovakia

Hungarians living in Slovakia form an autochthonous minority numbering around 600,000.[4] For a millennium the territories where Hungarians live formed an integral part of the Kingdom of Hungary. They came into existence as a minority as a consequence of the drawing of new borders based on strategic rather than ethnic principles. After the creation of the new multinational state, Czechoslovakia, thanks to the treaty on the protection of minorities concluded in 1919 in Saint-Germain-en-Laye, the Hungarian minority could retain some of their institutions, among them primary and secondary schools with Hungarian as the sole medium of instruction (though the Slovak language was taught as a subject).[5] The Hungarian language schools were all closed after 1945 when Hungarians were assigned collective guilt for the disintegration of the Czechoslovak state in 1938, and deprived of Czechoslovak citizenship, but shortly after the communist takeover in 1948 their Czechoslovak citizenship was restored and gradually the system of mother tongue primary and secondary schools was created.

The majority of Hungarians have lived and still live in territories along the 1918 Hungarian-Slovak border, mostly in areas where they are a numerical majority. This explains why despite language legislation aiming at the severe curtailment of minority languages, Hungarian is widely used in public life, albeit unofficially and predominantly orally.

Though the language of most written documents is Slovak, in effect being able to use Slovak for such 'official' purposes does not presuppose 'native-like' competence in Slovak. Since locally life can be conducted fairly well in Hungarian, for at least some strata of the population, 'native-like' competence in Slovak is not necessary for making one's way in society.

---

[4] According to the 1991 census, 567,296 people declared themselves Hungarian by nationality (which means 'ethnicity', not citizenship in Central Europe - they are all Slovak citizens!). They constitute 10.8% of Slovakia's overall population. At the same time the number of Slovak citizens who claimed Hungarian as their native language was substantially higher, 608,221, i.e. 11.5% of Slovakia's population.

[5] Nevertheless around 20% of Hungarians attended schools with exclusively Slovak medium instruction.

Language strategy for the Hungarian community in Slovakia

If being a functional bilingual in a society like that of Hungarians in Slovakia does not necessarily entail native-like command of both languages[6], nothing can justify that a 'native-like' command of both Hungarian and Slovak should be considered the ideal type of bilingualism for Hungarians in Slovakia. It has been long acknowledged that the form of bilingualism which most members of a community should aim at depends on the particular characteristics of the community (cp. Lewis, 1977, 8). In the case of Hungarians in Slovakia a very high degree of bilingualism is mostly necessary only for the intelligentsia and those Hungarians who live in localities inhabited predominantly by Slovaks. For the majority of the population the best type of bilingualism seems to be that of Hungarian dominance with a fairly good command of Slovak.

To remain Hungarian-dominant is vital for the community since there is a strong insistence on language maintenance. Hungarians are among the national groups for whom language is the central and indispensable component of their ethnic identity (cp. Lewis, 1977, 11, but see Kontra, this volume).

Taking this as the main goal we can say that schools with Hungarian as the language of instruction are more or less successful in producing functional bilinguals; if competence in Slovak is not as high as it is expected to be, it is mostly because of unrealistically high expectations. In spite of this Hungarian experts on educational matters are convinced that applying better methods of teaching Slovak as a second language could substantially improve the students' competence in Slovak without increasing exposure to the Slovak language by using it as a medium of instruction. This would be especially true if it were coupled with less restrictive language policies.

Arguments

The arguments used in refuting the 'alternative' education proposed by the authorities centered around two issues: a) the mother tongue as the most appropriate medium of instruction; b) 'alternative' education as being doomed to failure because of the way it is organized.

Mother tongue education has always been a 'self-evident rationale' (Cummins, 1991, 185) for the majority of Hungarians in Slovakia. In defending the 'language shelter-like' educational system, Hungarian writers, educators, and politicians in

---

[6] We will not tackle the delicate problem of what 'native-like command' of a language really is and whether it is at all realistic anywhere to talk about it, knowing that equal competence in two languages (balanced bilingualism) is an ideal which is in reality seldom achieved, since the two languages are at least partly used for different purposes in the bilingual communities.

Slovakia often referred to the famous 17th century Czech educationist Comenius (Jan Amos Komensky), especially to his tenet on mother tongue education as the best way of teaching children.

As more than 300 hundred years have passed since the formulation of Comenius's thesis, new arguments have been sought in the present day literature on bilingualism and bilingual education. The very first of such works referred to was Tove Skutnabb-Kangas's study (1977) in which she presented research conducted with Pertti Toukomaa providing empirical evidence that those children of Finnish immigrants in Sweden who attended classes with Finnish as the language of instruction achieved better results than those being instructed in Swedish - not only in Finnish, but also in other subjects, including the Swedish language. Another study by Skutnabb-Kangas that was used to argue for mother tongue education was her report written for the Minority Rights Group (1990) in which she presented a typology of education programmes, with the language shelter or maintenance programmes using the mother tongue as the language of instruction demonstrating a high degree of success for linguistic minorities (Skutnabb-Kangas, 1990a, 19).

There are certainly substantial differences between various minorities, the two end points on a continuum being immigrants using the state language in all domains of their life with the exception of the most private sphere, and autochthonous minorities living as a numerical majority and using their language in most public as well as private domains of language use. But in spite of the fact that the Hungarian minority in Slovakia falls closer to the latter end point, it is indisputable that at a community level it is the Slovak language which is dominant in the whole territory of Slovakia and Hungarian is the language (among other minority languages) which needs protection.

But what if the teaching of some subjects in the second language at some later stage in the process of schooling may help to develop better skills in the second language (learning language through content) without endangering the further development of the mother tongue?

In another study Skutnabb-Kangas (1994) elaborated a list of eight principles or conditions which have to be met for a bilingual program to be successful. Since the program offered by the Slovak education ministry met no more than one of them, this list became a major weapon in persuading the parents of Hungarian school children not to accept the kind of bilingual education the Slovak Ministry of Education was trying to impose on them, which entailed that:

- subjects to be taught in Slovak would be chosen according to 'parents' choice', with no consideration given to the research evidence on their suitability in relation to various phases in the students' developing Slovak competence;
- the teachers who would teach these Hungarian pupils were to be monolingual Slovaks without any special training;

- bilingual teachers of Slovak language and literature were to be replaced by monolingual Slovak teachers who were seen as a guarantee that Slovak nationalistic state ideology would be disseminated among minority pupils[7];
- for the social and natural sciences, the textbooks used in Slovak medium schools were to be used in 'alternative' schools, in spite of the fact that the project was said to be motivated by the fact that the Hungarian pupils' command of Slovak language was 'very poor';
- bilingual documentation was banned in all schools.

Fundamental linguistic human rights were also disregarded outside school, with a language law not allowing the use of minority languages in official contexts[8]. Skutnabb-Kangas (1994a, 31) regards an 'autonomy to administer matters internal to the groups, at least in the fields of culture, education, religion, information, and social affairs, with the financial means, through taxation or grants, to fulfill these functions to be part of linguistic human rights'. In Slovakia any type of autonomy or self-administration of minorities was and is rejected; the regulation of education at levels higher than the local schools was fully in the hands of the governing coalition, the representatives of the minorities had absolutely no influence on matters concerning their school system.

Comparing this situation with the 'Skutnabb-Kangasian' principles for successful bilingual education, it was clear that the proposed 'alternative' education would be disastrous for Hungarian pupils. It became evident that the only methodological principle this program relies on is what is aptly called the 'maximum exposure fallacy' by Skutnabb-Kangas (the neutral term being the 'time-on-task' hypothesis), i.e. the belief that 'the more the minority children are exposed to the majority language, the better they learn it (1990a, 16), which is definitely not true (Cummins, 1991, 187, 193).

Skutnabb-Kangas's works were often referred to when persuading parents to reject this type of bilingual education. And in the overwhelming majority of schools the parents did reject this 'alternative', so schools with Hungarian language of instruction have been saved.

Education was not the only issue in which Tove Skutnabb-Kangas's authority was used by Hungarians in Slovakia in arguing against linguistic discrimination; another one was language use. In the 'battles' in connection with the state language law Tove Skutnabb-Kangas participated not only 'spiritually', through her publications, but also directly, through her involvement in organising the world-wide protest of renowned linguists against the law. The benefits of this we are enjoying at present, as the new Slovak government, elected in October 1998, is

---

[7] As Skutnabb-Kangas states: 'A teacher, monolingual in L2, cannot make a really good L2- teacher. A good L2-teacher knows both languages and can teach contrastively' (1990a, 21; see also Skutnabb-Kangas, 1994a, 32).

[8] Skutnabb-Kangas (1990a, 21) stressed that it is important for minority members to be able to develop their language also outside school in formal contexts; otherwise formal registers of their languages will not have a chance to develop fully.

doing its best to develop a minority language law which should grant the use of minority languages in official contexts.

If I were pressed to give one word which is crucial for understanding the Skutnabb-Kangas phenomenon, I would have to choose a very 'unscholarly' one: love. Maybe I would prefer to hide this awkward 'term' into a metaphor; then I would say: fire. For those who create injustice, may it bring pain: being hit by the flames. For those who suffer injustice, may it bring warmth.

Giving Good Weight to Multilingualism in South Africa

Kathleen Heugh

For the better part of this century educators and commissions of enquiry into the state of education in Africa have concurred that the primary language of the school pupil is the language through which education, and primary education at the very least, should occur. As each formerly colonised territory in Africa has achieved independence, policy formulation for the newly independent state has been generated, as might be expected, by the new ruling elite. The last four decades have shown us that very often the articulation of policy, particularly language policy has more to do with a sense of political expediency than reasons of economic or educational development. Over the last ten years scholars on the continent have argued that language policy is not only too government or top-down in orientation, but that it should be integrated into the national plan for development (see Bamgbose and Chumbow in Alexander, 1992), of which economic development is a major component. Other scholars, such as Akinnaso, Siatchitema, and Tripathi point out that there is often a mismatch between policy and the plan for implementation, particularly with regard to language policy in education. Thus the implementation plan has little potential for achieving the goals of the policy. The situation in South Africa is one in which a matrix of contradictory threads, both supportive of multilingualism and antithetical to it, have become entangled despite the progressive commitment to equality of language rights in the country's recently crafted constitution.

From the early days of resistance to the segregationist policies of British colonial rule, followed under the Union of South Africa, African language speaking people identified English as a language of potential liberation. It represented access to international ideas and discourse as well as economic security. After the National Party came to power in 1948, it commissioned an enquiry into the educational needs of African people within a context of separate and unequal development. The result was the Bantu Education Act of 1953 which foregrounded 'mother-tongue instruction' for reasons other than those offered in the UNESCO study *The Use of Vernacular Languages in Education*, ironically published in the same year. Mother-tongue education under apartheid was to be used as an instrument for segregation and limiting access to higher education as well as political and economic power. Those few students who were able to reach secondary school were obliged to switch medium of instruction from a single 'mother-tongue' to two languages, English and Afrikaans (half of the subjects in each of these). It was the rigid implementation of this 50-50 policy in secondary school, interpreted as a mechanism to prevent adequate access to English, that precipitated the SOWETO student uprising of 1976. In understanding the unfolding developments in relation to language policy issues in South Africa, it is important to appreciate the extent to which English captured the imagination of disenfranchised people and assumed the status of a language of liberation.

Whereas elsewhere in Africa doubts about the role of English as an apparent vehicle for liberation were beginning to reverberate, it seemed obvious that English in South Africa needed to be identified as a lingua franca and predominant language of education. The turmoil in education and broader society, after a short respite following 1976, began to escalate in the early 1980s. The response from government was to proclaim a succession of 'state(s) of emergency' which engaged in extensive repression and intimidation. A number of radical educators and activists had in the meantime come together as The Education Co-ordinating Council of South Africa (ECCSA) in 1983. ECCSA spawned a number of educational initiatives, one of which was the National Language Project (NLP) which was established in 1986 as a community-based project, under the directorship of Neville Alexander. Initially, the NLP's purpose was to popularise language policy issues. In particular the focus was to popularise the notion of English as a 'linking language' and ensure that all students at school had adequate and appropriate access to the language. In addition the NLP strove to raise awareness about the importance of African languages in education, especially in relation to literacy and accessible second language programmes in these languages.

> English is going to play a pivotal role in the shaping of a new South Africa/Azania since it provides us with a convenient lingua franca/linking language through which the concepts of a new unified society may be transmitted.

> While it is the policy of the NLP to promote the notion of English as a lingua franca/linking language, it is also the policy of the NLP to promote all the languages of South Africa. People need to be able to communicate with one another through the languages spoken in the region in which they live... if one lives in Natal, one needs to communicate through English and Zulu. If one lives in the Western Cape... one needs to converse through Afrikaans, English and Xhosa.... The fundamental aim is effective communication (NLP, 1989 in Alexander, 1989, 69-70).

This amounted to bilingualism, at the very least for every South African, but preferably trilingualism. There had, of course, been an official policy of Afrikaans-English bilingualism, but African languages had never before been profiled in this way. Thus far, the teaching of African languages at tertiary institutions had been based on a grammar-translation approach to L1 speakers who would teach L1 learners. L2 pedagogy in African languages was sorely neglected. The early practical work of the NLP consequently was three-pronged: the development of a communicative approach to the teaching and learning of Xhosa (the African language of the region in which the NLP was based) as a second language; a communicative approach to teaching ESL to African language speakers; and L1 literacy to disadvantaged speakers of Afrikaans.[1] Since the intervention of activists in the mainstream education system was simply not possible during the 1980s, the NLP worked with community-based, church and trade union structures. Eventually by 1990 the NLP was able to trial a communicative ESL programme with Xhosa speaking learners in a disadvantaged school in an 'informal settlement'[2]. This intervention, like each of the NLP's other ESL programmes with various community-based organisations in the late 1980s, was to be a dismal failure. There seemed to be very little evidence of successful learning of English taking place.[3]

In the meantime, sociolinguists in the NLP were reviewing the relationship between language policy in education in South Africa against a backdrop of developments and critiques elsewhere in Africa and this brought about a significant shift of the thinking within the project. The inability of governments, in general, to articulate and implement policies which would ensure educational success for the majority of school pupils has formed a familiar pattern on this continent, as indeed it has elsewhere. Alexander recognised the significance of the critiques of Bamgbose and Chumbow and he, together with the NLP, refined a set of language planning proposals for post-apartheid South Africa. In these proposals, a triangulation of principles was foregrounded: language planning from below; the rehabilitation of the status and use of African languages in education; and the integration of language planning with the national development and economic plan.

The NLP, at the time, was the only organisation in South Africa which was primarily focused on language policy and planning initiatives. Most language practitioners, academics and activists had other immediate preoccupations, thus the developments in the NLP moved ahead of the language debates taking place elsewhere. The context in the mainstream discussions continued to give primacy to the role of English, on the one hand, and a protected status for Afrikaans from the powerful 'white' Afrikaans-speaking lobby.

Political developments were moving with great rapidity. The terrible repression of the mid-1980s had given way to an unbanning of many political organisations in 1990. The political movements were all attempting to formulate policies and

---

[1] The NLP is based in the Western Cape where the majority of people speak Afrikaans. Many of these are from severely disadvantaged communities unlike the majority of the 'white' Afrikaans-speaking community. Other literacy providers preferred to focus on literacy to adults, from the beginning in English as a second language. In reality, English was more akin to a foreign language for most learners.

[2] Also known as a 'squatter camp'.

[3] It needs to be stressed that the NLP staff were all well-trained, experienced teachers who were considered to be very good at their work.

positions prior to the beginning of formal political negotiations which would result in a shift of power.

The NLP had to look beyond South Africa in order to find some answers to the failure of its own ESL programmes and evidence of similar failure in mainstream education. By 1991 it became clear that the NLP was moving in the direction of proposing a multilingual model of education for schools. During a conference, 'The International Conference on Democratic Approaches to Language Planning and Standardisation'[4], which the NLP hosted in 1991, attention was repeatedly drawn to the terms, 'multilingual schools' and 'multilingual education'. Rama Kant Agnihotri, University of Delhi, demonstrated multilingual classroom strategies to a wide audience and this particular demonstration was to have significant reverberations in the country for the next several years. The conference also facilitated the establishment of useful links with educators and sociolinguists elsewhere on the continent.

The following year, 1992, was to prove to be the second major turning-point for the project. During the process of grappling for answers to both the project's failure with ESL programmes and its commitment to multilingual schooling, we discovered a powerful cocktail of work, notably Tollefson (1991) and the contributions to Skutnabb-Kangas and Cummins (eds., 1988), which had an extraordinary effect on the language in education debates inside the country immediately thereafter. The following words captured the collective essence of these scholars and riveted our imagination:

> Monolingualism is a psychological island. It is an ideological cramp. It is
> an illness, a disease which should be eradicated as soon as possible,
> because it is dangerous for world peace. It is a reflection of *linguicism.*
> (Skutnabb-Kangas, 1988, 13)

The connection, of course, between racism in this country and a language policy used to carry out the grand design of apartheid had all along been painfully apparent. The more covert linguicism in operation via the hegemonic drive of English monolingualism in South Africa, whilst frequently debated by educators, had not been closely examined from a structural point of view.

At exactly this time, the ANC commissioned, through an intermediary structure, a National Education Policy Investigation (NEPI). The NLP was considered by the ANC to be too left-wing and its participation in this exercise was consequently limited. However, the NLP co-operated with the process and liaised closely with NEPI researchers and referred them to Skutnabb-Kangas, Cummins and the work supported by the National Languages and Literacy Institute of Australia (NLLIA), particularly that of Joseph Lo Bianco and Jerzy Smolicz.

---

[4] The conference was held by the NLP in association with the Department of Linguistics at the University of Cape Town It was the first occasion when scholars from across the continent were able to attend a sociolinguistic conference in South Africa after a lengthy period of academic and other boycotts directed against the government.

By July 1992 both the NLP and the NEPI researcher working in this area, Kathy Luckett, had come to a similar conclusion. The majority of South African school children were failing in a system based on subtractive bilingualism for speakers of African languages. Speakers of English and Afrikaans, however, were in schools where additive bilingualism was facilitated. The only reasonable solution would be to promote additive bilingual schooling for all learners. This would mean the maintenance of the home language for each learner alongside the introduction of a second and possibly a third language. Heugh (1992, 1995) noted the relevance of Phillipson's analysis of the failure of policies for English learning in postcolonial settings, and Skutnabb-Kangas's insistence that minority children would fail in countries where bilingualism was not a goal. The goal in South Africa had become, by default, English, after 1977 when government dropped its insistence that African language speaking pupils learn through Afrikaans. English had become the only target. The mother tongue was retained as a language of learning only as far as the fourth year of school, thereafter all effort was directed at an unattainable target.

The notion of additive bilingualism took root, despite the odds against it in the mainstream environment. It was kept alive in the ANC language in education working group which followed the NEPI process during 1993. The powerful voices in the ANC, however, were far more committed to the use of English as the dominant language of education, as the following demonstrates:

> An education system with English-medium instruction and 10 years of free and compulsory State-funded schooling is envisaged by the African National Congress (Argus on Sunday, 4 April 1993).

Nevertheless, last minute constitutional negotiations between the National Party and the ANC resulted in the declaration of 11 official languages for the country by December 1993. In the meanwhile, Alexander had established the Project for the Study of Alternative Education in South Africa (PRAESA), at the University of Cape Town. Together with the NLP, this project focused on developing a comprehensive proposal for multilingual education. The core arguments hinged on the work of Cummins and Skutnabb-Kangas (see Heugh, Siegrühn, & Plüddemann, 1995). By the end of 1995 the Minister of Education began consulting the NGO sector on a language in education policy which would be in synchrony with the constitution. The conviction with which the arguments for additive bilingualism were made simply outweighed other arguments. Thus proposals for multilingual education and based on additive bilingualism became the foundation stones of a new language in education policy announced in mid-1997. The international weight given the arguments for additive bilingualism and the maintenance of the home language, particularly in the work of Tove Skutnabb-Kangas, cannot be overestimated in this regard. It is doubtful whether the work of the NLP in conjunction with PRAESA would have been so well received without it.

The task which now lies ahead, however, is to convince government to implement the new policy. Unfortunately, the history of education elsewhere in Africa demonstrates that this is extremely difficult to accomplish.

Education for All - In Whose Language?

Birgit Brock-Utne

African languages in the development discourse

One of the strategies in the globally unequal distribution of power and resources involves the invalidation of the non-material resources of dominated groups, including their languages and cultures. Non-material resources can be invalidated by making them invisible, as for instance African languages are in much development discourse, or by stigmatising them as handicaps or problems, rather than resources, as in minority discourses in Euro-American contexts.

The sociolinguists Tove Skutnabb-Kangas and Robert Phillipson (1996b) point out the striking fact that in much educational policy work, even in policies on education for all, the role of language is seldom considered. This myopia on the part of the donors and the researchers who guide them, they claim, continues a pattern set at the first UNESCO conference of African Ministers of Education, in 1961, which set a target for universal literacy, but gave little thought to the language in which literacy should be achieved. The same was true of a succession of British conferences held to 'assist' colonies to organise their education systems when they became independent states in the 1960s. Invariably language was given very little attention, and if raised, the focus was only on the learning of English (see Skutnabb-Kangas & Phillipson, 1996b; Phillipson, 1992; Brock-Utne, 2000).

African languages as languages of instruction

It has always been felt by African educationists that the African child's major learning problem is a linguistic one. Instruction is given in a language that is not normally used in the immediate environment, a

language which neither the learner nor the teacher understands and uses
well enough. (Obanya, 1980, 88)

Pai Obanya, who has for many years been the Head of the UNESCO office,
BREDA, in Senegal, belongs to the group of African educationists who are ardent
defenders of the use of African languages as languages of instruction. Unfortunately
there is also a large group of African educationists who favour the continued use of
the colonial languages as the language of instruction. This is so even though we
know that ninety percent of the population in Africa today speak only African
languages. Yet one talks about English-speaking, French-speaking, and Portuguese-
speaking Africa, according to the language of the former coloniser spoken only by a
small elite. And these former colonial languages are the languages of instruction in
secondary schools and all of the universities of Africa, and often even in the
primary schools.

Paulo Freire (1985) defined the practice of having a foreign language imposed
upon the learner for studying another subject as a violation of the structure of
thinking. Yet this is the situation most African children find themselves in today.

Tove Skutnabb-Kangas is concerned about the language death which is often
caused by western schooling introduced into Africa. She argues (1999a, 176) that
this schooling:

> has accelerated the death/murder of languages which without formal
> education had survived for centuries or millennia. One of the main agents
> in killing languages is thus the linguistic genocide which happens in
> formal education, every time indigenous or minority children or
> dominated group children, even if they are a majority in terms of
> numbers, are educated in a dominant language.

I have elsewhere looked into the educational language policies of several countries
in Sub-Saharan Africa (Brock-Utne, 2000). I note two distinct trends:

- a strengthening of dominant languages which, in the context of Africa, means
  the former colonial languages. I have analysed the role played by bilateral and
  multi-lateral donors, western scholars and the African elites.
- a growing concern among African ministers of education and some
  intellectuals for a preservation and revival of African languages as languages
  of instruction in at least the primary schools in Africa.

There is now a battle between these two trends all over Africa. In Tanzania English
has been strengthened to the detriment of Kiswahili in the secondary school system.
Some years after independence a reform was worked out for introducing Kiswahili
as the language of instruction throughout the secondary school system as well as at
the university level, beginning with Kiswahili as the language of instruction in two
subjects, Kiswahili and siasa (political education). But then implementation of the
reform was stopped. I have elsewhere described the politics behind this reversal,
where the British Council played a major role through its 'language-support
project' (Brock-Utne, 1993, 2000). Under the pressure of the introduction of multi-
party 'democracy', the subject 'siasa' has now been renamed and redefined as
'social science' and is taught in English. In Namibia the African languages lost their

position in school after independence and the introduction of English as the language of instruction (Brock-Utne, 1997). Madagascar, one of the very few countries in Africa that had succeeded in having an African language, Malagasy, as the language of instruction in secondary school, reverted to French in 1988 because there were no more textbooks in Malagasy. No donor would help them develop and print new textbooks in Malagasy but the Alliançe Française gave them new textbooks in French as a type of 'development aid'.

In the *World Declaration on Education for All*, which came out of the donor conference 'Education for All' held in Thailand in 1990, education through the mother tongue is mentioned just once, in the following sentence: 'Literacy in the mother tongue strengthens cultural identity and heritage' (Article 5).

At mid-term conferences to evaluate the progress of the Education for All initiative, some African Ministers of Education expressed concern, along with representatives of UNESCO, about lack of the use of African languages as languages of instruction (Brock-Utne, 2000). Quite recently several countries in Africa, among them Zambia, Uganda, Ghana, Niger, and Guinea, have defined new language policies where African languages are strengthened as languages of instruction.

The role of the World Bank

There has, over the last ten years, been a shift in the World Bank's rhetoric concerning the value of the use of the mother tongue as a language of instruction (ibid.). The pedagogical value of having the mother tongue as the language of instruction - at least in the first grades - is now acknowledged by the Bank. But to analyse the rhetoric of the Bank is not enough. As Jones (1997, 367), rightly notes, a key policy question facing analysts of World Bank operations is the issue of which practices the Bank is prepared to either support or reject, and how it backs its views with finance.

The World Bank claims that it cannot impose an educational language policy on any African country. Each country must itself determine the language policy it sees as best suited to local particularities. To this Alamin Mazrui (1997, 39) remarks:

> This same institution that has been coercing African governments into overhauling their educational structures virtually overnight, has suddenly become mindful of the national sovereignty of these countries and of their right to linguistic self-determination.

I have come across the same attitude among Nordic donors when I have maintained that the most important educational aid we could give to Africa would be help strengthen its own languages. I have then been told that educational language policy is an internal matter, one in which we should not intervene. This might be an appropriate attitude were it not for others like the British Council and French government aid bodies, as well as strong publishing interests in the North, already intervening, and if we consistently respected the same principle on other matters in the organization of the education system in Africa.

Mazrui's analysis shows that the World Bank merely pays lip-service to the claim that mother tongue instruction in Africa would be the preferable choice. In contrast to UNESCO, which holds that the use of the mother tongue ought to be extended to as late a stage in education as possible, the World Bank seems to see the use of African languages in the early grades of primary school as just a strategy for a smoother transition to the European languages as languages of instruction. The World Bank continues to place great emphasis on the reduction of government subsidies in education, though such subsidies are indispensable to the promotion of instruction in local languages.

It is easy to agree with Mazrui when he exclaims: 'In effect, the vaunted freedom of choice over education allowed to African nations by the democrats of the World Bank is no freedom at all!' (Mazrui, 1997, 40). He cites the example of a World Bank loan to the Central African Republic, supposedly intended to improve the quality and accessibility of elementary education, but which came with a package of conditions that required the nation to import textbooks (and even French language charts) directly from France and Canada. It has been estimated that due to similar World Bank projects and linkages, over 80% of schoolbooks in 'francophone' Africa are now produced in France.

The World Bank's policies not only position the West so that it retains control over the intellectual destiny of African children. They also continue to weaken and destroy infrastructural facilities, primarily publishing houses, for the technical production of knowledge locally. Textbooks are of crucial importance for the publishing and printing industry in Africa, as they represent 90 percent or more of the total book market in Africa. In terms of sheer cost effectiveness, western publishers would find it far more difficult to participate in this World Bank agenda if the languages of instruction in African countries were African rather than European languages. Mazrui claims that because of the Euro-linguistic policy of Western donors (and, I would like to add, much of the African elite), the intellectual self-determination of Africa has become more difficult. To quote Mazrui (1997, 46):

> For the time being, the prospects of a genuine intellectual revolution in Africa may depend in no small measure on a genuine educational revolution that involves, at the same time, a widespread use of African languages as media of instruction.

Language: A Diversity Category Beyond All Others

Ofelia García

The last four decades of the 20th century brought the world closer to recognizing and valuing its differences both globally and locally. In the United States, the ethnic boom of the 1960s resulted in executive actions and legislation guaranteeing civil rights and equal educational opportunity to groups who had been excluded previously, including people of color, women, those with different gender preferences and religious persuasions, the disabled, speakers of languages other than English (LOTEs) or of varieties of English that show non-standard features. Groups that had previously been oppressed demanded equal protection, and societal institutions, including schools, were forced to make accommodations to respect their individual rights.

But although all schools have found it comfortable to at least pay lip-service to teaching for diversity, it is the category of language that has remained, as we will see, most problematic. There are four reasons, discussed below, for the resistance to the inclusion of languages other than English (LOTEs) and varieties of English with non-standard features in U.S. schools:

- The teachers' conceptualization of language as simply an instrument for communication
- The schools' standard English identity
- The teachers' need for control of learning
- The schools' reluctance to reallocate resources.

Teachers learn early that language is simply an instrument for communication that can be used to help students develop knowledge or to control the class. But besides a utilitarian function, language links us to our identity because it connects us to our mother or initial caregiver. And although one develops a different identity from one's mother through schooling and socialization, the mother or caregiver's identity, outwardly manifested in the child's mother tongue or way of using language, remains a part of one's life, giving sense to oneself. Teachers who do not affirm the students' multiple language identities regardless of how well they speak, read, and/or write standard English, plunge them into self-oblivion and disconnect them from their relationship with parents, relatives, a community of speakers, and often a rich body of literature. Insisting that students of language minority background function as English monolingual speakers locks them into minority status. It robs them of their ability to connect to another place and time in which their other language identity was valued and worthy of majority status, was spoken by the rich and powerful, and was even used in schools.

U.S. public schools have taken a role in Americanizing and teaching English to the many immigrants who have come to our shores. But not all schools, all the time, have had an English-only language identity. There is also a historical tradition of languages other than English being used in the nation's schools. And in the last four decades, as immigration has increased dramatically especially from non-European and developing countries, at a time of globalization and increased need for a sophisticated technologically-enriched education, U.S. schools have used languages other than English for three distinct purposes. One, LOTEs have been used to accelerate familiarization with U.S. culture and English language acquisition. Two, using LOTEs enables the large number of U.S. English language learners to continue to be educated. Finally, developing U.S. citizens' literate uses of LOTEs will be an invaluable societal resource in the globalized market of the 21st century.

Another reason for the resistance of teachers to using LOTEs is that they have often been prepared to be in complete control of the classroom and of the students' learning. They have been educated to believe that their use of standard English, as measured by a test, should be the goal for an educated person. Thus, they set about eradicating all linguistic features that do not conform to their own and to those of the test. Allowing students to use their LOTEs and features of English with which teachers are not familiarized not only violates their sense of language correctness, but robs them of their presumed entitlement to be in total control of the classroom. Teachers who allow the use of the students' language in classrooms must suspend their authoritative role, must trust their students' ability to use language to make sense of their own world.

Finally, the teaching of a language other than English in schools or even the true understanding of some varieties of English requires bilingual or bidialectal personnel, people who can extend the children's world by making sense of their use of the other language. For example, without a bilingual teacher only static maintenance of a LOTE will result, with the development of biliteracy not possible. The same is true in many bidialectal situations where only someone deeply familiar with the ways of speaking and using language in a particular community will be able to extend the students' ways of using language.

It is clear then, that respecting language diversity and affirming the multiple language identities of U.S. students requires a difficult shift for teachers and schools alike. We turn now to what has been done in the recent past, before we consider what must be done to prepare for the new millennium.

Language diversity in U.S. classrooms: Where we've been

After the 1960s both special education and bilingual education were hailed as solutions to serve the disabled and the language minority population. In both cases, the educational approach was eventually mandated by judicial action, as the disabled and English language learners demanded equal educational opportunity. But for the most part, the educational programs that resulted took a deficit approach in educating these two groups, looking only at what the students did not have with regards to regular students. These students were seen as special, limited, and teachers were prepared only to notice their deficiencies, rather than their strengths. The categories for educational service and treatment became more and more medical in nature, an attempt to remedy the students' deficiencies.

Little by little the initial bilingual classrooms of the early 1970s where students who spoke languages other than English at home had been taught in English and Spanish in recognition of their multiple language identities started to disappear. This change was spurred by two societal changes. On the one hand, the pendulum had started to swing back in what Fishman has identified internationally as the rise and fall of the ethnic revival. The affirmation of the Spanish language identity of U.S. Latinos, and in particular, of those of Mexican American and Puerto Rican descent, was short-lived. 'Black is beautiful' or 'Brown is beautiful' became an outdated slogan of the 1960s, with whiteness and an English language identity slowly recovering its pre-1960 eminence. On the other hand, the U.S. bilingual and bidialectal landscape had become more complex, as the Immigration Act was amended in 1965, and immigration from other Spanish speaking countries increased, countries without the colonial or historical relationship to the United States of Puerto Rico and Mexico, as well as from countries where other languages or other varieties of English were spoken.

As language and ethnic diversity increased throughout the 1980s, bilingual classrooms became more remedial and transitional in nature, with the other language being used on a limited basis, for a short period of time, and only in educating those who were not proficient in English in an effort to remedy the situation. Bilingual teachers, who for the most part held monolingual and bilingual certification, were used only to teach in these remedial segregated settings. And although bilingual teachers were able to impart content knowledge to students in those classrooms, the goal of many bilingual education programs became solely to teach English, using professionals who spoke the child's language. From an educational program that started out respecting and affirming the language identities of the student, bilingual education often became the conduit to suppress the minority language identity, while maintaining the separateness of the group in question and excluding them from meaningful communicative interaction with students of language majority background.

In an effort to move beyond the remedial transitional model, two-way dual language programs of bilingual instruction made a very limited comeback in the late 1980s and 1990s, with English speaking and English language learners taught together and with bilingualism a goal.

However, as the new millennium approaches, the education of U.S. language minorities has become even more conflicted. In the last five years, we have seen the passage of Proposition 227 in California, effectively ending all kinds of bilingual instruction in that state. And an attempt to claim Ebonics as a variety of African-American English has met with strong opposition. As the country has increased in language diversity, the movement toward Standards has taken afoot, effectively denying language differences and expecting the same level of standard English language proficiency of all. For example, in New York State, passing the English Language Arts Regents which requires a commencement level of standard written English will now be a requirement for graduation.

Research on bilingual and bidialectal populations effectively concludes that these populations cannot be compared to monolingual populations who use the school's language at home. Those who use a different language at home or use the English language differently from the way it is used in school are doubly-taxed in school, and thus the development of their standard majority language takes time (usually five to seven years) and can only be achieved through a rigorous educational plan. In the case of adolescent or adult speakers of other languages, those who have been well educated in the other language will acquire English faster than those who have had limited schooling in their native language.

In moving toward Standards, the nation talks about high standards in English and minimum competence in LOTEs, promoting English as the only language identity of successful U.S. citizens. Standards has come to be identified with Standard English only. Although we must work harder to get language minority students to perform academically in standard English, not to affirm the multiple language identities of the students we teach is to effectively disenfranchise a large part of the population, and to rob U.S. society of an improved opportunity to communicate with the world at large.

Language diversity in the classrooms of the new millennium: Affirming multiple language identities

The classrooms of the new millennium must have teachers who have been trained to understand the role that language plays in identity and the importance that languages other than English and different varieties of English hold for the language minority child's development. Teachers must understand that bilingualism and bidialectism are not absolutes, but are continua, and that all of us, regardless of language background, can move a little bit in these continua. And all teachers must be responsible for moving students along the two axes of the bilingualism/bidialectism continuum, not only acting responsibly to ensure that all students acquire standard English and accommodating their instruction to meet the needs of those students, but also promoting the use of the students' other languages and other ways of speaking in the curriculum, regardless of their ability in standard English.

In the classrooms of the new millennium all teachers would be responsible for teaching all children, adapting instruction and assessment to meet their needs. Thus, the classroom teacher would be responsible for the growth in English of the English language learner, while the student would interact with other English speakers within the classroom. Of course, there would always be a need for an English as a Second Language or a Bilingual teacher, but that teacher would work mostly with the classroom teacher (except, of course, in cases where the bilingual teacher is the classroom teacher), recommending activities to further the students' development, adapting instruction, documenting their growth, and negotiating instruction. And although specialized pull-out ESL services would be needed, these services would not interfere with the student's participation in the inclusive classroom. Assessment in English language ability, however, would always be different for these students, allowing for the differences created by the different language circumstances at home.

In the classrooms of the new millennium all teachers would also feel comfortable encouraging children to speak, read, and write in languages other than English or in varieties of English other than the Standard. They would have significant collections of children's literature in the many languages of the children. And teachers would encourage children to read out loud in other languages, not only affirming the child's multiple identities, but also opening up a multilingual/ multidialectal world for the other children. As in the case above, there would be a need for bilingual teachers, sometimes of different language backgrounds, who would work with the classroom teacher, suggesting books and developing material in the students' native languages, and assessing the students' bilingual and biliteracy development. But there would also be a need for a bilingual teacher who would provide instruction in the school's most numerous language other than English. Although literacy in this language would be taught separately to those who speak that LOTE at home and those who do not, there would also be project-oriented sessions for all children where the language other than English would be used as a medium of instruction. Again, assessment for the two groups would be different.

All teachers must take responsibility to affirm the many different language identities of students in the United States, including the standard English one, as well as the LOTE or non-standard one. Leaving the acquisition and development of standard English only to traditional English as a Second Language, English language specialists, or bilingual teachers minimizes opportunities for interaction with native English speakers and for development and growth. Only if all teachers take responsibility for all students, and do so consistently throughout the curriculum, will the standard English literacy crisis in which we find ourselves as a nation be solved. Likewise, leaving the maintenance and development of the language other than English only to the bilingual teacher may affirm the fortunate few who may be in these specialized classes, but it leaves most bilingual speakers without any societal recognition. It also stigmatizes the use of the language other than English as a mark of minority membership and often just of non-English speakers, instead of promoting it as a societal resource from which both minorities and majorities would benefit.

We must insist then that affirming the multiple language identities of U.S. students becomes one of the Standards in the new millennium. In doing so, Standards becomes differentiated from standardization, recognizing differences which must be taken into account in the increased performance of different groups. While it may be impossible for an English language learner to meet the same standard in English as a native English speaker, it would be likewise impossible for a LOTE learner to achieve the same standard in a LOTE as a native speaker of that language. Differentiating language standards for majority and minority populations, while demanding that all teachers be responsible for helping both groups achieve higher standards, is the only way of affirming the multiple language identities of U.S. citizens and at the same time ensure the equity in education that Tove Skutnabb-Kangas has defended in her work.

'This Place Nurtures my Spirit': Creating Contexts of Empowerment in Linguistically-diverse Schools

Jim Cummins

The 'quotation' in the title is wishful thinking. It expresses what I and every other contributor to this volume would hope that schools might at least aspire to achieve. Instead, as Tove Skutnabb-Kangas' writing and presentations have powerfully articulated, schools frequently inculcate shame among culturally diverse students, constrict their identities and their minds, and leave them spiritually numb rather than vibrant. This reality emerges clearly from the study carried out by Mary Poplin and Joseph Weeres in four multicultural urban schools in southern California, termed *Voices from the Inside: A Report on Schooling from Inside the Classroom* (1992). Among the 24,000 pages of interview transcriptions, essays, drawings, journal entries, and notes that formed the data for this study was a poignant observation by one of the students: '*This place hurts my spirit.*' Poplin and Weeres reported that the schools exhibited 'a pervasive sense of despair' largely as a result of the problematic relationships that were the norm in these schools:

> Relationships dominated all participant discussions about issues of schooling in the U.S. No group inside the schools felt adequately respected, connected or affirmed. Students, over and over again, raised the issue of care. What they liked best about school was when people, particularly teachers, cared about them or did special things for them. Dominating their complaints were being ignored, not being cared for and receiving negative treatment. (Poplin & Weeres, 1992, 19)

Clearly, schools do not have to be like this. Yet, these kinds of relationships, however well-intentioned on the part of educators, tend to be the norm rather than the exception when the language or language variety that students bring to school is constructed as a problem to be resolved or fixed. We see too few examples, at least in North America, of schools that have taken as their starting point the conviction that linguistically diverse students have the *right* to maintain and develop their mother tongue within the context of the school and that their cultural identities are worthy of respect and nurturing. We also see too few schools that take as their starting point the conviction that the languages and cultures that students bring to school are *resources* for other students, teachers, and the society as a whole (Ruiz,

1988). Although the major reason for this is the prevalence of coercive relations of power in most spheres of human endeavor, the lack of knowledge of documented alternatives also contributes to the perpetuation of destructive forms of schooling.

In this paper, I attempt to redress this lack of knowledge of alternatives by sketching three school models that have clearly succeeded in 'nurturing students' spirits' as well as expanding their options for both academic achievement and identity formation. The schools come from three different continents and I have chosen them because they illustrate well what is possible when we as educators change our orientation from focusing on *language as problem* to a focus on *language as right* and/or *language as resource*. In describing each school, I first provide a summary of its main features in tabular form and then draw out some of the commonalities that characterize all three programs. In each case, I draw primarily on book-length documentation relating to the school so there is ample scope for those interested to pursue further details. All three programs were 'mature' at the time the reports were written, ranging from approximately 10-20 years of operation. The information is accurate as of the time of the publications cited; however, schools evolve and personnel change so it is quite likely that the portraits presented here do not fully represent these schools as they are now. The point, however, is that they illustrate what educators, students, and communities *can* achieve when the ideology that permeates the school challenges the constricting and devaluing ideology that subordinated groups have typically endured in the wider society.

Richmond Road School

Location: New Zealand (Auckland)
Languages: Cook Islands, English, Maori, Samoan
Students: Cook Islands L1, English L1, Maori L1, Samoan L1
L1/L2%:   Model A: 100% English
                Model B: 50% Maori, 50% English
                Model C: 50% Samoan, 50% English
                Model D: 50% Cook Islands, 50% English

Goals: To affirm and incorporate the languages and cultures of the students within the school.

Results: By the end of elementary school, students' reading attainment improved dramatically compared to their performance in the first few years of schooling. Most children (26/35) in the cohort analyzed longitudinally were performing at or above grade expectations compared to only 3/35 who were at or above grade norms on entry to school. This contrasts with the pattern in large scale studies which showed similar students in New Zealand far below grade level with the gap increasing as students progressed through the grades (Elley, 1992).

Comments: The classes are organized in vertical family groupings rather than according to chronological age. Peer tutoring and cooperative learning are central to the instructional approach. Students stay in the same program from 5 to 13 years old and parents are given the choice of which model to enter. Thus, children from English-speaking backgrounds also entered the bilingual (Maori) program (Cazden, 1989; May, 1994).

Oyster Bilingual School

Location: USA (Washington, DC)
Languages: English, Spanish
Students: Approximately 60% Spanish L1 (primarily Salvadorean), 40% English L1 (about half African-American, half Euro-American).
L1/L2 %:   Approximately 50% Spanish, 50% English; students read in both languages each day. Each class is taught by two teachers, one responsible for English-medium instruction and one for Spanish-medium instruction. This organization is achieved through larger class sizes and assigning ancilliary or resource teacher allocations to classroom instruction.
Goals: The development of students who are biliterate and bicultural.
Results: Grade 3 Reading, Mathematics, Language, and Science scores were 1.6-1.8 median grade equivalents above norms (percentiles 74-81); grade 6 grade equivalents were 4.4-6.2 above norms (percentiles 85-96) (1991 data).
Comments: Started in 1971, the school has evolved a *social identities project* (Freeman, 1998) that communicates strongly to students the value of linguistic and cultural diversity. In the words of one of the teachers: 'It's much more than language.'

The Foyer Model of Trilingual/Bicultural Education

Location: Belgium (Brussels)
Languages: Dutch, French, and one of the following: Arabic, Italian, Spanish, Turkish
Students: Students from the following backgrounds: Italian (2 schools), Spanish (2 schools), Turkish (1 school) and Moroccan (1 school)
L1/L2%:
   Nursery school (ages 3-5):
          50% L1 (L1 grouping),
          50% Dutch (integrated in multi-ethnic groups)

Primary school (ages 6-12):
    Year 1:
        60% L1 (reading, writing, mathematics)
        30% Dutch-medium (L1 grouping)
        10% Dutch-medium (multi-ethnic groups)
    Year 2:
        50% L1 (language, culture)
        20% Dutch-medium (L1 grouping)
        30% Dutch-medium (multi-ethnic groups)
    Year 3+:
        10% L1
        90% Dutch-medium + French lessons (multi-ethnic groups)

Goals:
1. To prepare *all* children and teachers to live together in a complex, multicultural society;
2. To enable migrant minority children to acquire fluency and literacy in three languages by the end of elementary schooling;
3. To increase migrant children's opportunities for integration in both the host country and in their parents' countries of origin;
4. To increase family involvement in the school and society in general;

Results: Project students develop better L1 knowledge than those in monolingual Dutch schools, although their L1 knowledge is less than that of students in their countries of origin. Students also develop a level of Dutch sufficient to enable them to keep up with subsequent classes at secondary school, although there are still differences between them and Dutch-L1 Belgian students.

Comments: Started in 1981 by Foyer (a non-governmental organization concerned with the well-being of immigrant communities in Brussels), the project assumed as axiomatic that children should be taught in part by teachers of the same origin as themselves in order to support their sense of identity (Byram & Leman, 1989, Reid & Reich, 1992). According to the evaluation report on Dutch proficiency 'children in the experimental group succeed in catching up on most of their arrears in proficiency in the course of primary school' (Jaspaert & Lemmens, 1989, 47).

The deep structure of educational change

At a superficial level, these three programs have obvious similarities and differences. Each has developed over a number of years and each has demonstrated sustained positive results. Each of the programs also incorporates instruction through the mother tongue for children from linguistic minority backgrounds. However, the amounts of L1 instruction differ considerably, as do the school organization and patterns of contact/integration with students from the dominant language background.

Similar surface structure variation could be found in bilingual and trilingual programs around the world. This is not at all surprising in view of the variation of sociolinguistic and sociopolitical contexts within and between countries. What appears to be crucial for the success of any program (monolingual, bilingual, trilingual) in reversing patterns of academic failure among students of bilingual/bicultural heritage is the extent to which the patterns of interaction between educators and students in the school (henceforth *micro-interactions)* actively challenge the historical and current patterns of relationship between dominant and subordinated communities in the wider society (henceforth *macro-interactions*). The framework in Figure 1 expresses this point.

The framework proposes that relations of power in the wider society (macro-interactions), ranging from coercive to collaborative in varying degrees, influence both the ways in which educators define their roles and the types of structures that are established in the educational system.

Coercive relations of power refer to the exercise of power by a dominant individual, group, or country to the detriment of a subordinated individual, group or country. For example, in the past, dominant group institutions (e.g. schools) have required that subordinated groups deny their cultural identity and give up their languages as a necessary condition for success in the 'mainstream' society. For educators to become partners in the transmission of knowledge, culturally-diverse students were required to acquiesce in the subordination of their identities and to celebrate as 'truth' the perspectives of the dominant group (e.g. the 'truth' that Columbus 'discovered' America and brought 'civilization' to its indigenous peoples).

Collaborative relations of power, by contrast, reflect the sense of the term 'power' that refers to 'being enabled', or 'empowered' to achieve more. Within collaborative relations of power, 'power' is not a fixed quantity but is generated through interaction with others. The more empowered one individual or group becomes, the more is generated for others to share, as is the case when two people love each other or when we really connect with children we are teaching. Within this context, the term *empowerment* can be defined as *the collaborative creation of power*. Students whose schooling experiences reflect collaborative relations of power participate confidently in instruction as a result of the fact that their sense of identity is being affirmed and extended in their interactions with educators. They also know that their voices will be heard and respected within the classroom. Schooling amplifies rather than silences their power of *self*-expression.

Educator role definitions refer to the mindset of expectations, assumptions and goals that educators bring to the task of educating culturally diverse students. Educational structures refer to the organization of schooling in a broad sense that includes policies, programs, curriculum, and assessment. While these structures will generally reflect the values and priorities of dominant groups in society, they are not by any means fixed or static. As with most other aspects of the way societies are organized and resources distributed, educational structures are contested by individuals and groups.

Educational structures, together with educator role definitions, determine the micro-interactions between educators, students, and communities. These micro-interactions form an interpersonal or interactional space within which the acquisition of knowledge and formation of identity is negotiated. Power is created and shared within this interpersonal space where minds and identities meet. As such, these micro-interactions constitute the most immediate determinant of student academic success or failure.

Micro-interactions between educators, students, and communities are never neutral; in varying degrees, they either reinforce coercive relations of power or promote collaborative relations of power. In the former case, they contribute to the disempowerment of culturally diverse students and communities; in the latter case, the micro-interactions constitute a process of empowerment that enables educators, students, and communities to challenge the operation of coercive power structures.

In short, the framework (Cummins, 1996) suggests that the deep structure of educational change reflects the extent to which educators individually and collectively challenge the coercive power structure of the wider society. In what ways do the three programs sketched above challenge coercive structures and promote collaborative relations of power?

The collaborative creation of power in three school programs

Some commonalities are immediately obvious. All three schools articulate the value for individual students and their families of developing strong L1 proficiency in both oral and written modes. In doing so, they are challenging the still pervasive devaluation and sometimes 'linguicidal' orientation towards the mother tongues of subordinated groups in the wider society (Skutnabb-Kangas, 1999b) The goals of these schools reflect both *language as right* and *language as resource* orientations.

Figure 1. Coercive and collaborative relations of power manifested in macro- and micro-interactions

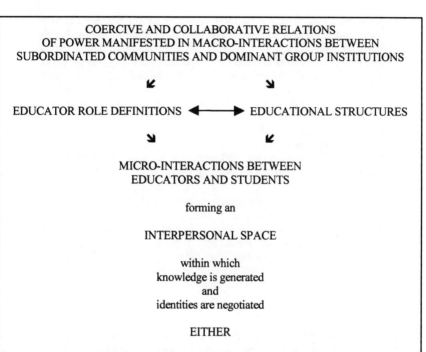

The following quotations from evaluation reports and other documentation illustrate other aspects of the deep structure of collaborative empowerment and willingness to challenge coercive relations of power that characterizes these schools.

Richmond Road. From Courtney Cazden's (1989) report come these quotes from teachers in Richmond Road that illustrate the ways in which identities are negotiated between teachers and students and among teachers from different backgrounds:

> We, as teachers, share our various ethnic backgrounds with each other. This helps to enrich us as a group working together. And not only that - the children also share their backgrounds with each other and with the teachers. The whole basis of the subject content matter of the school is who we are in *this* school. (p. 148)

I'm learning from the kids - their cultures, and not only that, their
languages as well. (p. 148)

It's taken a long time, but for me - like many people before - I think of
Richmond Road now as my *turangawaiwai* (a place to stand). It's the
place, and what it represents to me, in my mind and my heart. I left Fiji
with a chip on my shoulder, and I had nothing to do with Fijian people for
ten years. It's only by being involved with the philosophy here: we're
constantly telling people not to be sucked up in the system that says you
have to speak English and be like an English person before you can
succeed. And I realized that here *I* was, telling them to do these things,
and *I* wasn't even doing them myself. I had never spoken to *my* children
in Fijian. This was a big discovery to me. I felt good about myself before,
but as a *New Zealand* person. Whereas now, because of the experiences
that I had here, I feel totally different. (p. 149)

When I was a child, my mother never came near the school, because she
felt she didn't have a place in it. Here people come and feel they're
helping, and I think that's what's important-that everybody's got
something they can *do* for the school. If parents and children feel that
school is a special place for them, then the child benefits from this liaison.
When you, as a teacher, have the support of the parents who feel good
about the place, then there's nothing that can't be done for that child.
That's special about Richmond Road. And, of course, it's happening for
each ethnic group. (pp. 158-159).

When teachers who belong to groups with differential status in the wider society
share as equals within the school, this constitutes a challenge to the pattern of
coercive macro-interactions in the society. Similarly, when teachers *learn* from
their culturally diverse students, a shift in the pattern of power relations has
occurred. When the school creates a climate of two-way partnership with parents
from varied backgrounds and values the language and cultural resources they can
bring to school, collaborative empowerment is taking place.

Oyster Bilingual School. Rebecca Freeman provides detailed discourse
analyses that illustrate how the micro-interactions between educators and students
in Oyster bilingual school 'refuse' the discourse of subordination that characterizes
the wider society and most conventional school contexts. She points out that the
discourse practices in the school 'reflect an ideological assumption that linguistic
and cultural diversity is a resource to be developed by all students, and not a
problem that minority students must overcome in order to participate and achieve at
school' (1998, 233). Specifically, educators have *choices* in the way they organize
discourse practices and these choices entail significant consequences for both
language minority and majority students. The school *requires* all students to
become bilingual and biliterate in Spanish and English, and 'to expect, tolerate, and
respect diverse ways of interacting' (p. 27).

> Oyster's bilingual program has two complementary agendas that together challenge the unequal distribution of rights in mainstream US schools and society. First, the dual-language program is organized so that language minority and language majority students have the opportunity to develop the ability to speak two languages and to achieve academically through two languages. Second, the social identities project is organized so that language minority students gain experience seeing themselves as having the right to participate equally in the academic discourse, and the language majority students gain experience respecting that right. (p. 231)

In other words, the school 'aims to promote social change on the local level by socializing children differently from the way children are socialized in mainstream U.S. educational discourse' (p. 27).

> Rather than pressuring language minority students to assimilate to the positively evaluated majority social identity (white middle-class native English-speaking) in order to participate and achieve at school, the Oyster educational discourse is organized to positively evaluate linguistic and cultural diversity. ... this socializing discourse makes possible the emergence of a wide range of positively evaluated social identities, and offers more choices to both language minority and language majority students than are traditionally available in mainstream US schools and society. The Oyster educators argue that students' socialization through this educational discourse is the reason that [limited English proficient] language minority, and language majority students are all participating and achieving more or less equally. (p. 27)

There is an obvious congruence between Freeman's account of why and how the Oyster bilingual school succeeds so well and the framework presented in Figure 1.

The Foyer Model. A number of themes run through the various evaluation reports of the Foyer project. One is the necessity for schools to focus directly on issues of *identity* if they are to prepare students to thrive in a complex multilingual multicultural social context. In Brussels (and Belgium as a whole), French is the more prestigious language but Dutch is the majority language. Because of the similarity of languages, Spanish and Italian children often acquire French on the street and are frequently more fluent in French than their Dutch-speaking peers. These students speak their L1 in the home and frequently visit their countries of origin during the summer. So three languages permeate many aspects of their lives and constitute significant components of their *Belgian* identity.

At one level the school simply reflects and positively valorizes this multilingual and multicultural reality. However, the apparent logic and 'obviousness' of this approach masks its uniqueness and the challenge it constitutes to the educational status quo. Unlike more traditional schools that ignore and (implicitly or explicitly) devalue students' home language and culture, Foyer communicates to students (and their parents) the fact that their languages and cultures are *resources* that provide them with expanded options or *choices* with respect to both identity and future life choices (e.g. employment possibilities, place of residence, etc.).

Also clear from the Foyer case study is the fact that trilingualism can be developed at no cost to students' achievement in the dominant language of society and school (Dutch). Although the evaluation comparisons involve small numbers, it is clear that teachers, researchers, and parents consider the program to be highly successful with most students coming close to Dutch (L1) norms by the end of elementary school.

In short, the organizational structures of the project together with the ways in which educators have defined their roles or identities result in a pattern of micro-interactions that expand the identity options and academic opportunities available to language minority students. The *language as resource* orientation that permeates the ethos of the Foyer schools challenges and refutes the *language as problem/minorities as inferior* orientation that characterizes more typical educational contexts.

Conclusion

The three programs that have been reviewed suggest that the negotiation of identity in the interactions between educators and minority students is central to students' academic success or failure. An image of the society that students will graduate into and the kind of contributions they can make to that society is embedded implicitly in the interactions between educators and students. These interactions reflect both the organizational structures that have been implemented (e.g. L1 promotion or L1 suppression) and the ways in which educators have defined their roles with respect to the purposes of education in general and culturally diverse students and communities in particular. Are we preparing students to accept the societal status quo (and, in many cases, their own inferior status therein) or are we preparing them to participate actively and critically in their society as equal partners with those who come from dominant group backgrounds? This perspective clearly implies that in situations where coercive relations of power between dominant and subordinated groups predominate, the creation of interpersonal spaces where students' identities are validated will entail a direct challenge by educators (and students) to the societal power structure. School reform efforts that fail to challenge coercive relations of power rarely succeed because they do not address the causes of school failure.

Dual Language Models and Intergenerational Inspirations

Dawn Wink and Joan Wink

This chapter is written as a tribute to the Tove we know and love: philosopher, professor, writer, speaker, gardener, farmer, challenger of assumptions, and loving friend.

The perspective of this article will be based on the spirit of all that we have learned from Tove. For example, pre-Tove:

- we believed in the separation of the personal and the professional; now, we believe the personal and professional are parts of the whole which cannot be separated;
- we believed in linear-speak and the use of academic-ese; now, we believe in finding our own unique voice and crafting it to be meaningful for others;
- we believed in leaving our passion at home; now, we believe in living our passions;
- we believed that challenging assumptions would make us vulnerable girls; now, we believe that challenging assumptions makes us strong women;
- we believed that ambiguous contradictions should be clarified, cleaned up, or crushed; now, we believe that ambiguous contradictions are inherent in life and often can become a path which beckons to new ideas, insights, and more complex understandings;
- we believed that chaos was bad; now, we believe that chaos can be creative and eventually, productive;
- we believed that utopias were unattainable; now, we believe there are many utopias.

The purpose of this chapter is two-fold: to articulate differences among the immersion models; and, to demonstrate how the human interactions with Tove fostered a passion which joins the personal and professional for a Mom (Joan) and her daughter (Dawn). This specific study was conducted by Dawn and led her to question her assumptions – some of which were learned from Joan and Tove.

The various immersion models are often confused. Simultaneous and contradictory meanings result in misinformation. When misinformation is deliberately spread with deadly consequences for many language minority students, it becomes disinformation (Cummins, 1996). This immersion confusion makes it is easy for some who have an English-Only agenda to use misinformation and disinformation to further their own political goals. (For more thorough discussion of the latest research on dual language models of education, including the bilingual models, see Wink, J., 2000).

Dual language models of immersion

Bilingual (dual or two-way) immersion is designed to serve majority and minority students. The goals are bilingualism/biliteracy, high academic achievement, and positive intergroup relations in seven (K-6) years. The bilingual teachers are credentialed. French Canadian immersion is used in the US to refer to a dual language program which historically serves only language majority students. The goals and teachers' preparation is the same as in bilingual immersion. The French Canadian model is often cited as 'that immersion program in Canada which works'. It is effective for those enrolled: language majority students.

Structured English immersion is the opposite of the Canadian model. It is designed to serve *only* language minority students. The goal is English dominance within one year.

With the growing awareness of linguistic human rights, dual language immersion programs are often cited as the best manner to provide minority students with equitable education, as well as creating bilingualism in language majority students. Ideally, minority and majority students exit the program fully bilingual and achieving high levels of academic success in both languages. Gradually, researchers are beginning to challenge the assumption that *all* dual language immersion programs provide equity for minority students.

Reflecting on one research project

The following dialogue took place on a beautiful day as we were in the park with Dawn's two sons, Wyatt (age, 2½) and Luke (age 6 months). As Wyatt came barreling down the slide, his pant legs rose above his hiking books and revealed his wool, homemade socks which were a mixture of various shades of greens, grays, and maroons. These socks triggered the following conversation.

> 'Mom,' Dawn began, 'can you imagine Tove taking the time to make these little socks for Wyatt? They have come to exemplify Tove for me. Think of all of the writing, speaking, and teaching she is doing internationally, and yet, she takes time to knit these socks for Wyatt.'

This conversation of hand-knit socks and Tove led to our reflections on Dawn's research project about dual language immersion. We are constantly amazed at the power of the interconnections between our personal and professional lives.

Assumption number one: the one-size-fits-all myth

Dawn: Mom, you always taught me that bilingual immersion programs addressed the needs of both language groups: majority and minority. However, that was not true in my research project. Spanish was the medium of instruction, however the type of Spanish spoken was simplified to serve the English-dominant students. The data reflect that this modified Spanish did not foster development of high levels of literacies and cognitive development in the native Spanish-speakers. In the early grades, I found very few challenging language activities to meet the needs of the students who entered the program speaking Spanish as their first language.

Joan: Dawn, I also taught you that there are many ways to sabotage good pedagogy. Dual immersion is good pedagogy, but different groups of students have different sociocultural experiences and different academic needs at different times in their learning. Maybe the Spanish-dominant students in your study would have benefited from a more authentic and richer use of the language which demanded a higher level of proficiency?

So, what did you recommend?

Dawn: For true language enrichment and literacy development to occur, a dual language immersion program must have cognitively demanding and critically reflective processes built into the curriculum *at the very beginning* specifically for the language minority students (Wink, D., 1997, 72).

The data reflect that the Spanish-dominant students did not receive cognitively and linguistically demanding tasks in their own language from the very first day of school. Also, the Spanish-dominant students did not have access to oral language development in English. The parents' voice of the English-dominant students was more powerful with the decision makers at the district level, successfully silencing the wishes of the Spanish-dominant parents (ibid., 76).

Joan: Dawn, it seems you are finding a couple of different things in the data. First, when it comes to curriculum and pedagogy, one-size-does-not-fit-all. Second, there are many hidden (and, not so hidden) factors which affect teaching and learning.

Assumption number two: the equality myth

Dawn: Mom, I used to think that students act as peer language models for one another. However, the data reflect that even the Spanish-dominant students are so aware of the inequality of languages and power that they, too, begin using English as soon as possible, not only with the English-speaking students, but also with each other. This seems to be to be a perfect example of Tove's ideas about the hierarchy of languages. I also discovered that the Spanish-dominant students produced the least amount of writing in Spanish. Simply put: They knew more Spanish, and they wrote less than the English-dominant students.

Joan: Dawn, I also taught you that there are a lot of myths which drive pedagogy. In this case, let's call it the equality myth which goes something like this: This-is-America-and-all-kids-are-equal. However, Dawn, what did you recommend in this particular study?

Dawn: In my study, the Spanish-dominant students were very aware of the hegemony of English and could express it in multiple ways, but many adults involved with the program were unaware or, even more importantly, unwilling to acknowledge it. I recommended that all involved sit down and talk about this. This reality must be acknowledged and discussed by all participants so that the necessary actions can be taken toward creating a program which meets the needs of both groups of students. Treating language minority and majority students the same is treating them unequally.

Mom, I know that Tove believes that the wrong choice of medium of education is the main pedagogical reason for 'illiteracy' in the world. However, in my experience even the right choice can be sabotaged if bilingual immersion programs do not address the reality of the hierarchy of languages and power in the broader society in which the students live. It is exactly like Tove told me: Unless the needs of language minority students are specifically taken into consideration, even an 'ideal' program can reproduce unequal power relations through glorification, stigmatization, and rationalization.

In my study *glorification* of the dominant group took place as the parents of the English-dominant children were the main people involved in policy making which placed the needs of the majority over the needs of the minority. *Stigmatization* of the minority students was evident as Spanish-dominant parents were effectively excluded from active participation by sending home information in English and conducting family meetings in English. Even the Spanish-dominant students soon refused to speak Spanish with each other because of the stigmatization of their language and culture. *Rationalization* was seen as the language minority students' lack of academic success and their parent's lack of school involvement which is blamed on their own disinterest, socioeconomic standing, and cultural stereotypes. Language majority policy makers prefer to 'blame the victim', rather than look at the true nature of the immersion program. The fact that language minority students receive education through the medium of their own language is used to rationalize the continuation of unequal power structures. However, we must reflect critically and take action so that language minority students aren't in dual language programs to (*de facto*) serve as language models for the majority students, rather than to enhance their own academic and social achievement.

Conclusion

Based on this research project and our combined lived-experiences, we recommend that these three concepts (glorification, stigmatization, and rationalization) serve as an ideal method for the deconstruction of hidden (and, not so hidden) hegemonic processes which glorify the language majority group; stigmatize the language minority group; and rationalize the actions of the majority so that it appears to help the minority.

Previously, we avoided the use of the word, minority, because of the connotations of 'less' which are inherent in the word. Freire (Freire & Macedo, 1987) called our attention to this initially by clarifying that in the U.S. context 'minority' often refers to the majority of people who are not part of the dominant class. In reality, as with many other words, the semantic alteration of the term 'minority' serves to hide the many myths that are part of the mechanisms sustaining cultural dominance (ibid., 124-125). However, once again Tove calls on us to challenge our assumptions. She cuts through 'well-meaning intentions' by pointing out that by ceasing to use the word 'minority' we actually rob minority students of their only protection under international law. Unlearning is not always easy (Wink, J., 2000; see Cummins, 1996, for more on the use of majority and minority).

Since Tove is the one who taught us to always seek our own utopias, we still believe that dual immersion programs have the potential to be a viable part of the academic agenda for the 21st century - but, only if there is courageous, moral leadership at the local level which will create a safe place where majority and minority together can challenge their own assumptions, speak honestly, and create a program which serves the diverse needs of both groups of students.

Integrative Comment: Living with Vision and Commitment

Robert Phillipson

Critical intellectuals

This book is a distillation of the experience and vision of many people who work with languages and who share a belief in the capacity of the human spirit to transcend some of the injustice and inhumanity that are all too present in the contemporary world. The words, the language, black symbols on white paper, mean that we can glimpse what each contributor stands for. The medium is the familiar one of print. Pointing this out can serve as a reminder that at the time of the transition from the medieval period to industrialisation and modernity, printing was one of the central preconditions for the establishment of 'national' languages and 'nation' states. In the global age the technologies, transnational links and 'international' languages that are part of our contemporary lives and identities have very different forms and functions, which is why a study of rights and language should be approached globally – in the sense of both the full geographical extent of our world and the full range of scholarly approaches.

The book itself may be a traditional product, but in bringing it to life the relatively new medium of electronic mail was indispensable. This means of communication will hopefully also facilitate follow-up: the addresses of authors have been included in the brief professional biographies so as to promote dialogue. And much still needs to be done to work for a more equitable world linguistic order.

The book is largely in the academic genre of scholarly papers, but the use of a variety of types of text - some integrating the personal and the professional, poems, narratives, simulated or recreated dialogues - demonstrates that different genres capture an intensity that is often absent in scholarly works. Thus while poems should ideally be experienced through sound, having access to them in written, visible text can allow for a variety of performance and experience. We are now able to read the first chapter in the book, on language as a 'treasure of knowledge', but when the text was initially delivered orally at a Nordic-Chilean Intercultural meeting in Santiago in March 1997, it was not for Kerttu Vuolab a question of reading or narrating how her mother passed on the cultural knowledge of an aboriginal pastoral community. Kerttu was acting the story, as she puts it. The imagery of her tale is also integral to her message and to the importance of language in our culture. The arrow symbolises the tongue, the power of the tongue, and the tongue as the source of food for survival in the world.

The tongue, our languages, our mother tongues, the other tongues, and the right to linguistic and cultural diversity, are at the heart of this book. Tove Skutnabb-Kangas, like the creative writer Ngũgĩ wa Thiong'o, 'dreams to change the world'. The vision of the critical intellectual and the novelist is fundamentally similar, even if their medium and audience may differ. The role of the intellectual, in the brilliant analysis of the Palestinian-American, Edward Said, is

> to raise embarrassing questions, to confront orthodoxy and dogma (rather than to produce them), to be someone who cannot easily be co-opted by governments or corporations... someone whose whole being is staked on a critical sense, a sense of being unwilling to accept easy formulas, or ready-made clichés, or the smooth, ever-so-accommodating confirmations of what the powerful or conventional have to say, and what they do. (1994, 9, 17)

Living by this ideal requires of us an attitude of openness to the approaches of many disciplines in the social sciences and the humanities. Several contributors see themselves as working in critical applied linguistics, critical discourse analysis, and critical pedagogy, actively striving for professional change, multi-disciplinarity and social responsibility. Sociolinguistics is at its most powerful when informed by this spirit, by anthropology, sociology, and postcolonial studies, and when the perspectives of 'the Other' are integrated into our scholarly approaches. Cultures must be understood on their own terms. We may see them as dichotomously contrasting with what 'we' are most familiar with, as non-western (aboriginal, Indian), non-oral (Sign languages), or non-national (Esperanto), but their validity, their alternative world view, their means of communication need to be understood in their own right.

Critical scholarship will often involve a merging of research, applied work, and advocacy, as in Maffi's presentation of Terralingua, an NGO linking scholars working for linguistic diversity. We need to be attuned to the complexities and paradoxes inherent in globalization and diversity (Rassool, Martel), so as to rigorously analyse the problems of our contemporary world, and for instance expose the imposition of western 'science' on alien cosmologies and different cultures, as in the case of Sign languages globally and locally (Branson & Miller), or the way conceptual frameworks that ignore political and cultural realities masquerade in 'authoritative' reference works, as in the coverage of Kurdish and the Kurds (Hassanpour).

The role of the critical intellectual also means working with the heart as well as the brain (Sanchez). Being passionate is not a question of personality and commitment, though these are of course essential, but rather of being in touch with the ongoing struggles of ordinary people, functioning as an organic intellectual in Gramsci's sense, processing people's basic sense of their place in the world, situating these gut feelings historically (in Tove's case, perceptions of linguistic injustice) and converting them into a solid scientific position (which Gramsci elaborates in his 'Passage from Knowing to Understanding and to Feeling and vice versa from Feeling to Understanding and to Knowing', 1971, 418). This process of the cross-fertilisation of personal experience and insight with scientific rigour is characteristic of many of the papers in this book (among them Huss, Taylor, Wink & Wink, ...). It permeates those which document the struggle for minority rights in Sweden (Lainio, Municio-Larsson, Peura), where scholars work with and for minority groups in a reciprocal learning process. Such interaction is essential in defining what needs investigation, in the conduct of research and advocacy, and in results not being 'owned' by the scholar but being common property.

This is not romanticising. For the critical intellectual it is a question of being willing to see things afresh (Beutel), of drawing on alternative sources of knowledge as a means of counteracting unsustainable modernisation and the scientific sets of mind it entails (Fettes), and releasing the creativity that is present in all of us. This presupposes a willingness to be challenged, to be aware of the epistemological and political dimensions of one's professionalism, and to dialogue on its strengths and weaknesses.

Being challenged is an uncomfortable but productive process. Thus language specialists tend to be well informed about linguistic forms, language teachers to have favoured ways of organising language learning, but they might be different people if they heeded Ivan Illich (1973, 41): 'A language of which I know only the words and not the pauses is a continuous offence. It is as the caricature of a photographic negative. It takes more time and effort and delicacy to learn the silence of a people than to learn its sounds'.

Real communication involves so much more than sounds, words, signs, symbolic systems. Effective communication involves the right to be well informed (Hamelink). It implies not being deprived of access to key communicative uses of language and discourses (van Dijk). It implies classrooms that nurture the spirit of learners and empower collaboratively (Cummins), in programmes that serve majority and minority fairly. Inter-ethnic communication and cross-cultural understanding are challenges that require openness and a willingness to see one's own culture in perspective and relationally (Menk). Members of the A-Team can understand themselves and their own professional practices only if they can see things from the B-Team point of view.

The challenge then is to ensure that our own work is firmly anchored in cultural, economic, and political realities and to transcend these. Working in an ecology of language paradigm, imbued with principles of language rights, is a starting-point. Tove Skutnabb-Kangas has demonstrated for decades the capacity to diagnose language policy matters in a critical and independent way, to develop theoretical frameworks for analysing them, and to propose and pursue courses of action tenaciously. This has clearly been a source of inspiration to many. For instance the concept linguicism has been readily comprehensible to the linguistically oppressed. It was therefore no surprise that the term was adopted in official post-apartheid South African language planning.[1] At a more personal level her influence was expressed vividly by an elderly Sikh after a lecture in Britain in 1983: 'you spoke our soul'.

Issues of scientific approach

Research that can facilitate 'changing the world' must tread new ground. Researchers do not follow a linear, smooth path from idea or plan to product and goal. Their choice of topic is determined by a multitude of personal, non-scholarly factors, just as our capacity to function as academics is influenced by a range of personal factors other than purely scientific or methodological ones. The need for rigour, and awareness of methods remains, but paradigm shifts are triggered in unpredictable ways. People with real commitment and clear vision are key catalysts in such processes.

Tove Skutnabb-Kangas was fortunate in being able to work closely in the 1960s at a formative stage of her professional development with Einar Haugen, an enlightened pioneer in bilingualism studies and language planning. It is no surprise that towering figures in the sociology of language like Haugen and Joshua Fishman are people with hybrid cultural and linguistic identities (Norwegian-American, Jewish-American; Norwegian-English; Yiddish-English). Tove Skutnabb-Kangas has added to her original bilingual Finnish-Swedish identity the immigrant experience of living in a Danish-speaking environment and the cross-cultural experience of sharing her domestic and professional life with someone who happens to have the globally imperialist language, English, as his/my mother tongue. All of which enhances one's awareness of cultural and linguistic diversity, one's appreciation of language learning and the silences of language, and one's sensitivity to hierarchies of language and the interlocking of language and power, and one's joy in passing on more than one language to the next generation.

Bringing existential involvement into one's professional remit goes well beyond playing the kind of intellectual games that a lot of would-be scholarship seems to be. Commitment to the rights of oppressed groups is, of course, not incompatible with producing hard science, which many papers demonstrate. At the practical level being independent and outspoken can mean not having a secure professorial position, marginalisation, and not being able to attract research funding from the

---

[1] *Towards a national language plan for South Africa* from the Language Plan Task Group, LANGTAG, established by the Ministry of Arts, Culture, Science and Technology, 8 August 1996, chair Neville Alexander.

establishment. This happens even in countries like Sweden (Lainio) and Denmark (Hussain), that pride themselves on their democratic credentials and champion the cause of human rights internationally. The alternative to honestly declaring one's epistemological credentials is to conform to conventional norms, 'not rocking the boat, not straying outside the accepted paradigms or limits, making yourself marketable and above all presentable, hence uncontroversial and unpolitical and "objective"' (Said, 1994, 55). This conformity is enforced, often in subtle hegemonic ways, by dominant-group power-holders, some of whom may be self-proclaimed 'liberals' or 'left-wing' scholars who are dogmatically convinced of the superiority of their analytical tools and judgement, for instance Marxist fundamentalists in Germany (Menk), whose influence effectively makes it more difficult for research at the behest of minorities and carried out by minorities to break into the public sphere and academic discourse.

The fact that debates on the significance of ethnicity could take this turn in western European countries reinforces the case for research that connects economic and cultural oppression locally and globally, that clarifies processes of hegemonic dominance and legitimation, and the role of linguicism in societal hierarchisation. It is not surprising that scholars in language policy and globalization are influenced by class theory and Bourdieu's concepts cultural and linguistic capital, which are useful and productive in the study of power and linguistic inequality. Linguistic injustice is generally existentially obvious to those suffering from linguistic oppression, such as immigrants worldwide, and Hungarians in Slovakia in recent years (Lanstyak) but its more subtly coercive traits throughout the western world may be less transparent (Cummins), and the factors that can trigger conflict not completely predictable (Kontra). Often the writing is on the wall, however, and even in the statute book: in Serbia, laws were passed restricting minority language rights long before evil forces of cultural tribalization (Hamelink) were unleashed and violent conflict erupted. As many chapters show, the violation of linguistic human rights in education and public services is in fact widespread, even if injustice is hidden behind a smokescreen of liberal rhetoric. Hence the imperative need for studies of linguicism to focus on the two interlocking constituents - ideologies, attitudes, and beliefs on the one hand, and material resources, structure and power on the other. Democracies do permit alternatives (Peura), and taking language issues out of mainstream political discourse might lead to an even worse position for linguistic diversity (Clyne). There is an expanding literature on linguistic human rights and many aspects of linguistic diversity (see the papers in Kontra et al, eds., 1999, and Skutnabb-Kangas, 2000), to which an increasing number of critical intellectuals are committed.

At the personal level,

> to be as marginal and as undomesticated as someone who is in real exile is for an intellectual to be unusually responsive ... to the provisional and risky rather than to the habitual, to innovation and experiment rather than the authoritatively given *status quo*. The *exilic* intellectual does not respond to the logic of the conventional but to the audacity of daring, and to representing change, to moving on, not standing still. (Said, 1994, 47)

At root this builds on a quest for truth, for universal values, for moral principles. One can be 'exilic', a critical or dissenting intellectual, in South and North, as a local or an immigrant. Many such 'exilic intellectuals' have contributed descriptions of the types of struggle they have been involved in:

- maintaining bilingualism within the family and the immigrant community despite the insensitivity and ignorance of the dominant group (Huss, Lainio, Leporanta-Morley),
- explaining the self-imposed 'exile' of those who have adopted Esperanto (Dasgupta, Fettes), a language of 'inter-local communication', a democratic inter-ethnic, non-ethnic language founded on a universalism that is in total contrast to what globalization and nationalism mostly stand for,
- combating the scourge of subtle everyday racism in the media in the west, and the complicity of journalists with state policies (Hussain), and political discourse that deprives marginalised people of voice (Rassool) or access (van Dijk), fields where research involves detailed micro-level textual analysis that is linked to macro-societal structures,
- denouncing western cultural and linguistic imperialism in the postcolonial world and creating alternatives that strengthen local languages (Ngũgĩ),
- counteracting the blindness of linguistics to particular communities and their languages (Mühlhäusler), the blindness of Saussurean 'internal linguistics' to the social reproduction of language and to its own cultural biases (Branson & Miller), and the blindness of scholarship that seeks to eliminate personal commitment so as to conform to a norm of academic 'objectivity' - which, as Hassanpour rightly points out, is itself a major political statement.

Monolingualism in a global age

Ariel Dorfman, the Chilean-American writer, in his wonderful book *Heading South, looking North: a bilingual journey'* (1998), analyses his personal experience of bilingualism, language loss, and re-acquisition in a vivid portrait of a turbulent life in the U.S. and Chile. The book is a *New York Times* Notable Book. When Dorfman, who holds a professorial chair at a prestigious US university, wrote a short article in this newspaper entitled 'If only we could all speak two languages', he was at the receiving end of a torrent of denunciation and hate mail. Evidently to suggest that Americans might benefit by being bilingual (which, of course, is what millions of minority language speakers have been throughout the history of the U.S.) can be seen as un-American and can trigger a McCarthyite response.

If monolingualism is a curable disease, to borrow one of Tove's old but still provocative metaphors, it is a disease that much of the population does not know it is suffering from. The disease is particularly widespread in 'big' states that have seen themselves as monolingual and linguistically self-sufficient. A significant development in western Europe in the 1990s has been that the member states of the

European Union have endorsed the desirability of schoolchildren acquiring competence in at least two foreign languages, an achievement that is quite common in 'small' countries such as The Netherlands and the Nordic countries but rare in France, Germany, and the United Kingdom. French policy-makers (in the Haut Conseil de la Francophonie) have called foreign language learning 'a disaster of planetary proportions', implying that there is a poor return on the massive investment in education.

Tove Skutnabb-Kangas published an article in 1984 entitled 'Why aren't all the children in the Nordic countries bilingual?', pleading for Europeans to learn from the immersion experience in North America, and pointing out that majority group members as well as minorities could become multilingual if education policy was organised appropriately. In fact immersion education has taken off in some parts of Europe since then, particularly in Catalonia and Finland. The book *Multilingualism for all* (Skutnabb-Kangas, ed., 1995), in particular the concluding chapter written with Ofelia García summarising general principles, analyses the evidence from a great deal of experience of multilingual education worldwide, and specifies what criteria need to be met for success. The vision underlying the book is that majorities and minorities need to become multilingual together, in programmes that are geared towards the needs of both groups, and that multilingual citizens hold the key to a peaceful future. It is therefore important that elites themselves have the experience of becoming bilingual or multilingual (a point made earlier by Joshua Fishman).

In the European Union there is a definite trend towards increased multilingual competence among the younger generation, with the possible exception of those from 'English-speaking' countries. The dominance of English in commerce, scientific communication, the media, youth culture, military liaison, and a host of domains, and not least its ubiquity as a foreign language in continental European classrooms, has accelerated the acquisition of English. In principle the 15 member states of the European Union accord equal rights to 11 official languages in the supra-national institutions of the Union (the Commission and Council of Ministers in Brussels, the European Parliament), but in reality there is a pecking order of languages, with English at the top and French near the top. Endorsing a rhetoric of strengthening linguistic diversity and multilingualism represents a changed political awareness of what 'Europeanisation' involves, but lack of an explicit language policy in member states and in the European Union as a supra-national entity means that there is a major risk of English expanding at the expense of other languages. Serious study of the language policy issues in the European Union has not been undertaken, though there have been some empirical studies and some programmatic analysis[2].

---

[2] There is a substantial literature documenting small empirical studies and identifying a number of the problems, see, for instance, the annual International Handbook of European Sociolinguistics *Sociolinguistica*. The most sophisticated starting-point for a study of the language policy issues of the European Union is a conference report published in 1999 by the European Cultural Foundation, 'Which languages for Europe?'. Information on http://www.eurocult.org

Eliminating monolingualism through additive language learning will take time, and resistance to multilingualism needs better clinical diagnosis before one can envisage a linguistic health system that reaches the entire population. And as in all good treatment, what is essentially needed is to create the conditions that permit bodies and minds to cure themselves rather than relying on a pharmaceutical fix, though for some conditions drugs can of course be necessary and life-saving. Just as peace is far more than the absence of war, linguistic health involves far more than the mere survival of our linguistic diversity. It means creating the conditions that permit language groups to develop their cultures and languages along lines that they wish, to modernise in ways that suit their cosmologies and that allow users of a language to adapt it in sustainable ways in response to local and global pressures. Adequate typologies of language policy and language defence situations are needed so that the diagnostic description rests on a solid theoretical base (Fishman & Fishman) and can lead to prescriptions that are proactive and preventive.

The general drift of the last 20 years in the U.S. away from policies that celebrate linguistic diversity (García) makes it very important to publicise how it is that successful bilingual education policies operate. The experience of the Finnish minority schools in Sweden (Peura) is that very high levels of linguistic competence in two languages are achieved. The evidence from this type of schooling, from the cases presented by Cummins, and in Skutnabb-Kangas, ed., 1995, would suggest therefore that when García has a vision of schools in the USA in the future building on the multiple linguistic identities of the schoolchildren, it would not be necessary for learners to aim at less competence in either language than monolinguals.

It is impossible to ignore the power of English in the modern world, and several chapters address the issue of 'reducing English to equality', to adapt a memorable phrase first used by Neville Alexander in relation to Afrikaans. Whether English is learned additively or subtractively in education is a key theme in all postcolonial settings, which South African language planning is addressing (Alexander, Desai, Heugh). English has retained its privileged status in India, with the effect that its prestige counteracts the development of the full range of Indian languages, though reliance on English can also serve to curb dominant regional languages (Annamalai). Legally enforceable language rights are relevant at a range of levels in India, and many factors, political, economic, and ethnic, influence whether language rights are pursued actively or not, and affect the transition from normative legislation to implementation. What is decided on in education has a major impact on the power structure internally in postcolonial countries, and as English is the key external link language, its local status is inextricably linked with its global role. In each local context there is a massive need to educate the general public, and policy-makers in particular, about the challenges and implications of language policies (Alexander) and the practical implications for schooling in a multilingual society (Desai). This task is equally important, and much neglected, in modern nation-states that have seen themselves as 'monolingual'.

Seeing language dominance afresh

Ammon raises the issue of the rights of L2 users of English as a language of science. Calling English a lingua franca serves to conceal the inequalities inherent in a system that is supposed to serve native speakers and non-natives equally well, but which manifestly serves some better than others, as a consequence of 'market forces'. However it also needs to be recalled that being confined to operating in a single language, however diverse and varied, is limiting. Some Danish multilingual scholars are convinced that they are in a better position than people who are monolingual in English (Phillipson & Skutnabb-Kangas, 1999), and many scholars who use English as an L2 in their professional work report that they have not experienced discrimination.

Oda also documents how the dominant language English serves to constrain rather than promote learning, and that the root problem is the native speaker teachers of English and their narrow cultural and linguistic horizons. It appears that the English teaching profession (ELT, TESOL) is still 'imposing an ethnocentric ideology and inadvertently supporting the essentializing discourse that represents cultural groups as stable or homogeneous entities' (Spack, 1997, 773). Some bilingual education programmes fail to appreciate that majority and minority pupils have very different needs (Wink & Wink). Such practices perpetuate a colonialist world view in which orientalism operates to position the Other in education:

> When students are considered to have cultures, these tend to be fixed and deterministic. Thus, it is common to talk in terms of Asian, Japanese or Hispanic etc. students having certain characteristics as if these emerged from some preordained cultural order. This tendency to ascribe fixed (and often, though not always, negative) characteristics by dint of membership to a certain culture can be explained in terms of the colonial construction of the Other.... Culture has become a category of fixity rather than an engagement with difference. (Pennycook, 1998b, 188-189)

Exactly the same point is made by Hussain in relation to media and political discourse in western Europe. The same attitudes were also the norm in earlier times vis-à-vis aboriginal cultures. The experience of a Japanese student in London rejecting the way her culture was defined in the dominant educational discourse (Oda) has affinities with the way resistance to learning is used as a weapon by aboriginals to avoid cultural submersion, for instance Mayan refugees from Guatemala refusing to learn English in Canada:

> As they acquired Spanish, they increasingly lost control of their lives. As Mayans acquired Spanish, they lost their land... The language teacher, in our culture, specializes in the ranking of speech, actively discouraging some forms and praising others... these learners reject the standard calculation of languages' utility: to accept this calculation is to accept the forces which have shattered the contexts-of-use which formerly indemnified the threatened speech... To give English priority in language study is to accept the forces which erased the utility of native

> speech....Mastery of English does not necessarily entail mastery of their
> own lives, and they have had long and deep experience of the
> consequences of forfeiting control to outsiders. (Giltrow & Colhoun,
> 1992, 53-54)

Resistance by aboriginals, in past and present, permeates Gaski's paper, reflecting on what happens to cultural products in new contexts of consumption and appreciation. There is a striking affinity between his presentation of ethnocriticism as dialogic rather than oppositional, and Pattanayak's plea for an Indian intellectual approach which differs markedly from the neat binary oppositions of western scholarship, which he claims are fundamentally flawed.

I cannot help wondering how widespread the kind of experience narrated in Oda's and Ammon's articles is. I have been contacted by postgraduate students in Britain and Denmark who have experienced discrimination because their thesis supervisors defined PhD topics narrowly, along lines that they were able to supervise rather than those that were relevant in the context that the foreign student came from. What seems to be in place is a kind of educational and academic censorship, with gate-keeping and agenda-setting masquerading as quality control, and an academic 'old boys network' stifling more critical voices. From my own experience when submitting material (articles, book reviews, rebuttals of attacks on my work), I know that some journal editors publish articles which have not been through any peer review (albeit in a 'peer review journal'), and some editors have attempted to dissuade me from publishing, by a variety of subtle and not so subtle means. When this happens to someone with a well-established international reputation, and a native speaker of English, it is not implausible to suspect that less fortunately placed people experience difficulty in breaking into the market. This applies particularly to dissenting intellectuals and to scholars from South countries (the academic B team?).

A more practical aspect of the issue of the role of English, at least for me as editor of this book, has been the fact that two thirds of the contributors do not have English as a mother tongue. For some, the burden of needing to write in a foreign language has been considerable, which reinforces the point made by several contributors about equity and access. As editor the question arises of how far ensuring that the language conforms to 'standard' English norms also means changing the distinctive discourse style of scholars whose work derives from a different scientific tradition. Clearly what is important in the final reckoning is the quality of what is written, and while there is considerable variation among native speakers, just as there is among non-native speakers, the fact that all of us are not operating on a level playing field ought to lead to codes of practice that address this aspect of linguistic inequality. This applies both to written scholarly production and to participation in conferences.

In the summer of 1996 I attended two 'international' conferences, a Language Rights conference in Hong Kong (see Benson, Grundy, & Skutnabb-Kangas, eds., 1998), and a language policy symposium in Prague as part of the Universal Esperanto Association 81st World Congress (see Fettes & Bolduc, eds., 1998). At the Hong Kong conference, English was virtually the sole means of communication. In the question time of one of the plenary sessions, a South African participant expressed surprise at why those whose competence in English was less than ideal, particularly Asians who had great difficulty in expressing themselves in English, accepted the unequal communication rights imposed on them by the conference organizers. The answer was that the organizers, mainly British, had not given the matter any thought, and the non-native speakers were too polite to protest. A couple of weeks later at the Esperanto symposium it was amazing to experience participants from all over the world communicating confidently in a shared international language, among them a number of Asians who were manifestly at no disadvantage. As this event was my first experience of Esperanto in action (with interpretation provided for us non-Esperantists), it was a vivid and memorable way of seeing at first hand that Esperanto is not merely utopian but a reality for those who have chosen to make it part of their lives, domestic, national, and international. The juxtaposition of the experience of English working badly and inequitably – and for once this being discussed openly in public - and Esperanto working well provides appetising food for thought.

There is a tendency for those not familiar with Esperanto to reject it without seriously investigating whether it might be a more efficient and equitable solution to some problems of international communication or making foreign-language learning in schools more effective (because of its simple, regular, productive grammar). The scholarly study of international communication, and practical proposals for the solution of the major problems of international bodies, ought to take into consideration the use of Esperanto as an alternative to the juggernaut English, which rides roughshod over the rights of many non-native users of the language. There is an extensive literature on Esperanto, see, for instance, Tonkin (ed.) 1997, which has opened my eyes in recent years to the potential and the reality of this democratic language.

In this volume, multilingualism can be glimpsed through the reproduction of a few of the original Finnish and Swedish texts, so as to make the point that shifts between home language and dominant language can permit subtlety and depth but may impose a major emotional burden. For elites, bilingualism of this sort is primarily a source of joy and enrichment, whereas for others the risk is semilingualism, which Toukomaa is at pains to clarify conceptually. Semilingualism has tended to be misunderstood, despite the fact that Tove Skutnabb-Kangas devotes an entire chapter in her 1984 book *Bilingualism or not: the education of minorities* (Swedish version, 1981) to the genealogy of the concept, and the uses and abuses to which it was put. Some of the international debate on the topic ignored her clear position: 'I do not consider semilingualism to be a linguistic or scientific concept at all. In my view it is a political concept, so far at a pre-scientific stage of development' (1984, 249). She relates the debate in Scandinavia about the validity of the concept to conflicting paradigms, the one more quantitative and positivistic, the other more qualitative and ideologically explicit. She was particularly concerned about the risks for minority children of a deficit theory that would use 'monolingual white middle-class norms in a markedly ethnocentric fashion to force those norms on bilingual immigrant working-class children, and then to label them as inferior, deficient, or at least different' (ibid.).

Sadly, the parlous state of bilingualism in mainstream education, despite a great deal of evidence that both majority and minority children can benefit from bilingual education, including the Deaf (Jokinen), shows that deficit theories are still widely serving to ensure that a lot of children do not succeed in education as well as they could. Likewise, there is a major task to raise awareness about the way inequalities and a-symmetry in 'international communication' places non-native users of English lower on a hierarchy of norms of communication than native English-speakers, and tends to ignore 'Other' cultures and languages, or to see them as deficits. Even our concepts serve to maintain this inequality: natives are the norm, non-natives are defined negatively in relation to the norm. Addressing and solving these problems should not be the exclusive responsibility of those who happen not to be born with English as their mother tongue. It is often the native speakers who are the problem, not least because they are unaware of hierarchical linguistic ordering, structural inequality, and the rationalisation processes that lead us to accept inequality. This linguistic ethnocentricity and linguicism largely go unchallenged. To move from a changed awareness to strategies to implement more equitable and symmetrical communication is a central challenge for language policy in the coming years. The European Union is therefore a test case for the implementation of policies that respect linguistic human rights. The scientific community worldwide ought to show a lead in tackling such issues in its own communicative discourses.

Economic gospels

Language policy and education function in a world which is increasingly dominated by commerce, by market principles that strengthen the rich and further impoverish the poor globally and locally. The fact that many of the poor may be culturally and multilingually rich does not count on the balance sheets of states and transnational corporations. As economic rationales are a present reality, it is essential to understand how economists think, and to dialogue with those working in the economics of language, who can clarify relationships between resources, output, and certain types of justice and efficiency, while reminding us that approaches in economics are not independent of value judgements, nor is 'equity' an absolute standard but a principle requiring different goals and means in varying contexts (Grin & Vaillancourt). Relying exclusively on 'market forces' is theoretically and politically suspect. Less powerful languages can become victims of linguicide as much from economic forces, the 'laws' of the market, as state policies (Hassanpour).

On the other hand corporations are in some respects sensitive to non-economic variables. The internet is potentially a powerful force for democratisation (Beutel) and for combating 'monolingual stupidity', a concept which is Skutnabb-Kangas shorthand for those whose voluntary monolingualism confines and unnecessarily condemns them to seeing the world through a single lens. A monolingual world view is one of the pillars underpinning the massive pressures that are imposing cultural and linguistic homogenization worldwide (Rassool, Hamelink).

Globally the trend is towards larger corporations (backed up by the World Trade Organization), bigger alliances (for instance an expanding NATO with a much wider mandate), and supra-statal groupings (such as the European Union, which the North American Free Trade Agreement and other American regional groupings are seeking to emulate). In most of these supra-national fora the globalization agenda is accepted without much questioning, and language policy is invisible and covert except for the provision of minimalistic rights to certain types of interpretation or translation. The interlocking of language with the global economy has not yet been adequately explored in depth, though there are inspiring books that lay bare what is happening globally (e.g. Mander & Goldsmith, 1996, Pilger, 1998), which can serve as a useful starting-point. The issue of alternatives to global capitalism, and the characteristics of a sustainable economy that builds on local languages and cultures, is a serious language policy concern that has only been explored indirectly in this volume. There is a comparative study of how English functions in such different contexts as the Philippines and Australia (Smolicz & Secombe), but much more detailed empirical investigation and comparative study would be needed so as to unravel something of the complexity of globalization and English in the contemporary world[3].

Researchers are not helpless victims of economic forces, even if, as Clyne and Municio-Larsson show, the constraints on what is possible sway in the political winds. Even political systems that articulate a rhetoric of grounding social policy on a foundation of rational analysis of the evidence, as does Sweden, may choose to ignore scientific findings. When arguments are heeded, and enlightened policies formed, the central issue becomes whether implementation of the policy actually takes place (Heugh). Adequate funding is essential if appropriate language policies are to go beyond rhetoric and posturing.

The World Bank has a decisive influence on the funding of basic education in postcolonial contexts, and currently provides investment that strengthens the former colonial languages, and particularly English, while deviously adopting a rhetoric of support for local languages (Brock-Utne). It is therefore not surprising that one issue that cuts across many of the themes of this book is the relationship between English, the language par excellence of the economic forces that have propelled it

---

[3]   There is a considerable body of research on 'world English' and its propagation, but much remains to be clarified. See Phillipson, 1992, Pennycook, 1994, Fishman, Conrad & Rubal-Lopez (eds.) 1996 (reviewed in Phillipson, 1999a), Graddol & Meinhof (eds.) 1999, Phillipson & Skutnabb-Kangas, 1996, 1997, 1999, Ricento (ed.) forthcoming. Crystal (1997) is in my view unlikely to support the cause of linguistic diversity, as it has an underlying triumphalist tenor; for a detailed review article, see Phillipson, 1999b.

forward, and local languages. A key issue in language policy in general is whether it is local politicians setting the agenda (South African language policy has been characterised by an eminently democratic consultation process) or the transnational corporations which are imposing a late capitalist world order that relegates peripheral countries, economies and languages to a subordinate position. In this scenario elites need to be proficient in English in order to serve their own and 'global' interests, and local languages must facilitate internal policing of an export-oriented economy, and attempt to limit social unrest so that this economy can persist. The same corporations are muscling in on education systems, particularly in North America, but also elsewhere, including Europe, particularly at higher education level through research funding. Education is in fact central to the entire globalization process (Spring, 1998), this development reflecting the predominant interest of corporations in producing consumers rather than critical citizens. It is only through maintaining the vitality of all our languages that we may be able to force corporations to function multilingually and consolidate our cultural diversity. The maintenance of linguistic diversity, and analysis of the forces that constrain and promote it, are central themes in Tove Skutnabb-Kangas's book *Linguistic genocide in education - or worldwide diversity and human rights* (2000). Full details of her publications are accessible on her home page http://babel.ruc.dk/~tovesku/

Hopeful ways forward

There are many pointers in this book for ways to take more equitable language policies forward in principled ways. Some promisingly suggest that utopias are not wishful thinking but are firmly rooted in the real world:

- examples of peaceful language emancipation in various historical periods in the Nordic countries, and how increased language rights are integrated into more general socio-political developments (Lindgren);
- examples of language policy efforts contributing substantially to peaceful transition in post-communist states: greater respect for minority language rights in Slovakia (Lanstyak), and a changed hierarchy of languages in Latvia through policies to remedy historic injustice and revitalise the local language while respecting the linguistic human rights of a relatively recent settler group, the political goal being to forge a civic nation that all groups can identify with and are equipped linguistically to function in (Druviete);
- The People's Communication Charter (Hamelink) exemplifies critical scholarship and advocacy moving into a phase with a thrust in two directions: to give cultural and communication rights greater prominence in the public domain, not least in influential bodies in the media world, and to provide an instrument for grassroots activism, ideally a tool for empowering people so that

they both are better informed and can resist some of the massive pressures of cultural homogenization and McDonaldization;

- the encouraging fact that in international law, several recent developments suggest that language rights are being formulated more strongly, in ways that indicate that the political world and lawyers now accept that respect for linguistic human rights is increasingly important (de Varennes), which could represent a small step towards policy-makers being accountable to ethical principles, and human rights declarations being implemented for a larger section of humanity;

- many examples of multilingual educational policy meeting the need, in contexts requiring action in favour of language 'defence', for improved theory-based understanding (e.g. permissive, active, or proactive policies, collaborative rather then coercive relations), of equitable language policies, in this as in any other 'applied' scientific activity (Fishman & Fishman, Cummins);[4]

- given nature's life-giving processes (symbolized in Liukka's image of birch trees), and the dynamic interaction of linguistic, biological, and cultural diversity, it is through giving children appropriate multilingual education that a more just, sustainable world will be built.

Personally I have found living with Tove Skutnabb-Kangas, working with her, and trying to live up to her boundless sense of commitment and vision an immensely stimulating, challenging and productive process. Hopefully this book can serve not merely as a tribute to her achievements but as a source of inspiration for all those involved in championing the rights of speakers of all languages, for equitable policies, appropriate education, and the power to implement such language rights.

---

[4] Fishman's approach can be supplemented by means of the grid categorising the extent to which language rights are observed in language legislation along two parameters, degree of overtness, and degree of prohibition, toleration or promotion (Skutnabb-Kangas & Phillipson, 1994b).

Contributors

Neville Alexander is at present Director of the Project for the Study of Alternative Education in South Africa at the University of Cape Town, where he co-ordinates research on models of multilingual education, focuses on language planning and policy issues at national and provincial levels and also advises government on language policy in education. nalexan@education.uct.ac.za

Ulrich Ammon is Professor of the linguistics of German with a focus on sociolinguistics, University of Duisburg. He has also been visiting professor at universities in Australia, Japan, and the USA. He has published widely on dialects, mother-tongue teaching, pluricentric languages, and languages in international communication. He is a co-editor of the handbook *Sociolinguistics* (1987/88) and the yearbook *Sociolinguistica*. His three latest monographs are: 'Die internationale Stellung der deutschen Sprache' (1991), 'Die deutsche Sprache in Deutschland, Österreich und der Schweiz' (1995), and 'Ist Deutsch noch internationale Wissenschaftssprache?' (1998). ammon@uni-duisburg.de

E. Annamalai studied linguistics in India and the USA, specializing in syntax and semantics. At the Central Institute of Indian Languages, Mysore, as Professor and then Director, he primarily worked on issues of language conflicts, language in education, and the development of aboriginal languages. He served on committees advising the Government of India on language policies. His publications include 'Language movements in India' (1979), and 'Multilingual management: Languages planning and use in India' (1999). anianamm@giasbga.vsnl.net.in

Constance Beutel worked for more than 30 years in the telecommunications industry, the last 12 of which were spent in bringing innovative academic programs to working professionals for Pacific Bell. She was the interim Executive Director of the Buckminster Fuller Institute in Santa Barbara, California, has been attached to Menlo College, Atherton, California, and is currently Assistant Professor in the School of Technology and Industry at Golden Gate University, San Francisco. Her research and application focus is on using technology to extend learning and teaching. Her passion is about the future and our human potential to live compassionately and sustainably on the planet. cmbeutel@worldnet.att.net

Jan Branson is Director of the National Institute for Deaf Studies and Sign Language Research at La Trobe University in Melbourne, Australia. Her research has focused on the comparative understanding of processes of social and cultural discrimination and oppression, the impact of formal education on the reproduction of inequalities based on gender and class in both Australia and Indonesia, and comparative studies of the economic and political roles of women in Australia and Indonesia. She has also developed courses in Women's Studies, and has for the last decade been involved in the study of the cultural construction of 'the disabled' leading to intensive study of the language and culture of Deaf communities in Australia, Indonesia and Thailand. branson@latrobe.edu.au

Birgit Brock-Utne is Professor of International Education at the Institute for Educational Research, University of Oslo, Norway. She has qualifications from Norway, Germany, and the USA in the humanities and social sciences, and a doctorate in peace studies (Oslo). From 1987 to 1992 she worked at the University of Dar es Salaam, Tanzania. She has written extensively in the fields of educational innovation and action research, women and education, peace education, and education in Africa. She is active in ongoing support to education in many African countries, particularly South Africa. birgit.brock-utne@ped.uio.no

Michael Clyne is Professor of Linguistics and Director, Language and Society Centre, Monash University, Melbourne. He was previously Associate Professor of German at Monash, where he obtained his PhD. Member of the Order of Australia, Fellow of the Academy of Social Sciences in Australia and of the Australian Academy of the Humanities, Austrian Cross of Honour for Science and the Arts, Honorary Doctorate, University of Munich, Grimm Prize 1999. Research interests: multilingualism, sociolinguistics (especially of German), inter-cultural communication, second language acquisition. He has written 24 books and over 250 articles. michael.clyne@arts.monash.edu.au

Jim Cummins teaches in the Department of Curriculum, Teaching and Learning of the University of Toronto. He has published widely in the areas of language learning, bilingual education, educational reform, and the implications of technological innovation for education. Among his publications are 'Brave new schools: Challenging cultural illiteracy through global learning networks' (with Dennis Sayers, 1995) and 'Negotiating identities: Education for empowerment in a diverse society' (1996). jcummins@oise.utoronto.ca

Probal Dasgupta, a graduate of the University of Calcutta (majoring in linguistics, 1973) and of New York University (1980 PhD in generative syntax, on Bangla). An author of several books on linguistics and a translator from Bangla into Esperanto, he has taught in New York, Melbourne, Calcutta, Pune, and (as Professor of Applied Linguistics) at the University of Hyderabad since 1989. He co-edits *Language Problems and Language Planning* and *The Yearbook of South Asian Languages and Linguistics* and is a member of the Akademio de Esperanto. pdgalts@uohyd.emet.in

Zubeida Desai is a Senior Lecturer specialising in language in education in the Faculty of Education at the University of the Western Cape in South Africa. She is also currently the chairperson of the Pan South African Language Board, an independent statutory body set up by the post-apartheid government to promote multilingualism and the development of African languages. zdesai@uwc.ac.za

Teun van Dijk was for many years Professor of Discourse Studies at the University of Amsterdam before moving to the University of Barcelona. After earlier work in literary theory, text grammar, the psychology of text processing and news analysis, his work took a more social and critical direction, focussing especially on the reproduction of racism through a variety of discourses. His current research program involves the development of a multidisciplinary theory of ideology. He was founder editor of *Text, Discourse & Society,* and *Discourse Studies.* For publications see: www.hum.uva.nl/teun   teun@let.uvan.nl

Ina Druviete has a doctorate and is Professor of General Linguistics at the University of Latvia, Head of the Department of Sociolinguistics at the Latvian Language Institute, and Head of the Latvian Language Council. Corresponding member of the Latvian Academy of Sciences. Fields of specialisation: sociolinguistics, language policy, history of linguistics. Author of more than 140 scientific publications. Visiting scholar at Stockholm, Oslo, and Roskilde Universities, Fulbright scholar at the University of Pittsburgh (1996-1997). latv@ac.lza.la

Mark Fettes has worked on language policy issues with Canadian Aboriginal organizations, the Canadian Centre for Linguistic Rights, the Centre for Research and Documentation on World Language Problems, and the Esperantic Studies Foundation. His PhD dissertation 'The Linguistic Ecology of Education' (University of Toronto, 1999) develops a theory of situated language use to guide community-based policy-making in language education. mfettes@magi.com

Gella Schweid Fishman is President of the 'Friends of the Yiddish Secular Schools of America Collection', Stanford, California, founder of the 'Yiddish Secular Schools of America Collection' at special collections, Stanford University Libraries, at which she is also Special Consultant. She is a published Yiddish poet and has taught Yiddish at every level (from nursery to college and teacher training courses) for 55 years. gellafsysa@aol.com

Joshua A. Fishman is Emeritus Distinguished University Research Professor of Social Sciences at Yeshiva University, Visiting Professor of Linguistics and Education at Stanford University, Adjunct Professor of Language Learning and Teaching at New York University and Visiting Professor of Linguistics at the graduate center of City University in New York. His most recent books are 'Reversing Language Shift' (1991, under revision), 'In Praise of the Beloved Language' (1997), 'Handbook of Language and Ethnicity' (1999) and he is currently preparing a 'Handbook of Language and Religion'. fishman@csli.stanford.edu

Ofelia García is Dean of the School of Education at the Brooklyn Campus of Long Island University. She was a professor of bilingual education at City College of New York for almost twenty years. García has been a Spencer Fellow of the National Academy of Education, a Fulbright Scholar, and was the first recipient of the Ofelia García Spirit of the Community Award for her vision in adult education. She has published extensively in the area of bilingual education, the education of language minorities, the sociology of language, and Spanish in the U.S. ogarcia@hornet.liunet.edu

Harald Gaski is Associate Professor of Sámi Literature at the University of Tromsø, Norway, and has been a visiting professor at universities in Australia, Greenland, and the USA. He has written and edited several books on Sámi literature and culture, including translations into English, and has played a pivotal role in establishing Sámi literature as an academic subject. His latest books are the anthologies 'In the shadow of the midnight sun', and 'Contemporary Sámi prose and poetry', both published by the Sámi press, Davvi Girji in Norway, and available internationally through the University of Washington Press, Seattle. harald.gaski@hum.uit.no

François Grin took his PhD in economics at the University of Geneva and has held research and teaching positions at the Universities of Montreal, Washington (Seattle), Fribourg, and Geneva. He is currently Acting Director of the European Centre for Minority Issues in Flensburg, Germany, as well as interim Associate Professor at the Department of Economics, University of Geneva. François Grin has published extensively on the economic approaches to language, ethnicity, and language policy, as well as in education economics. françois.grin@ecopo.unige.ch

Cees Hamelink is Professor of International Communication at the University of Amsterdam. He studied moral philosophy and psychology at the University of Amsterdam and obtained his PhD degree in 1975. He is the editor-in-chief of the *International Journal for Communication Studies: Gazette*. He is adviser on various communication projects for UNESCO, UNRISD, and the International Baccalaureate. He is also Honorary President of the International Association for Media and Communication Research. He has authored 14 books on international communication, culture, human rights and information technology. Major publications are 'Cultural Autonomy in Global Communications' (1983), 'Finance and Information' (1983), 'The Technology Gamble' (1988), 'Trends in World Communication' (1994), and 'The Politics of World Communication' (1994). hamelink@mail.antenna.nl

Amir Hassanpour is Assistant Professor in the Department of Near and Middle Eastern Civilizations, University of Toronto, Canada. He studied linguistics

(Tehran University) and communications (University of Illinois) and has taught media studies at the University of Windsor and Concordia University. His published research includes papers on the language, culture and politics of Kurdistan, language and television, and communications in Canada. amirhp@chass.utoronto.ca

Kathleen Heugh is a language policy and planning researcher and teacher educator with the Project for the Study of Alternative Education in South Africa, at the University of Cape Town. She is also a member of the Pan South African Language Board, a statutory body established to promote the development of previously marginalised languages as well as multilingualism in South Africa. kh@education.uct.ac.za

Leena Huss is Associate Professor and Research Fellow at the Centre for Multiethnic Research, and a lecturer at the Department of Finno-Ugric Languages, Uppsala University, Sweden. Her PhD was on child bilingualism, and has authored a book (1999) on minority languages and linguistic revitalization in northern Scandinavia and Finland. For publications see http://www.multietn.uu.se/ leenahuss@hotmail.com

Mustapha Hussain migrated from Pakistan to Denmark in 1973. He graduated in social sciences from the University of Lund, Sweden, where he is nearing completion of a doctoral thesis in sociology. He has been involved in a series of research projects in Denmark, and in anti-racist training for the police. mustafa.hussain@get2net.dk

Markku Jokinen is a graduate in education from the University of Jyväskylä, where he is Coordinator in the Programme for Finnish Sign Language Users, and has undertaken postgraduate studies in Linguistics, Psycholinguistics and Sign Language Linguistics at the University of Rochester, NY, USA. He is President of the Finnish Association for the Deaf, Vice-President of the European Union of the Deaf, and serves as an expert for the World Federation of the Deaf on Deaf Education, Sign Language and Deaf Culture. markku.jokinen@kl-deaf.fi

Miklos Kontra is Professor of English Applied Linguistics at József Attila University, Szeged, and head of the Department of Sociolinguistics in the Linguistics Institute, Hungarian Academy of Sciences, Budapest. He has coedited 'Hungarian Sociolinguistics' (1995) and 'Language: a right and a resource' (1999), and has edited a special issue on Central Europe of *Multilingua* (2000). kontra@nytud.hu

Jarmo Lainio emigrated as an infant from Finland to Sweden. He studied modern languages and wrote a doctoral study on the language of adult Sweden Finns. He has held posts at the Department of Finno-Ugric Languages (Uppsala University), the Department of Finnish and the Centre for Research on Bilingualism (both at Stockholm University). He has published some 50 articles/books on sociolinguistics, language policy, minority languages, Finnish in a minority position, and the sociology of language. jarmo.lainio@finska.su.se

Istvan Lanstyak was born in Slovakia, studied in Debrecen, Hungary, and after several years of secondary school teaching, completed a PhD in 'modern non-Slavonic philology' in Slovakia, where he is assistant professor at Comenius University, Bratislava. Research interests: Hungarian dialectology, Hungarian-Slovak bilingualism, especially contact phenomena and language planning. lanstyak@fphil.uniba.sk

Pirkko Leporanta-Morley works in the pre-school sector in Sweden, and is currently an advisor on multi-ethnic pre-schools in Rinkeby. As well as publishing poetry she has written scholarly papers on the multicultural pre-school, for UNESCO-99's 'Comparative perspectives on language and literature'. p.leporanta@telia.com

Anna-Riitta Lindgren is Professor of Finnish at the University of Tromsø. Her PhD dealt with linguistic aspects of Kven dialects. She has written widely on the Kven language, the sociology of language, Sámi, trilingualism, and minority languages in northern Scandinavia. anna-riitta.lindgren@hum.uit.no

Lilja Liukka, born in 1920 in northern Finland, lives in Rinkeby, Sweden, the suburb with the largest percentage of minorities in Sweden. After 6 years of formal education she worked in hospitals in both countries and as the secretary of the Finnish Association in Rinkeby. She has mainly worked with children, youth and women, organising after-school activities, summer camps, courses (e.g. in zone therapy, bakery, assertion training). She has been actively involved in negotiating and organising Finnish-medium day care, pre-schools, classes, and schools - and a strike. The Sweden Finnish school in Järva, Stockholm, has been named Lilja school in her honour. She was awarded the first ever Finnish Language Day Prize. She has published poems, and is writing the history of the Finnish Association.

Luisa Maffi holds a BA in Linguistics from the University of Rome and a PhD in Anthropology from the University of California at Berkeley. She is currently attached to the Smithsonian Institute, Washington, DC. She has conducted field research in Somalia, East Africa and Chiapas, Mexico. She has published on Somali and Mayan linguistics, color categorization, ethnomedicine, ethnoecology, and the relationships between linguistic, cultural, and biological diversity. The book 'Language, Knowledge and the Environment: The Interdependence of Biological and Cultural Diversity' is currently under review. Maffi is co-founder and President of the international NGO Terralingua: Partnerships for Linguistic and Biological Diversity, which is devoted to research, information, education, applied work and advocacy on the world's linguistic diversity and its relationships with biodiversity. maffi@nwu.edu

Angéline Martel is Professor of Sociolinguistics and Languages at Télé-université. She is editor of the electronic journal *DiversCité Langues* at http://www.uquebec.ca/diverscite. Her research interests deal with minority constitutional rights, with activism, and technology in language teaching and learning. amartel@teluq.uquebec.ca

Antje-Katrin Menk studied linguistics and psychology and is Professor of Linguistics and German as a second and foreign language. Research interests: multilingualism, minority languages, language policy. menk@uni-bremen.de

Don Miller is Head of Anthropology at Monash University in Melbourne, Australia and a Research Fellow with the National Institute for Deaf Studies and Sign Language Research at La Trobe University. He has worked on the relationship between religion and the reproduction of structured social inequalities in India and Indonesia, and has worked jointly with Jan Branson on the role of education in the reproduction of structured social inequalities in Australia and Indonesia, on the cultural construction of 'the disabled' in the West, and currently on the language and culture of Deaf communities in Australia, Indonesia and Thailand. don.miller@arts.monash.edu.au

Ingegerd Municio-Larsson received her PhD in Political Science from the University of Stockholm. Currently she holds a position as Professor at Södertörn University College, Sweden. Her research interests include a constructivist approach to policy analysis (education and family policy), a feminist approach to policy making, interpretive methods, and comparative European politics. ingegerd.municio@sh.se

Peter Mühlhäusler was born and educated in Freiburg. He studied Germanic languages, linguistics, and Pacific linguistics at Stellenbosch, Reading, and the Australian National University. On completion of his PhD in 1976 he lectured on linguistics at the Technical University of Berlin and from 1979 to 1992 was University Lecturer in General Linguistics and a Fellow of Linacre College at the University of Oxford. Since 1992 he has been Foundation Professor of Linguistics at the University of Adelaide (South Australia). His research interests include Pidgin and Creole linguistics, the preservation of the language of Norfolk Island, the indigenous languages of Australia and the Pacific, pronominal grammar, and the relationship between language and the environment. pmuhlhau@arts.adelaide.edu.au

Ngũgĩ wa Thiong'o. As well as pursuing an academic career he is a key figure in post-colonial writing. He was a successful novelist in English in the 1960s and 1970s who chose to write plays in Gĩkũyũ when he was a professor at Nairobi University, Kenya. This led to imprisonment, during which time he wrote a novel in Gĩkũyũ. He has been obliged to live in exile for many years. He has written a series of non-fiction works analysing the decolonisation of the mind, cultural imperialism, cultural freedom, and related topics. He is currently Professor of Comparative Literature and Performance Studies at New York University. nwt1@is9.nyu.edu

Masaki Oda has a PhD in Applied Linguistics from Georgetown University, USA, where he also taught Japanese. He is an associate professor of linguistics at Tamagawa University in Tokyo, and teaches courses in sociolinguistics, language pedagogy, Japanese and English. Research interests include sociopolitical aspects of language teaching and societal multilingualism. oda@tamagawa.ac.jp

D. P. Pattanayak was founding director the Central Institute of Indian Languages in Mysore, India, after doing a doctorate in linguistics at Cornell University, USA. He has been involved in a succession of national policy documents on language policy, education, and culture. His most influential book is 'Multilingualism and mother tongue education' (1981). He now lives in productive retirement in his native Orissa.

Markku Peura was born in Finland, and studied political science in Stockholm. He was a Lecturer and researcher at the Department of Political Science and at the Center for Research in International Migration and Ethnic Relations, University of Stockholm, 1973-1992. Currently chair of the Sweden-Finnish archives, and Principal of the Sweden-Finnish school at Upplands Väsby. He jointly edited 'Man kan vara tvåländare också' (One can be bi-countrial too) with Tove Skutnabb-Kangas. markku.peura@sverigefinskaskolan.se

Robert Phillipson studied at Cambridge and Leeds Universities, and has a doctorate from the University of Amsterdam. He worked for the British Council in Algeria, Yugoslavia and London before emigrating to Denmark in 1973. For publications, including several books and over 50 articles written with Tove Skutnabb-Kangas, to whom he is married, and with whom he lives on and off the land, see www.ruc.dk/~robert   robert@ruc.dk

Naz Rassool teaches in the School of Education at the University of Reading where she is Director of the MA in Primary Education. She has published within the field of the sociology of technology in education, literacy for development, language rights, and gender issues in education. Recent publications include 'Literacy for Sustainable Development in the Age of Information' (1999); 'School Effectiveness: Fracturing the Discourse'(1999), co-authored with Louise Morley; 'Nationalisms Old and New' (1999), co-edited with Kevin Brehony. n.rassool@reading.ac.uk

Margaret Secombe is a Senior Lecturer in the Graduate School of Education at the University of Adelaide, formerly Head of the School, and is currently Co-ordinator for International Students and Chair, Equal Opportunity Board's

Multicultural Group. She was earlier Deputy Principal of Port August High School and Volunteer Teacher in Tanzania. margaret.secombe@adelaide.edu.au

Jerzy J. Smolicz is Director of the Centre for Intercultural Studies and Multicultural Education at the University of Adelaide. He holds a Personal Chair in the Graduate School of Education at Adelaide, and is an Honorary Professor at the University of Santo Tomas in the Philippines. He is Chair of the Ministerial Advisory Committee on Multicultural Education and Fellow of the Academy of Social Sciences in Australia. His most recent book is 'On Education and Culture', 1999. jerzy.smolicz@adelaide.edu.au

Shelley Taylor has conducted research on educational linguistics in Denmark, Turkey and Canada on issues ranging from language and power to the development of bi-/multilingualism. She taught in an MA Bilingual Education program at the University of Utah and presently has a joint appointment in the French Department and in the Faculty of Education at the University of Western Ontario, Canada. taylor@julian.uwo.ca

Pertti Toukomaa studied social sciences and has a PhD in Psychology from the University of Tampere. He has worked as a clinical psychologist and in vocational counseling in Finland and Sweden, been a lecturer at several Finnish universities, and is currently Professor of Educational Psychology at the University of Oulu. Research interests: educational policy and minority education, for which he has served as a UNESCO expert. ptoukoma@ktk.oulu.fi

François Vaillancourt took his PhD in economics from Queen's University (Ontario). He has been visiting professor at universities in Canada and Australia and is currently full Professor and Acting Director of the Centre for Research and Development in Economics at the University of Montreal. He is a specialist in fiscal policy and tax systems and a frequent consultant for international organisations in this field, has published widely on taxation issues, education economics and language economics. vaillanf@ere.umontreal.ca

Fernand de Varennes is a Senior Lecturer in international law and human rights at Murdoch University, Perth, Australia. He holds law degrees from the Université de Moncton in Canada, the London School of Economics, and Political Science and a doctorate from the Universiteit Maastricht. He has published world-wide, in eight languages, in the area of language, minorities and human rights. Research interests: international law, minority rights, and ethnic conflicts. fernand.devarennes@eruac.edu

Kerttu Vuolab is a Sámi author and artist and currently works as a commissioning editor for a publishing company specialising in books in the Sámi language. kerttu@davvi.com

Dawn Wink has taught in bilingual and immersion elementary programs in California for six years. She has her Master's in bilingual education from California State University, Sacramento. She is presently staying at home with her three small children and pursues academic interests by writing and reading. dawnwm@yahoo.com

Joan Wink is a Professor of Education at California State University, Stanislaus. Her area of interest is the relationship between languages, literacies, and learning in a pluralistic context, see the second edition of her book 'Critical pedagogy: Notes from the real world'. She has 30 years of experience in public education, pre-K through higher education, in multiple contexts in the US. jwink@toto.csustan.edu

Bibliography

Alexander, Neville (1989). *Language Policy and National Unity in South Africa/Azania*. Cape Town: Buchu Books.

Alexander, Neville (1992). Language planning from below. In Herbert, Robert K. (ed.) *Language and Society in Africa. The Theory and Practice of Sociolinguistics*. Johannesburg: Witwatersrand University Press, 143-149.

Alexander, Neville (1999). An African Renaissance without African languages? Paper delivered at the Goedgedacht Social Responsibility Forum, 16 July 1999, Newlands, Cape Town.

Alexandre, Pierre (1972). *An Introduction to Language and Languages in Africa*. London: Heinemann.

Ammon, Ulrich (1989). Die Schwierigkeiten der deutschen Sprachgemeinschaft aufgrund der Dominanz der englischen Sprache. *Zeitschrift für Sprachwissenschaft* 8(2), 257-272.

Ammon, Ulrich (1990). German or English? The Problems of Language Choice Experienced by German-Speaking Scientists. In Nelde, Peter (ed.). *Language Conflict and Minorities*. Bonn: Dümmler, 33-51.

Ammon, Ulrich (1991). *Die internationale Stellung der deutschen Sprache*. Berlin & New York: de Gruyter.

Ammon, Ulrich (1998). *Ist Deutsch noch internationale Wissenschaftssprache? Englisch auch für die Lehre an den deutschsprachigen Hochschulen*. Berlin & New York: de Gruyter.

Andersen, Benedict (1980*). Imagined Communities: Reflections on the Origin and Spread of Nationalism*. London: Verso.

Annamalai, E. (1998). Language Choice in Education: Conflict Resolution in Indian Courts. In Benson et al. (eds.), 29-43.

Annamalai, E. (forthcoming). Emergence of Dominant Languages. In Annamalai. E. *Multilingual Management: Languages Planning and Use in India*. New Delhi: Sage.

Appadurai, Arjuna (1993). Disjuncture and difference in the global cultural economy. In Williams, Patrick & Chrisman, Laura (eds.). *Colonial Discourse and Post-Colonial Theory*. New York: Harvester Wheatsheaf, 324-339.

Arnberg, Matts, **Ruong**, Israel & **Unsgaard**, Håkan (1969). *Jojk – Yoik*. Stockholm: SR förlag.

Auld, William (1980). *La infana raso: poemo en 25 chapitroj*. La Laguna: Stafeto 3rd edition, first 1956).

Auld, William (ed.) (1984). *Esperanto Antologia*. La Laguna: Stafeto (Rotterdam: Universala Esperanto-Asocio, second edition, first 1958).

Baker, Colin & **Jones**, Sylvia Prys (1998). *Encyclopedia of Bilingualism and Bilingual Education*. Clevedon, UK: Multilingual Matters.

Bautista, M.L.S. (ed.) (1996). *Readings in Philippine Sociolinguistics*. Manila: De la Salle University Press.

Benson, Phil, **Grundy**, Peter & **Skutnabb-Kangas**, Tove (eds.) (1998). Language Rights. Special Issue, *Language Sciences* 20(1).

Bloomfield, Leonard (1927). Literate and illiterate speech. *American Speech* 2, 432-439. [Reprinted in Hymes, Dell (ed.) (1964). *Language in culture and society*. New York: Harper & Row Publishers].

Bordie, John (1978). Kurdish dialects in Eastern Turkey. In Jazayery, Mohammad Ali et al. (eds.), *Linguistic and Literary Studies in Honour of Archibald A. Hill, Vol. II, Descriptive Linguistics*. The Hague: Mouton, 205-212.

Bourdieu, Pierre (1991). *Language and Symbolic Power*. London: Polity Press.

Branson, Jan & **Miller**, Don (1992). Linguistics, Symbolic Violence and the Search for Word Order in Sign Language. *Signpost*, the International Sign Linguistics Association, Summer, 14-28.

Branson, Jan & **Miller**, Don (1993). Sign language, the Deaf, and the epistemic violence of mainstreaming. *Language and education* 7(1), 21-41.

Branson, Jan & **Miller**, Don (1998). Nationalism and the linguistic rights of Deaf communities: Linguistic imperialism and the recognition and development of sign languages. *Journal of Sociolinguistics* 2(1), 3-34.

Branson, Jan, **Miller**, Don & **Marsaja**, I Gede (1996). Everyone Here Speaks Sign Language Too: A Deaf Village in Bali, Indonesia. In Ceil, Lucas (ed.) *Multicultural Aspects of Sociolinguistics in Deaf Communities*. Washington, D.C.: Gallaudet University Press, 39-57.

Branson, Jan, **Miller**, Don & **Marsaja**, I Gede (1999). Sign Languages as a Natural Part of The Linguistic Mosaic: The Impact of Deaf People on Discourse Forms in North Bali, Indonesia. In Ceil, Lucas (ed.). *Sociolinguistics in Deaf Communities*. Washington, D.C.: Gallaudet University Press.

Brass, Paul (1974). *Language, Religion and Politics in North India*. London: Cambridge University Press.

Brock-Utne, Birgit (1993). Language of instruction in African schools - a socio-cultural perspective. *Nordisk Pedagogik*. 4, 225-247.

Brock-Utne, Birgit (1997). Language of instruction in Namibian schools. *International Review of Education* 43(2/3), 241-260.

Brock-Utne, Birgit (2000). *Whose Education for All? The recolonization of the African mind?* New York & London: Falmer.

Byram, Michael & **Leman**, J. (eds.) (1990). *Bicultural and trilingual education*. Clevedon: Multilingual Matters.

Cajete, Gregory (1994). *Look to the Mountain. An Ecology of Indigenous Education*. Skyland, NC: Kivaki.

Campbell, George (1991). Kurdish. *Compendium of the World's Languages. Vol. 1*. London: Routledge, 769-773.

Castells, Manuel (1996). *The Networked Society*. Oxford: Basil Blackwell.

Castells, Manuel (1997). *The Information Age: Economy, Society and Culture, Volume II : The Power of Identity*. Oxford : Basil Blackwell.

Castro, Max J. (1992). On the Curious Question of Language in Miami. In Crawford, James, (ed.) *Language Loyalties: A Sourcebook on the Official English Controversy*. Chicago: University of Chicago Press, 178-186.

Cazden, Courtney B. (1989). Richmond Road: A multilingual/multicultural primary school in Auckland, New Zealand. *Language and Education*, 3, 143-166.

Charny, Israel W. (1994). Toward a generic definition of genocide. In Andreopoulos, George (ed.), *Genocide: Conceptual and Historical Dimensions*. Philadelphia: University of Pennsylvania Press, 64-94.

Clyne, Michael (1987). Cultural Differences in the Organization of Academic Texts. *Journal of Pragmatics* 11, 211-247.

Clyne, Michael, **Fernandez**, Sue, **Chen**, Imogen Y. & **Summo-O-Connell**, Renata (1997). *Background Speakers. Diversity and its Management in LOTE Programs*. Canberra: Language Australia.

Cobarrubias, Juan (1983). Ethical issues in language planning. In Cobarrubias, Juan & Fishman, Joshua A. (eds.). *Progress in Language Planning: International Perspectives*. Berlin: Mouton de Gruyter, 41-85.

Coulmas, Florian (1987). Why Speak English? In Knapp, Karlfried, Enninger, Werner & Knapp-Potthoff, Andrea (eds.) *Analyzing Intercultural Communication*. Berlin: Mouton de Gruyter, 93-107.

Crystal, David (1997). *English as a Global Language*. Cambridge: Cambridge University Press.

Cummins, Jim (1991). The Politics of Paranoia: Reflections on the Bilingual Education Debate. In García, Ofelia (ed.) *Bilingual Education: Festschrift in honor of Joshua A. Fishman on the occasion of his 65th birthday*. Amsterdam & Philadelphia: John Benjamins, 183-199.

Cummins, Jim (1996). *Negotiating Identities. Education for Empowerment in a Diverse Society*. Ontario, CA: California Association for Bilingual Education.

Cummins, Jim (1997). Minority status and schooling in Canada. *Anthropology and Education Quarterly* 28(33), 411-430.

Dasgupta, Probal (1987). Toward a dialogue between the sociolinguistic sciences and Esperanto culture. *Language Problems and Language Planning* 11(3), 305-334. (Reprinted in Tonkin (ed.) 1997, 139-171).

Dasgupta, Probal (1998). Oitihaasiker aabossok bhaasaa. *Oitihaasik* 7(1-2), 113-128.

de Bot, Kees (1997). Nelde's Law Revisited: Dutch as a Diaspora Language. In: Wölck, Wolfgang & de Houwer, Alex (eds.), *Recent studies in contact linguistics*. Bonn: Dümmler, 51-59.

Diachkov, Mark (1998). A Vision of National Unity and Interests of Ethnic Minorities. In Vçbers, E. (ed). *Pilsoniskâ apzióa* [Civic Consciousness]. Riga: Mâcîbu apgâds, 176-182.

Di Pietro, Robert J. (1990). Review of Ulrich Ammon (ed.) 'Status and Function of Languages and Language Varieties'. *Language Problems and Language Planning* 14, 298-291.

Dittrich, Eckhard J. & **Radtke**, Frank-Olaf (eds.) (1990). *Ethnizität. Wissenschaft und Minderheiten*. Wiesbaden: Westdeutscher Verlag.

Dorfman, Ariel (1998). *Heading South, looking North: a bilingual journey*. New York: Penguin.

Druviete, Ina (1998a). Republic of Latvia. In Paulston, Christina Bratt & Peckham, Donald (eds.), *Linguistic Minorities in Central & Eastern Europe*. Clevedon, UK: Multilingual Matters, 160-183.

Druviete, Ina (1998b). La situation sociolinguistique de la langue lettone. In Terminogramme, Juillet 1998. *Les politiques linguistiques des pays baltes*. Numéro préparé sous la direction de Jacques Maurais. Québec: Office de la langue française, 105-149.

Einejord, Jon Eldar (1975). *Innhald i joiken Luotti - juoigos - dajahus* [Luotti - juoigos - dajahus. The content, melody and lyrics of the Sámi yoik]. Hovedfagsoppgave i Sámisk. Oslo: Universitetet i Oslo.

Elley, Warwick (1992). *How in the world do students read? IEA study of reading literacy*. The Hague: The International Association for the Evaluation of Educational Achievement.

Falk, Richard (1995). *On Humane Governance. Toward a new global politics*. Pennsylvania: Pennsylvania State University Press.

Fettes, Mark & **Bolduc**, Suzanne (eds.) (1998). *Towards Linguistic Democracy*. Rotterdam: Universala Esperanto Asocio.

Fishman, Joshua A. (ed.) (1968). *Readings in the Sociology of Language*. The Hague: Mouton.

Fishman, Joshua A. (1991). *Reversing Language Shift: Theory and Method of Assistance to Threatened Languages*. Clevedon, UK: Multilingual Matters.

Fishman, Joshua A. (1997). *In Praise of the Beloved Language: A Comparative View of Positive Ethnolinguistic Consciousness*. Berlin: Mouton de Gruyter.

Fishman, Joshua A. (ed.) (1999). *Handbook of Language and Ethnic Identity*. New York & Oxford: Oxford University Press.

Fishman, Joshua A., **Conrad**, Andrew W. & **Rubal-Lopez**, Alma (eds.) (1996). *Post-Imperial English. Status Change in Former British and American Colonies, 1940-1990*. Berlin & New York: Mouton de Gruyter.

Forster, E. M. (1965). What I Believe. In Forster, E. M. *Two Cheers for Democracy*. Harmondsworth: Penguin Books.

Freeman, Rebecca D. (1998). *Bilingual education and social change*. Clevedon, UK: Multilingual Matters.

Freire, Paulo (1985). *The Politics of Education: Culture, Power and Liberation*. South Hadley, MA: Bergin & Garvey.

Freire, Paulo & **Macedo**, Donaldo (1987). *Literacy: Reading the word and the world*. South Hadley, MA: Bergin & Garvey.

Friedrich, Paul (1985). *The Language Parallax. Linguistic Relativism and Poetic Indeterminacy*. Austin: University of Texas Press.

Gal, Susan (1979). *Language Shift: Social Determinants of Linguistic Change in Bilingual Austria*. New York: Academic Press.

Gaski, Harald (1993). The Sámi People: The 'White Indians' of Scandinavia. *American Indian Culture and Research Journal* 17(1), 115-128.

Gaski, Harald (1997). Voice in the Margin: A Suitable Place for a Minority Literature. In Gaski (ed.), 199-220.

Gaski, Harald (ed.) (1997). *Sámi Culture in a New Era. The Norwegian Sámi Experience*. Kárášjohka/Karasjok: Davvi Girji.

Giddens, Anthony (1990). *The Consequences of Modernity*. Cambridge: Polity Press.

Giddens, Anthony (1991). *Modernity and Self-Identity. Self and Society in the Late Modern Age*. Cambridge: Polity Press.

Giltrow, Janet & **Colhoun**, Edward R. (1992). The culture of power: ESL traditions, Mayan resistance. In Burnaby, Barbara & Cumming, Alastair (eds.) *Socio-political aspects of ESL*. Toronto: The Ontario Institute for Studies in Education, 50-66.

Gogolin, Ingrid (1994). *Der monolinguale Habitus der multilingualen Schule*. Münster & New York: Waxman.

Gomes de Matos, Francisco (1998). Learners' Pronunciation Rights. *Braz-TESOL Newsletter* (September), 14-15.

Gonzales, Andrew (1996a). Bilingual Communities. National/Regional Profiles and Verbal Repertoires. In Bautista (ed.), 38-62.

Gonzales, Andrew (1996b). Language and Nationalism in the Philippines: An Update. In Bautista (ed.), 228-239.

Graddol, David (1997). *The Future of English? A Guide to Forecasting the Popularity of the English Language in the 21st Century*. London: British Council.

Gramsci, Antonio (1971). *Selections from the Prison Notebooks of Antonio Gramsci*, edited and translated by Q. Hoare and G. Nowell Smith. London: Lawrence & Wishart.

Grin, François. (1992). Towards a Threshold Theory of Minority Language Survival. *Kyklos* 45, 69-97.

Grin, François (1999). Economics. In Fishman (ed.), 9-24.

Grin, François & **Vaillancourt**, François (1997). The economics of multilingualism: overview and analytical framework. In Grabe, William (ed.) *Multilingualism. Annual Review of Applied Linguistics*, 17, 43-65.

Grin, François & **Vaillancourt**, François (1998). *Language revitalisation policy: an analytical survey* (Part I). Report to the Treasury, Wellington (N.Z.). [<http://www.treasury.govt.NZ>].

Haberland, Hartmut (1989). Whose English, Nobody's Business. *Journal of Pragmatics* 13, 927-938.

The Hague Recommendations Regarding the Education Rights of National Minorities & Explanatory Note; for the use of the OSCE High Commissioner on National Minorities, Max van der Stoel (1996). The Hague: Foundation on Inter-Ethnic Relations. [<http://arts.uwaterloo.ca/MINELRES/osce/hagrec.htm>].

294   Bibliography

Hallahan, Daniel P. & **Kauffman**, James M. (1991). *Exceptional children* (5ᵗʰ ed.). Englewood Cliffs, N.J.: Prentice-Hall International.

Hamel, Rainer Enrique (ed.). (1997). Linguistic Human Rights from a Sociolinguistic Perspective. *International Journal of the Sociology of Language* 127.

Hansegård, Nils-Erik (1968). *Tvåspråkighet eller halvspråkighet?* [Bilingualism or semilingualism?]. Stockholm: Aldusserien 253.

Hansegård, Nils-Erik (1990). *Den norrbottenfinska språkfrågan. En återblick på halvspråkighetsdebatten.* [The question of the Finnish language in Norrbotten. Looking back on the semilingualism debate]. Uppsala Multiethnic Papers 19. Uppsala: Centre for Multiethnic Research, Uppsala University.

Harmon, David (1996a). The converging extinction crisis: Defining terms and understanding trends in the loss of biological and cultural diversity. Paper presented at the colloquium 'Losing Species, Languages, and Stories: Linking Cultural and Environmental Change in the Binational Southwest'. Arizona-Sonora Desert Museum, Tucson, AZ, April 1-3, 1996.

Harmon, David (1996b). Losing species, losing languages: Connections between biological and linguistic diversity. *Southwest Journal of Linguistics* 15, 89-108.

Harrison, Shirley (1985). The Social Setting of Norfolk Speech. *English World-Wide* 6(1), 131-153.

Hartshorne, Ken (1995). Language policy in African education: a background to the future. In Mesthrie (ed.), 306-318.

Hassanpour, Amir (1992). *Nationalism and Language in Kurdistan, 1918-1985.* San Francisco: Mellen Research University Press.

Heryanto, Ariel (1995). Language Development and Development of Language: The Case of Indonesia. *Pacific Linguistics*, Series D - 86. Canberra: Department of Linguistics, Research School of Pacific and Asian Studies, The Australian National University.

Heugh, Kathleen (1992). Enshrining elitism: the English connection. *Language Projects' Review* 7(3), 2-4.

Heugh, Kathleen (1995). Disabling and enabling: implications of language policy trends in South Africa. In Mesthrie (ed.), 329-350.

Heugh, Kathleen, **Siegrühn**, Amanda & **Plüddemann**, Peter (eds.) (1995). *Multilingual Education for South Africa.* Johannesburg: Heinemann.

Huss, Leena (1999). *Reversing Language Shift in the Far North: Linguistic Revitalization in Northern Scandinavia and Finland.* Uppsala: Acta Universitatis Upsaliensis. Studia Uralica Upsaliensia 31.

Huss, Leena & **Lindgren**, Anna-Riitta (1999). *Scandinavia.* In Fishman (ed.), 300-318.

Hussain, Mustafa, **Ylmaz**, Ferruh & **O'Connor**, Tim (1997). *Medierne, minoriteterne og majoriteten.* [The media, minorities and the majority]. København: Nævnet for Etnisk Ligestilling.

Hyltenstam, Kenneth (1986). *Politik, forskning och praktik.* [Politics, research and practice]. In Invandrarspråken - ratad resurs? [Immigrant languages - a rejected resource]. Källa 25. Stockholm: Forskningsrådsnämnden, 6-16.

Hyltenstam, Kenneth & **Tuomela**, Veli (1996). Hemspråksundervisningen [Home language teaching]. In Hyltenstam, Kenneth (ed.). *Tvåspråkighet med förhinder?* [Bilingualism prevented?]. Lund: Studentlitteratur.

Illich, Ivan (1973). *Celebration of awareness.* Harmondsworth: Penguin.

Illich, Ivan (1981). Taught mother language and vernacular tongue. In Pattanayak, D. P. *Multilingualism and Mother-Tongue Education.* Delhi: Oxford University Press, 1-39.

Jalava, Antti (1988). Nobody could see that I was a Finn. In Skutnabb-Kangas & Cummins (eds.), 161-166.

Janulf, Pirjo (1998). *Kommer finskan i Sverige att fortleva?* [Will Finnish in Sweden survive?]. Acta Universitatis Stockholmiensis. Studia Fennica Stockholmiensia 7. Stockholm: Almqvist & Wicksell.

Jaspaert, Koen & **Lemmens**, Gertrud (1989). Linguistic evaluation of Dutch as a third language. In Byram, Michael & Leman, Johan (1990). *Bicultural and trilingual education.* Clevedon, UK: Multilingual Matters, 30-56.

Jones, Phillip W. (1997). The World Bank and the literacy question: Orthodoxy, heresy and ideology. *International Review of Education* 43(4), 367-375.

Joutselainen, Marjo (1991). *WFD Survey of Deaf People in the Developing World.* WFD Publications. Helsinki: Offsetpiste.

Jucquois, Guy (1996). Aspects de la diversité dans les sociétés contemporaines occidentales. *DiversCité Langues.* [<http://www.uquebec.ca/diverscite>].

Kachru, Braj B. (1982). Models for Non-Native Englishes. In Kachru (ed.), 31-57.

Kachru, Braj B. (ed.) (1982). *The Other Tongue. English Across Cultures.* Oxford: Pergamon.

Karklins, Rasma (1998). Language Policy for Multi-Ethnic Societies. In Harris, Peter & Reilly, Ben (eds.) *Democracy and Deep-Rooted Conflict: Options for Negotiators.* IDEA Handbook Series, 243-251.

Kipp, Sandra, **Clyne**, Michael & **Pauwels**, Anne (1995). *Immigration and Australia's Language Resources.* Canberra: Australian Government Publishing Service.

Kloss, Heinz (1977). *The American Bilingual Tradition.* Rowley, MA: Newbury House. (Republished in 1998 by the Center for Applied Linguistics, Washington, D.C., ed. Terrence Wiley).

Kontra, Miklos (1995/1996). English Only's Cousin: Slovak Only. *Acta Linguistica Hungarica* 43, 345-372.

Kontra, Miklós, **Phillipson**, Robert, **Skutnabb-Kangas**, Tove & **Várady**, Tibor (eds.) (1999). *Language: a Right and a Resource. Approaching Linguistic Human Rights.* Budapest: Central European University Press.

Krausneker, Verena (1999). Sign languages and Minority Languages. Handout at European Union of the Deaf General Assembly, Wageningen, Netherlands, May 29, 1999.

Kreyenbroek, Philip G. (1994). Kurdish. *The Encyclopedia of Language and Linguistics.* Oxford: Pergamon Press, 1880-1881.

Krupat, Arnold (1992). *Ethnocriticism. Ethnography, History, Literature.* Berkeley: University of California Press.

Kuure, Olli (1997). *Discovering traces of the past. Studies of bilingualism among school pupils in Finland and in Sweden.* Oulu: Acta Universitatis Ouluensis, E 23.

Kuurojen Liitto r.y. (1998). *Kuurot kehitysyhteistyössä. Kumppanuudella kestävään kehitykseen* [The Deaf in development cooperation. Towards sustainable development with the help of companionship]. Helsinki: Libris.

Lainio, Jarmo (ed.) (1996). *Finnarnas historia i Sverige, del 3. Tiden efter 1945.* [The history of the Finns in Sweden, Part 3. The period after 1945]. Helsinki & Stockholm: Suomen Historiallinen Seura & Nordiska Museet.

Lainio, Jarmo (1997). Swedish minority language treatment and language policy. Positive public rhetoric vs. grassroot struggle. *Sociolinguistica* 11, 29-42.

Lambert, Wallace E. (1979). The social psychology of language: perspective for the 1980's. In Giles, Howard & Robinson, W. Peter (eds.). *Language - social psychological perspective.* Oxford: Pergamon Press, 415-424.

Lenhart, Gero (1990). Ethnische Indentität und sozialwissenschaftlicher Instrumentalismus. In Dittrich & Radtke (eds.), 191-213.

Lewis, E. Glyn (1977). Bilingualism in Education - Cross-National Research. *International Journal of the Sociology of Language* 14, 5-30.

Lindgren, Klaus (1997). From class languages to national languages: The language shift from Swedish to Finnish among the educated classes of Finland during the Russian era (1809-1917). Paper presented in European graduate school for training in economic and social historical research (ESTER).

Lo Bianco, Joseph (1987). *National Policy on Languages.* Canberra: Australian Government Publishing Service.

Luckett, Kathy (1992). *National Additive Bilingualism.* NEPI Working Paper. Unpublished report.

Lummis, C. Douglas (1996). Equality. In Sachs, Wolfgang (ed.) *The Development Dictionary.* London: Zed, 38-52.

MacKenzie, David N. (1961). *Kurdish Dialect Studies, Vol. 1.* Oxford: Oxford University Press.

MacKenzie, David N. (1986). Kurds, Kurdistan. V. Language. *The Encyclopaedia of Islam.* New Edition, Vol. 5. Leiden: E. J. Brill, 479-480.

Maffi, Luisa (1998). Language: A resource for Nature. Nature and Resources. *The UNESCO Journal on the Environment and Natural Resources Research* 34(4), 12-21.

Maffi, Luisa (ed.) (in press). *Language, Knowledge and the Environment: The Interdependence of Biological and Cultural Diversity.* Washington, D.C.: Smithsonian Institution Press.

Maffi, Luisa, **Skutnabb-Kangas**, Tove & **Andrianarivo**, Jonah (1999). Linguistic diversity. In Posey (ed.). 21-56.

Magga, Ole Henrik (1994). The Sámi Language Act. In Skutnabb-Kangas & Phillipson (eds.), 1994a, 219-234.

Mander, Jerry & **Goldsmith**, Edward (eds.) (1996). *The case against the global economy and for a turn toward the local.* San Francisco: Sierra Club.

May, Stephen (1994). *Making multicultural education work*. Clevedon, UK: Multilingual Matters.

Mazrui, Alamin (1997). The World Bank, the language question and the future of African education. *Race & Class. A Journal for Black and Third World Liberation* 38(3), 35-49.

Mazrui, Ali & **Mazrui**, Alamin (1998). *The Power of Babel*. Cape Town: David Philip.

McCarus, Ernest (1958*). A Kurdish Grammar: Descriptive Analysis of the Kurdish of Sulaimaniya, Iraq*. New York: American Council of Learned Societies.

McCarus, Ernest (1992). Kurdish. *International Encyclopedia of Linguistics*, Vol. 2. New York: Oxford University Press, 289-94.

Mesthrie, Rajend (ed.) (1995). *Language and Social History. Studies in South African Sociolinguistics*. Cape Town & Johannesburg: David Philip.

Millikan, Ruth G. (1984). *Language, Thought, and Other Biological Categories: New Foundations for Realism*. Cambridge, MA: MIT Press.

Moilanen, Irma & **Myhrman**, Antero & **Kuure**, Olli (1989). Linguistic problems of return migrant children. In Niemi, Jussi (ed.) *Papers from the 11th Scandinavian Conference of Linguistics. Studies in Languages* 14(2). Joensuu: University of Joensuu, Faculty of Humanities, 580-592.

Monatagut, Abel (1993). *Poemo de Utnoa*. Vienna: Pro Esperanto.

Municio, Ingegerd (1987). *Från lag til bruk – hemspråksreformens genomförande*. [From law to use - implementation of the home language reform]. Stockholm Studies in Politics 31. Stockholm: University of Stockholm, Department of Political Studies.

Murray, Heather & **Dingwall**, Sylvia (1997). English for Scientific Communication at Swiss Universities: 'God helps those who help themselves.' *Babylonia* 4, 54-59.

Mühlhäusler, Peter (1996). *Linguistic Ecology: Language change and linguistic imperialism in the Pacific Region*. London: Routledge.

Mühlhäusler, Peter (1998). How Creoloid can you get? *Journal of Pidgin and Creole Languages* 13(2), 355-372.

Nauclér, Kerstin (1997). *Den uppgivna läroplanen - tvåspråkighet i förskolan*. [The abandoned syllabus - bilingualism in the pre-school]. In Svenska som andraspråk och andra språk. Festskrift till Gunnar Tingbjörn. [Swedish as a second language and other languages. A Festschrift for Gunnar Tingbjörn]. Göteborg: Institutionen för svenska språket. Göteborgs universitet, 283-294.

Navarro, Richard (1997). Commentary. *Anthropology & Education Quarterly* 28(3), 455-462.

Nelson, Cecil (1982). Intelligibility and Non-Native Varieties of English. In Kachru (ed.), 58-73.

Ngũgĩ wa Thiong'o (1981). *Decolonising the mind. The politics of language in African literature*. London: James Currey.

Niemi, Einar (1997). Sámi history and the frontier myth: A perspective on the northern Sámi spatial and rights history. In Gaski (ed.), 62-85.

Nylenna, Magne, **Riis**, Poul & **Karlsson**, Yngve (1994). Multiple Blinded Reviews of the Same Two Manuscripts. Effects of Reference Characteristics and Publication Language. *The Journal of the American Medical Association* 272(2), 149-151.

Obanya, Pai (1980). Research on alternative teaching in Africa. In: Yoloye, E.A. & Flechsig, Hans-Jürgen (eds.) *Educational Research for Development.* Bonn: Deutsche Stiftung für Internationale Entwicklung, 67-112.

Oksaar, Els (1978). Människan och tvåspråkighet [The individual and bilingualism]. In Stedje, Astrid & Trampe, Peter (eds.) *Tvåspråkighet.* [Bilingualism]. Föredrag vid det Andra Nordiska Tvåspråkighetssymposiet, 18.-19 May 1978. Stockholm: Akademilitteratur, 51-65.

Pennycook, Alastair (1994). *The cultural politics of English as an international language.* Harlow: Longman.

Pennycook, Alastair (1998a). The right to language: towards a situated ethics of language possibilities. In Benson et al. (eds.), 73-88.

Pennycook, Alastair (1998b). *English and the discourses of colonialism.* London: Routledge.

Phillipson, Robert (1992). *Linguistic imperialism.* Oxford: Oxford University Press.

Phillipson, Robert (1998). Globalising English: Are linguistic human rights an alternative to linguistic Imperialism? In Benson et al. (eds.), 101-112.

Phillipson, Robert (1999a). Review of 'Post-imperial English: Status change in former British and American colonies, 1940-1990', ed. Fishman, Joshua, Conrad, Andrew W., & Rubal-Lopez, Alma. *Language,* 75(2), 375-378.

Phillipson, Robert (1999b). Voice in global English: unheard chords in Crystal loud and clear. Review article on 'English as a global language' by David Crystal. *Applied Linguistics* 20(2), 265-276.

Phillipson, Robert & **Skutnabb-Kangas**, Tove (1996). English Only Worldwide, or Language Ecology. *TESOL Quarterly,* Special Topic Issue: Language Planning and Policy, eds. Ricento, Thomas & Hornberger, Nancy, 429-452.

Phillipson, Robert & **Skutnabb-Kangas**, Tove (1997). Lessons for Europe from language policy in Australia. In Pütz, Martin (ed.). *Language Choices. Conditions, constraints and consequences.* Amsterdam & Philadelphia: John Benjamins, 115-159.

Phillipson, Robert & **Skutnabb-Kangas**, Tove (1999). Englishisation: one dimension of globalisation. In Graddol, David & Meinhof, Ulrike H. (eds.) *English in a changing world. AILA Review* 13. Oxford: The English Book Centre, 19-36.

Pilger, John (1998). *Hidden Agendas.* London: Vintage.

Piron, Claude (1994). *Le défi des langues: du gâchis au bon sens.* Paris: L'Harmattan.

Poplin, Mary & **Weeres**, Joseph (1992). *Voices from the inside: A report on schooling from inside the classroom.* Claremont, CA: The Institute for Education in Transformation at the Claremont Graduate School.

Posey, Darrell A. (ed.) (1999). *Cultural and spiritual values of diversity.* A complementary contribution to the global diversity assessment. London: Intermediate Technology Publications, for the United Nations Environmental Programme.

Rattansi, Ali & **Westwood**, Sallie (eds.) (1994). *Racism, Modernity & Identity: on the Western front.* Cambridge: Polity Press.

Reed, Edward S. (1996). *Encountering the World: Toward an Ecological Psychology.* Oxford: Oxford University Press.

Reid, Euan & **Reich**, Hans (eds.) (1992). *Breaking the boundaries: Migrant workers' children in the EC.* Clevedon, UK: Multilingual Matters.

Ricento, Thomas K. (ed.) (forthcoming). *Ideology, politics and language policies.* Amsterdam: John Benjamins.

Ruiz, Richard (1988). Orientations in language planning. In McKay, Sandra L. & Wong, Sau-Ling Cynthia (eds.) *Language diversity: Problem or resource?* New York: Newbury House, 3-25.

Runblom, Harald (1995). Swedish multiculturalism in a comparative European perspective. In Gustavsson, Sven & Runblom, Harald (eds.) *Language, Minority, Migration.* Yearbook 1994/1995 from the Centre for Multiethnic Research. Uppsala Multiethnic Papers 34. Uppsala: Uppsala University, 199-218.

Said, Edward W. (1994). *Representations of the intellectual.* London: Vintage.

Schierup, Carl-Ulrik (1993). *På kulturens slagmark.* [On the battlefield of culture]. Esbjerg: Sydjysk Universitetsforlag.

Schiffman, Harold F. (1996). *Linguistic Culture and Language Policy.* New York: Routledge.

Seufert, Günter (1997). *Politischer Islam in der Türkei. Islamismus als symbolische Repräsentation einer sich modernisierenden muslimischen Gesellschaft.* Wiesbaden: Steiner.

Simonnot, Philippe (1998). *Trente-neuf leçons de théorie économique.* Paris: Gallimard.

Skutnabb-Kangas, Tove (1977). Language in the process of cultural assimilation and structural incorporation of linguistic minorities. In Elert, Claes-Christian, Eliasson, Stig, Fries, Sigurd & Ureland, Sture (eds.) *Dialectology and Sociolinguistics.* Essays in honor of Karl-Hampus Dahlstedt. Umeå: Umeå University, 191-203 (reprinted in 1979 by the National Clearinghouse for Bilingual Education: Rosslyn, Virginia).

Skutnabb-Kangas, Tove (1982). Gastarbeiter oder Immigrant - verschiedene Arten eine Unterschicht zu reproduzieren. *Deutsch lernen* 1, 59-80.

Skutnabb-Kangas, Tove (1984a). *Bilingualism or not: The education of minorities.* Clevedon, UK: Multilingual Matters.

Skutnabb-Kangas, Tove (1984b). Why aren't All the Children in the Nordic Countries Bilingual? *Journal of Multilingual and Multicultural Development* 5, 301-315.

Skutnabb-Kangas, Tove (1987). Are the Finns in Sweden an Ethnic Minority? Finnish parents talk about Finland and Sweden. Research Project on The

Education of the Finnish Minority in Sweden, Working Paper No. 1. Roskilde: Roskilde University Centre.

Skutnabb-Kangas, Tove (1988). Multilingualism and the education of minority children. In Skutnabb-Kangas & Cummins (eds.), 9-44.

Skutnabb-Kangas, Tove (1990a). *Language, Literacy and Minorities*. London: The Minority Rights Group.

Skutnabb-Kangas, Tove (1990b). *Minoritet, sprog og racisme* [Minorities, language and racism]. København: Tiden.

Skutnabb-Kangas, Tove (1990c). Wer entscheidet, ob meine Sprache wichtig für mich ist? Minderheitenforschung zwischen Sozialtechnologie und Selbstbestimmung. In Dittrich & Radtke (eds.), 329-351.

Skutnabb-Kangas, Tove (1994a). Educational challenges in multilingual Western Europe. In Phillipson, Robert & Skutnabb-Kangas, Tove (eds.) *Papers from the Round Table on Language Policy in Europe, April 22, 1994*. Roskilde: Roskilde Universitetscenter, 30-40.

Skutnabb-Kangas, Tove (1994b). Linguistic Human Rights in Education. In *Language Policy in the Baltic States*. Conference papers. Riga, December 17-18, 1992. Riga: Garâ pupa, 173-191.

Skutnabb-Kangas, Tove (1995). Introduction. In Skutnabb-Kangas (ed.), 7-20.

Skutnabb-Kangas, Tove (ed.) (1995). *Multilingualism for All*. Lisse: Swets & Zeitlinger.

Skutnabb-Kangas, Tove (1996a). The colonial legacy in educational language planning in Scandinavia: from migrant labor to a national ethnic minority? *International Journal of the Sociology of Language* 118, 81-106.

Skutnabb-Kangas, Tove (1996b). Educational language choice - multilingual diversity or monolingual reductionism? In Hellinger, Marlis & Ammon, Ulrich (eds.) *Contrastive Sociolinguistics*. Berlin & New York: Mouton de Gruyter, 175-204.

Skutnabb-Kangas, Tove (1997). Bilingual education for Finnish minority students in Sweden. In Cummins, Jim & Corson, David (eds.) *Bilingual education. Encyclopedia of Language and Education. Vol. 5*. Dordrecht: Kluwer Academic, 217-227.

Skutnabb-Kangas, Tove (1998). Human rights and language wrongs - a future for diversity. In Benson et al. (eds.), 5-27.

Skutnabb-Kangas, Tove (1999a). The Globalization of Language Rights. In Brock-Utne, Birgit & Garbo, Gunnar (eds.). *Globalization - on whose terms?* Oslo: Institute for Educational Research, 168-199.

Skutnabb-Kangas, Tove (1999b). Education of minorities. In Fishman (ed.), 42-59.

Skutnabb-Kangas, Tove (1999c). Linguistic Human rights - are you naive or what? *TESOL Journal*, 8/3, One World, Many Tongues, Special Issue on Language Policies and the Rights of Learners, eds. de Villar, Robert A. & Sugino, Toshiko, 6-12.

Skutnabb-Kangas, Tove (2000). *Linguistic Genocide in Education - or Worldwide Diversity and Human Rights?* Mahwah, NJ: Lawrence Erlbaum Associates.

Skutnabb-Kangas, Tove & **Bucak**, Sertaç (1994). Killing a mother tongue. How the Kurds are deprived of linguistic human rights. In Skutnabb-Kangas & Phillipson (eds.), 1994a, 347-370.

Skutnabb-Kangas, Tove & **Cummins**, Jim (eds.) (1988). *Minority Education: from Shame to Struggle.* Clevedon, UK: Multilingual Matters.

Skutnabb-Kangas, Tove & **Peura**, Markku (eds.) (1994). *Man kan vara tvåländere också. Sverigefinnarnas väg från tystnad til kamp* [You can be bi-countrial too. Sweden Finns on the road from silence to struggle]. Stockholm: Sverigefinländarnas arkiv.

Skutnabb-Kangas, Tove & **Phillipson**, Robert (1989). *Wanted! Linguistic Human Rights.* ROLIG-papir 44. Roskilde: Roskilde Universitetscenter.

Skutnabb-Kangas, Tove & **Phillipson**, Robert (eds., in collaboration with Mart **Rannut**) (1994a). *Linguistic Human Rights. Overcoming Linguistic Discrimination.* Berlin & New York: Mouton de Gruyter (paperback 1995).

Skutnabb-Kangas, Tove & **Phillipson**, Robert (1994b). Linguistic human rights, past and present. In Skutnabb-Kangas & Phillipson (eds.), 1994a, 71-110.

Skutnabb-Kangas, Tove & **Phillipson**, Robert (1996a). Linguicide and Linguicism. In Goebl, Hans et al. (eds.) *Kontaktlinguistik/ Contact Linguistics/ Linguistique de contact.* Vol. I. Berlin & New York: de Gruyter, 667-675.

Skutnabb-Kangas, Tove & **Phillipson**, Robert (1996b). The possible role of donors in a language policy for all. In Brock-Utne, Birgit & Nagel, Tove (eds.). *The role of aid in the development of education for all.* Report 8. Oslo: Institute for Educational Research, 161-202.

Skutnabb-Kangas, Tove & **Phillipson**, Robert (1997). Linguistic Human Rights and Development. In Hamelink, Cees (ed.) *Ethics and Development.* Kampen: Kok, 56-69.

Skutnabb-Kangas, Tove & **Phillipson**, Robert (1998). Language in Human Rights. *Gazette: The International Journal for Communication Studies* 60(1), 27-46.

Skutnabb-Kangas, Tove & **Toukomaa**, Pertti (1976). *Teaching migrant children's mother tongue and learning the language of the host country in the context of the socio-cultural situation of the migrant family.* Research Reports 15. Tampere: Department of Sociology and Social Psychology, University of Tampere. (Also published by UNESCO, 1976, as ED-76/CONF.713/COL.5-6).

Smith, Dorothy E. (1990). *The Conceptual Practices of Power: A Feminist Sociology of Knowledge.* Toronto: University of Toronto Press.

Smolicz, Jerzy J. & **Nical**, Illuminado (1997). Exporting the European Idea of a National Language: Some Educational Implications of the Use of English and Indigenous Languages in the Philippines. *International Review of Education* 43(5-6), 1-21.

Spack, Ruth (1997). The Rhetorical Constructions of Multilingual Students. *TESOL Quarterly* 31(4), 765-774.

Spivak, Gayatri Chakravarti (1987). *In Other Worlds.* London: Methuen.

Spring, Joel (1998). *Education and the Rise of the Global Economy.* Mahwah, NJ: Lawrence Erlbaum Associates.

Stölting-Richert, Wilfried (1994). Sozialdemokratische Bildungspolitik unter der Annahme 'sprachlich-kultureller Behinderung'. In Gogolin, Ingrid (hrsg.). *Das nationale Selbstverständnis der Bildung*. Münster: Waxmann, 147-160.

Stölting-Richert, Wilfried (1996). Die Sprachlichkeit von Menschen in der Migrationsgesellschaft und die Interkulturelle Pädagogik. *Deutsch lernen* 3, 238-248.

Tarkiainen, Kari (1993). *Finnarnas historia i Sverige, del 2. Inflyttarna från Finland och de finska minoriteterna under tiden 1809-1944*. [The history of the Finns in Sweden, Part 2. The Immigrants from Finland and the Finnish minorities in the period 1809-1944]. Helsingfors & Stockholm: Suomen Historiallinen Seura & Nordiska Museet.

Taylor, Charles (1998). Entretien de DiversCité Langues avec Charles Taylor. *DiversCité Langues*. [<http://www.uquebec.ca/diverscite>].

Taylor, Shelley K. (1993). Preliminary findings of an investigation into the trilingual educational experience of Mi'kmaq children in French immersion. Paper presented at the British Association of Applied Linguistics Seminar on 'Bilingual Classroom Discourse'. Lancaster University, Lancaster, U.K. (July, 1993).

Taylor, Shelley K. (1996). Policy and planning concerns for the future. Championing sustained minority language development. Paper presented at the AILA '96 symposium 'Current Issues and Future Prospects in the Study of Language Policy and Planning.' University of Jyväskylä, Jyväskylä, Finland (August, 1996).

Taylor, Shelley K. (1997). 'I treat them all the same': Educator role definitions and child multilingualism in a minority. In Jørgensen, Jens Norman & Holmen, Anne (eds.) *The Development of Successive Bilingualism in School-Age Children*. Københavnerstudier i tosprogethed 27. København: Danmarks Lærerhøjskole, 159-185.

Taylor, Shelley K. & **Skutnabb-Kangas**, Tove (1997). Sleights of hand (and of pen): A reply to Yagmur. *TESOL Matters* 6(6), 19.

Terralingua (1999). Learn about Terra Lingua. <http//:cougar.ucdavis.edu/nas/terralin/>.

Tollefson, James W. (1991). *Planning Language, Planning Inequality*. Harlow: Longman.

Tombiah, Stanley J. (1996). The Nation-State in Crisis and the Rise of Ethnonationalism. In McAllister, Patrick N. (ed.) *The Politics of Difference*. Chicago & London: The University of Chicago Press, 124-143.

Tonkin, Humphrey (ed.) (1997). *Esperanto, Interlinguistics, and Planned Language*. Lanham: University Press of America.

Topolinska, Zuzanna (ed.) (1998). Sociolinguistics in the Republic of Macedonia. *International Journal of the Sociology of Language* 131.

Touraine, Alain (1997). *Pourrons-nous vivre ensemble? Égaux et différents*. Paris: Fayard.

Truchot, Claude (1990). *L'anglais dans le monde contemporain*. Paris: Robert.

UNESCO (1953). *The use of the vernacular languages in education.* Monographs on fundamental education VIII. Paris: UNESCO.

UNICEF (1999). The State of the World's Children 1999 [UNICEF Homepage, <http//:www.unicef.org/crc/>].

Valadez, Concepción, **Martinez**, Corrine & **MacSwan**, Jeff (1997). Toward a new view of low achieving bilinguals: Syntactic competence in designating 'semilinguals'. Paper presented at the Annual Meeting of the American Educational Research Association (AERA), March 24-29, 1997. [<http://www.public.asu.edu/~macswan/>].

Valkeapää, Nils-Aslak (1984). *Ett sätt at lugna renar.* [A way of calming reindeer]. Café Existens No. 24. Göteborg.

de Varennes, Fernand (1996). *Language, Minorities and Human Rights.* The Hague: Martinus Nijhoff.

van Djik, Teun A. (1996). Discourse, Power and Access. In Caldas-Coulthard, Carmen Rosa & Coulthard, Malcolm (eds.) *Texts and Practices: Readings in critical discourse.* London: Routledge, 84-104.

van Dijk, Teun A. (1997). *Ideology. A Multidisciplinary Approach.* London: Sage.

Vandenbroucke, J. P. (1989). On not Being Born a Native Speaker of English. *British Medical Journal* 298, 1461-1462.

Wingstedt, Maria (1998). *Language Ideologies and Minority Language Policies in Sweden. Historical and Contemporary Perspectives.* Stockholm: Centre for Research on Bilingualism.

Wink, Dawn (1997). Bilingual Immersion: Variables for Language Minority Student Success. Unpublished Master's thesis. Sacramento: California State University.

Wink, Joan (2000). *Critical Pedagogy: Notes from the Real World.* (2nd ed.). New York: Longman.

Winsa, Birger (1998). Language Attitudes and Social Identity. Oppression and revival of a minority language in Sweden. Occasional Paper No 17. Canberra: Applied Linguistics Association of Australia.

Index